COMMUNICATING IN GROUPS: APPLICATIONS AND SKILLS

• • • • • • • • • • • • • • • • • •

COMMUNICATING IN GROUPS: APPLICATIONS AND SKILLS

SECOND EDITION

GLORIA J. GALANES
Southwest Missouri State University

JOHN K. BRILHART
Southwest Missouri State University

Madison, Wisconsin • Dubuque, Iowa • Indianapolis, Indiana
Melbourne, Australia • Oxford, England

Book Team

Executive Editor *Stan Stoga*
Developmental Editor *Kassi Radomski*
Production Editor *Peggy Selle*
Photo Editor *Karen Hostert*
Permissions Coordinator *Gail I. Wheatley*
Visuals/Design Developmental Consultant *Marilyn A. Phelps*
Visuals/Design Freelance Specialist *Mary L. Christianson*
Publishing Services Specialist *Sherry Padden*
Marketing Manager *Carla J. Aspelmeier*
Advertising Manager *Jodi Rymer*

WCB Brown & Benchmark

A Division of Wm. C. Brown Communications, Inc.

Executive Vice President/General Manager *Thomas E. Doran*
Vice President/Editor in Chief *Edgar J. Laube*
Vice President/Sales and Marketing *Eric Ziegler*
Director of Production *Vickie Putman Caughron*
Director of Custom and Electronic Publishing *Chris Rogers*

Wm. C. Brown Communications, Inc.

President and Chief Executive Officer *G. Franklin Lewis*
Corporate Senior Vice President and Chief Financial Officer *Robert Chesterman*
Corporate Senior Vice President and President of Manufacturing *Roger Meyer*

Cover design and illustration by Julie Anderson.

Opener 1: © Alan Carey/The Image Works; Opener 2: Michael J. Okoniewski/
The Image Works; Opener 3: © Jean-Claude Lejeune; Fig. 4.1, Opener 4:
© James Shaffer; Opener 5: © Nita Winter/The Image Works; Opener 6, 7, 8:
© James Shaffer; Opener 9: © Steve Takatsuno; Opener 10: © James Shaffer;
Opener 11: © Alan Carey/The Image Works; p. 260, Opener 12: © James Shaffer.

Printed in the United States of America by Wm. C. Brown Communications, Inc.,
2460 Kerper Boulevard, Dubuque, IA 52001

10 9 8 7 6 5 4 3 2 1

CONTENTS

PREFACE xi

PART ONE

Orientation to Small Group Systems

CHAPTER ONE

Small Groups as the Heart of Society 2

Groups in Your Life 6
Groups as Problem Solvers 6
Participating in Groups 7
Groups versus Individuals as Problem Solvers 8
When a Group Is a Good Choice 9
When a Group Is Not a Good Choice 10
Groups, Small Groups, and Small Group Theory 11
Group 11
Small Group 12
Group Dynamics 13
Communication 13
Small Group Communication 14
Classifying Groups by Their Major Purpose 14
Primary or Secondary Groups 14
Primary Groups 15
Secondary Groups 15

Types of Secondary Groups 16
Learning Groups 16
Organizational Groups 16
The Participant-Observer Perspective 19
Summary 20
Review Questions 21
Bibliography 21
References 21

CHAPTER TWO

Groups as Structured Open Systems 24

Overview of General Systems Theory 26
The Small Group as a System 27
Definition of a System 28
Concepts Vital to Understanding Systems 28
Inputs 28
Throughput Processes 31
Outputs 32
Environment 33
Characteristics of Systems 33
Open and Closed Systems 33
Interdependence 35
Feedback 36
Multiple Causes, Multiple Paths 36
Life Cycles in the System 37
Organizations as Systems of Groups 38

Summary 40
Review Questions 41
Bibliography 42
Reference 42

PART TWO

Foundations of Small Group Communicating

CHAPTER THREE

Interpersonal Communication
Principles for Group Members   44

Communication: What's That? 47
Myths about Communicating 51
**Listening: Receiving, Interpreting,
    and Responding to Messages from
    Other Group Members 52**
Listening Defined 53
The Effects of Culture on the
    Communication Process 54
Habits of Poor Listeners 58
Listening Actively 61
Focused Listening 63

Summary 64
Review Questions 65
Bibliography 65
References 66

CHAPTER FOUR

Verbal and Nonverbal
Messages   68

**Creating Messages in a Small
    Group 70**
Levels of Meaning 71
**Using Language to Help the Group
    Progress 71**
Follow the Rules 72

Adjust to the Symbolic Nature of
    Language 73
Use Emotive Words Cautiously 75
Organize Remarks 77
Make Sure the Discussion Question is
    Clear and Appropriate 80

**Nonverbal Signals in Small Group
    Communication 84**
Principles of Nonverbal
    Communication 84
Functions of Nonverbal
    Signals 86
Categories of Nonverbal Signals 87
    Appearance 87
    Space and Seating 88
    *Facial Expressions and Eye
        Contact 89*
    Movements 90
    Voice 90
    Timing 91

Summary 92
Review Questions 93
Bibliography 93
References 93

CHAPTER FIVE

Critical Thinking in the Small
Group   94

What Makes Thinking "Critical"? 96
Attitudes 98
Gathering Information 100
    Assessing Information Needs 101
    Collecting Needed Resources 102
Evaluating Information 103
    *Determining the Meaning of What Is
        Being Said 104*
    *Distinguishing Fact from Opinion and
        Inference 106*
    *Identifying and Clarifying Ambiguous
        Terms 106*
    *Evaluating Opinions by Determining
        the Credibility of the Source 107*
    *Assessing the Accuracy and Worth of
        the Information 108*

Checking for Errors in Reasoning   110
   Overgeneralizing   110
   Attacking a Person Instead of the
     Argument   111
   Confusing Causal Relationships   112
   Either-Or Thinking   112
   Incomplete Comparisons   113
Asking Probing Questions   114

**Behaviors Counterproductive to
Critical Thinking   115**
Impulsiveness   116
Overdependence on Authority Figures   116
Lack of Confidence   116
Dogmatic, Inflexible Behavior   117
Unwillingness to Make the Effort to Think
   Critically   118

Summary   118
Review Questions   119
Bibliography   119
References   120

PART THREE

Understanding and Improving Group Throughput Processes

CHAPTER SIX

Becoming a Group   122

**Primary, Secondary, and Tertiary
Tensions   124**
Managing Tensions   126
**Phases in the Development of a
Group   128**
Rules and Norms   129
Development of Group Norms   130
Enforcement of Group Norms   132
   Dealing with Deviants   133
Changing a Group Norm   135
Group Roles   136
Types of Roles   136
Role Functions in a Small Group   137

   Individual Roles and the Hidden
     Agenda   139
The Emergence of Roles in a Group   140
**Development of the Group's
Culture   141**
Fantasy Themes   142
Group Climate   144
   Trust   144
   Cohesiveness   145
   Supportiveness   146

Summary   147
Review Questions   148
Bibliography   149
References   149

CHAPTER SEVEN

Perspectives on Leading Small
Groups   152

Leadership and Leaders   155
Leadership   155
   Sources of Power in the Small
     Group   156
Leaders   158
   Designated Leader   158
   Emergent Leader   161

Myths about Leadership   162
Current Ideas about Leadership   166
The Functional Concept of Group
   Leadership   166
   Leader as Completer   167
The Contingency Concept of Group
   Leadership   168
   Leadership Adaptability as the Key to
     Effectiveness   170

Summary   172
Review Questions   173
Bibliography   174
References   174

CHAPTER EIGHT

Applying Leadership Principles   176

What Groups Expect Leaders to Do 178

Administrative Duties 179
  Planning for Meetings 179
  Following Up on Meetings 181
Leading Group Discussions 181
  Initiating Discussions 183
  Structuring Discussions 183
  *Equalizing Opportunity to
    Participate 185*
  Stimulating Creative Thinking 187
  Stimulating Critical Thinking 187
  *Fostering Meeting-to-Meeting
    Improvement 188*
Developing the Group 189
  Establishing a Climate of Trust 189
  *Developing Teamwork and Promoting
    Cooperation 190*
Managing the Group's Written
  Communication 191
  Personal Notes 192
  Group Records 193
  Written Notices and Visuals 195
  Reports and Resolutions 195

**Group-Centered Democratic
  Leadership: A Special Case 197**
Summary 201
Review Questions 201
Bibliography 201
References 202

CHAPTER NINE

Procedures for a Problem-Solving
Group 204

**Scientific Method as the Basis for
  Problem Solving 208**
Characteristics of Problems 209
Definition of *Problem* 209
Problem Solving versus Decision
  Making 210
Problem Characteristics 210
  Task Difficulty 211
  Solution Multiplicity 211
  Intrinsic Interest 211
  Member Familiarity 211
  Acceptance Level 211

Area of Freedom 212
**The General Procedural Model for
  Problem Solving 213**
1. Describing and Analyzing the
  Problem 214
2. Generating and Explaining Possible
  Solutions 216
3. Evaluating Possible Solutions 217
  Criteria for Evaluating Solutions 217
  *Narrowing a Long List of Proposed
    Solutions 218*
  Charting the Pros and Cons 219
4. Deciding on a Solution 219
  *Different Ways to Make Decisions in
    Groups 220*
5. Planning How to Implement the
  Solution 221
**Applications of the General
  Procedural Model for Problem
  Solving 223**
Summary 223
Review Questions 226
Bibliography 226
References 226

CHAPTER TEN

Managing Conflicts Productively 228

What Is Conflict? 231
Myths about Conflict 231
Groupthink 234
Symptoms of Groupthink 235
Preventing Groupthink 237
Managing Conflict in the Group 240
Conflict Management Styles 240
  Avoidance 240
  Accommodation 241
  Competition 242
  Collaboration 243
  Compromise 243
Expressing Disagreement 245
Steps in Principled Negotiation 247
Breaking a Deadlock 249
  Mediation by the Leader 249
  Third Party Arbitration 252

Summary 252
Review Questions 253
Bibliography 254
References 254

PART FOUR

Special Techniques for
Small Groups

CHAPTER ELEVEN

Group Techniques in Organizations
   256

**Generating Information and Ideas
   259**
Brainstorming 259
Focus Groups 262
Buzz Groups 263

Identifying Problems 265
Problem Census 265
RISK Technique 267

**Solving Problems and Making
   Decisions Effectively 268**
Nominal Group Technique 269

Implementing Group Solutions 272
PERT 272

**Improving Organizational
   Effectiveness 273**
Quality Circles 273
Self-Managed Work Teams 276

**When Members Cannot Meet
   Face-to-Face 277**
Delphi Technique 277
Teleconferencing 279
Summary 280
Review Questions 281
Bibliography 281
References 282

CHAPTER TWELVE

Techniques for Observing
Problem-Solving Groups 284

The Role of the Observer 287
**Observation Instruments and
   Techniques 290**
Verbal Interaction Analysis 290
Content Analysis Procedures 290
SYMLOG 292
Member/Observer Rating Scales 296
   *Rating Scales for General
      Evaluation 298*
   Postmeeting Reaction Forms 298
   Evaluating Individual Participants 301
   Evaluating Group Leadership 301

Summary 308
Review Questions 308
References 309

INDEX 311

PREFACE

"People can be motivated to be good not by telling them that hell is a place where they will burn, but by telling them it is an unending committee meeting. On judgment day, the Lord will divide people by telling those on His right hand to enter His kingdom and those on His left to break into small groups."

Rev. Robert Kennedy

This quote was given to us by one of our students. It expresses precisely how many people feel about participating in groups. In fact, Gloria's original interest in small groups came about because she found herself frequently asking, "Why do group meetings have to be such torture?" On the other hand, Jack's experience with small groups had been a positive one. Accustomed to making decisions on his own, Jack's initial group experiences showed him that the small group experience can be rewarding and group decisions can be better than individual ones. Eventually, Gloria participated in some "good" groups and Jack participated in some "bad" ones. Both of us have had considerable experience with a wide variety of groups. Our academic study of small groups has been enriched by our participation in these numerous groups. We have *seen* the theories in operation. We have made our own mistakes, but we also have used what we know about groups to improve the process of small group problem solving. We share a philosophy of participatory democracy as an ideal model for organized human society. For both of us, "to lead" is to serve, not to use. "To follow" does not mean subservience to other individuals but cooperative work for the common good.

One of our friends, who recently returned from a camping and white-water rafting trip down the Colorado River, described her group experience as "life-changing." Members of her team learned to rely on each other in a healthy way, to pull their own fair share of the load, and to be responsible to and for the group. Although this book deals primarily with the kinds of problem-solving groups found in business and industry, education, nonprofit organizations, and government, these everyday groups can achieve that same bonding and transcendence as our friend's outdoor group. This process starts with members who are productive and leaders who are effective. The skills and behaviors needed to have an effective group can be learned, and both of us are strong advocates for education and training in this area. We hope this book will teach you what usually happens when people join to form a small group and to anticipate what can go wrong and why. We hope to take you from theoretical understanding to application of the information. We hope you will use the information we provide to change your own behavior when you are part of a small group, whether you are the leader or a member. That is why we have included numerous principles, suggestions, and guidelines for effective group communication. These guidelines are a type of "operator's manual" for group participants.

The theme that runs through all the chapters of *Communicating in Groups* is that solving problems in groups is too important to be left to chance. Group members must learn to apply critical thinking skills to the vital business of group problem solving. This highly *practical* orientation most clearly differentiates *Communicating in Groups* from our other small group text, *Effective Group Discussion,* which is designed to meet the academic needs of undergraduate students, most of whom are communication majors. Such students are interested not only in practical applications but also in the summaries of research by small group communication scholars. *Communicating in Groups* has the same research *foundation* as *Effective Group Discussion,* but we report the research in much less detail, with more synthesis and distillation of the findings, fewer footnotes, and less evaluation of competing theories. This allows the readers to focus on what is usually most important to them—practical applications of the research.

We think *Communicating in Groups* is an appropriate textbook for freshman-level small group courses in departments of communication. We think it is the most appropriate textbook available for small group courses in community colleges and technical institutes, and for practical small group courses in departments of business, education, engineering, health sciences, political science, psychology, sociology and social sciences, and urban affairs. In addition, we think the book will be a helpful guide to nonstudent practitioners. Whether you belong to a quality control circle at your factory, chair a government or military task force, serve on a school board, or participate in a study group at church, you need to know how to operate effectively as a small group participant/leader.

We have done a number of things in the book to make it useful to a variety of readers. First, each chapter begins with a story that illustrates the main theme in the chapter. Some of the stories will be familiar to you, such as the ill-fated group decision to launch the space shuttle *Challenger* in 1986. These introductory stories come from examples our students have shared with us, from personal experiences, and from materials we have read. Second, numerous actual examples throughout the book illustrate the theoretical points we present and demonstrate that small groups have relevance to *you*. These examples are not meant to limit you but to remind you of your *own* examples and experiences.

Third, the major points of the chapters are summarized in figures provided in the text so they will be easy to understand and retain. We have tried to make our points visually as well as verbally. Finally, we use an informal writing style that comes close to the kind of speech you are likely to hear in many small groups.

For example, we have referred to ourselves—Gloria and Jack—throughout the book. We think this illustrates a major point about small group communication, which is that members of groups usually do not call each other "Mr." or "Dr." or "Mrs." Likewise, we think of you, our readers, as individuals with whom we are on a first-name basis and we encourage you to think of us in the same way.

We have arranged the chapters of *Communicating in Groups* so that many chapters build on information presented in earlier ones. However, after Part One you can change the sequence in which you study them without loss of understanding because the order in which instructors prefer to study the topics in small group communication varies widely.

This second edition has been reorganized according to suggestions provided by teachers who have used the text. We have tried to add key information without increasing the length of the book by removing redundant or less useful material. Information about communication theory is presented earlier. Material from the previous chapter on group members has been distributed elsewhere or consolidated with related information. The section about nonverbal communication has been expanded, and material on intercultural communication as it affects small groups has been included. We have also updated the stories that begin each chapter and added important information about how various group techniques have been used successfully by numerous organizations. And we have retained the focus on critical thinking.

Part One provides basic information you need to understand how groups function. Chapter 1 introduces you to some of the basic terms you will encounter throughout the book and shows you how to classify groups according to their major purpose. In chapter 1, you will learn to identify the types of problems for which groups are best suited. Chapter 2 presents general systems theory as a framework for understanding the complexity of group communication. We view the group as an open living system that receives inputs from the environment, transforms them via throughput processes, and produces outputs. We provide specific illustrations of these concepts throughout the rest of the book.

Part Two provides the foundation for understanding communication in groups. Chapter 3, which may present review material for some readers, discusses basic communication theory. You will learn what communication is, what constitutes effective listening and how people interpret what they see and hear. Chapter 4 discusses the specifics of verbal and nonverbal communication. You will also learn how to create messages that are clear and helpful, and how to evaluate nonverbal messages in a group. Chapter 5 discusses critical thinking skills. We see critical thinking as the heart of the group problem-solving process, so we show you how to gather information, evaluate it, and check for errors in reasoning. No matter how committed and conscientious the group, decision making will be flawed if members fail to do this.

Part Three focuses on the group's throughput processes. Chapter 6 explains how a group develops into a team from an initial collection of individuals. Knowing what is natural and appropriate in the development of a group can prevent you from becoming too impatient with a process that should not be cut short. You will learn how norms develop in a group and what you can do to change ineffective norms, how roles form, and how each group creates its own culture and climate. Chapters 7 and 8 discuss leadership. In chapter 7 we present theoretical principles that serve as the foundation for the practical guidelines and suggestions we supply in chapter 8. Chapter 9 discusses group problem-solving. We show you how to analyze a problem and give you an all-purpose problem-solving model you can adapt to virtually any problem. Chapter 10 explains why group conflicts occur and how they can be managed so that the group benefits instead of suffers. Without some conflict, it is possible that the group has fallen into *groupthink,* a state that prevents a group from using critical thinking skills. We explain how to help prevent this.

In Part Four we discuss special techniques that you can use for a variety of purposes. Chapter 11 focuses on group techniques that are useful to small groups in larger organizations. We provide detailed guidelines for employing such procedures as brainstorming, the problem census, the nominal group technique, quality circles, and PERT. These procedures can be modified to fit hundreds of different organizational needs. Chapter 12 gives you a number of tools you can use to observe problem-solving groups, help them diagnose problems, and provide suggestions for solving those problems. We explain in detail such techniques as verbal interaction analysis, content analysis procedures, SYMLOG, postmeeting reaction forms, and rating scales.

Additionally, we have provided numerous pedagogical aids to help readers get maximum benefit from their study. There is a detailed outline at the beginning of each chapter, a list of key terms and concepts, and several questions to guide and focus your reading. Each chapter concludes with a summary of the major points, a list of review questions, and references to guide further study.

Also, we have augmented the pedagogical aids for instructors who use the text. We have expanded the *Instructor's Manual* by updating and adding to the suggested exercises and learning activities for each of the chapters. In addition, we have added a new section about using the videotape ancillaries available for this text, along with other video materials. We ourselves are quite excited about this aspect of the *Instructor's Manual.* We have been using video case studies in our classes for several semesters and have been pleased with the way students have responded. We think teachers who are looking for updated and vivid ways of teaching small group concepts will particularly appreciate this section.

We have designed this book to be of practical use to you. The suggestions and information we have provided are backed by scholarly research, but we have chosen to emphasize the practical application, not the academic research. We hope the reading of this book will give you all the tools you need to become a more productive group member and an effective leader when you next have the opportunity.

Acknowledgments

We wish to thank the reviewers, all of whom did a conscientious job of reading the manuscript and providing helpful suggestions. We have incorporated many of the suggestions in this second edition:

Dale Basler
Western New Mexico University

Madeline Keaveney
California State University-Chico

Robert E. Nofsinger
Washington State University

Nancy L. Ruda
Columbus State Community College

Brant Short
Idaho State University

PART ONE

Orientation to Small Group Systems

Part One introduces you to the study of small groups. In chapter 1 we define many of the terms you will need in your study of small groups. We discuss the types of small groups you are likely to experience and we explain the participant-observer perspective used throughout the book. Chapter 2 presents you with a framework, general systems theory, to help organize the many concepts important to understanding how groups function.

CHAPTER ONE

Small Groups as the Heart of Society

CHAPTER OUTLINE

Groups in Your Life
Groups as Problem Solvers
Participating in Groups
Groups versus Individuals as Problem Solvers
When a Group Is a Good Choice
When a Group Is Not a Good Choice
Groups, Small Groups, and Small Group Theory
Group
Small Group
Group Dynamics
Communication
Small Group Communication
Classifying Groups by Their Major Purpose
Primary or Secondary Groups
Primary Groups
Secondary Groups
Types of Secondary Groups
Learning Groups
Organizational Groups
Committees
Quality Control Circles
Self-Managed Work Teams
The Participant-Observer Perspective

KEY TERMS AND CONCEPTS

Committee
Communication
Group
Group Dynamics
Learning Groups
Organizational Groups
Participant-Observer (Perspective)
Primary Groups
Quality Control Circle
Secondary Groups
Self-Managed Work Team
Small Group
Small Group Communication
Work Team

STUDY QUESTIONS

1. Why is it important for everyone to have a working knowledge of how problem-solving groups develop and function?
2. How do small groups compare with individuals as solvers of various types of problems?
3. Why do groups produce superior solutions when they function at their best?
4. How are the terms *group, small group, group dynamics,* and *small group communication* used in *Communicating in Groups*?
5. How do the basic purposes of primary and secondary groups differ?

Things looked grim for General Motors in the 1980s.[1] Not only had GM's share of the U.S. car market dropped from 46 percent to 32 percent, but in 1989 the automaker's North American operations barely broke even. Competition from Japanese cars had really hurt. Furthermore, several embarrassing fiascos involving poorly designed, defective and underpowered cars, and an unflattering quasi-documentary (*Roger & Me*) about GM chairman Roger Smith, had nearly destroyed GM's image with the public. The company needed to do something drastic to improve its performance and regain public trust.

GM executives decided to place their hopes on the Saturn, a small car designed to compete directly against Japanese imports. But GM couldn't afford to make the kinds of mistakes with the Saturn that had been made with its other cars, so executives decided to use a revolutionary (for GM) design and manufacturing procedure for the Saturn: the company would use teamwork at all stages of the manufacturing process. In addition to using the best of available technology and manufacturing/operations systems, the Saturn division was established as the mutual responsibility of labor and management to run as they jointly saw fit.

A team of 99 people, including representatives from the United Auto Workers and GM, traveled the world to find the best processes and procedures for use in the new Saturn company. This team designed the new company. One of the most significant decisions was to organize the Saturn Corporation as a set of interdependent small groups—work teams—with authority to control their work procedures. Saturn employees receive an annual salary rather than an hourly wage, but a part of the salary is contingent on the success and profitability of the company.

The company is run by 165 work teams, averaging ten members each, which decide how to run their own areas. The teams have the authority to screen applications, interview applicants, and hire new members for the team. They also determine their own budgets, choose suppliers, and even selected the advertising agency handling Saturn—all team decisions are made by consensus. Team members must be committed to decisions that affect them before the decisions are implemented. The teams have the responsibility for ensuring that the quality of the automobiles produced will stand up to Japanese competition, and they also have the authority they need to carry out their work.

The company represents participatory democracy at its finest. At Saturn, everyone believes that workers know best how their jobs can be done most effectively. Even design decisions are made collaboratively. The Saturn car was developed using simultaneous engineering, where teams of marketers, engineers, suppliers, production workers, accountants, and salespeople contributed their expertise to the design. To make all this collaboration work, GM invests considerable time and money training employees. New workers receive five days of training on how to work in teams and build consensus. This is followed by anywhere from 100 to 750 hours of training in all aspects of the business, including conflict resolution and finance. The Saturn labor agreement calls for workers to spend 12 or 13 days each year in class.

Is it working? So far, critics say the Saturn is built with solid workmanship and will be competitive against Japanese cars. *Consumer Reports* magazine recently reported that Saturns have compiled a reliability record that is much better than average in their first year of production, a landmark for a domestic model. Did teamwork alone make the difference? Of course not. The Saturn division combines the best of modern technology, contemporary inventory and manufacturing operations practices, and a well-designed product with teamwork. All have contributed to Saturn's success. However, the people skills have been essential. In the recruitment of Saturn workers, the interpersonal skills, including those necessary to work effectively in groups, were more important than technical skills.

The Saturn story highlights a principle you must learn to succeed: you've got to be able to work well in teams, task forces, committees, and all kinds of special problem-solving groups if you want to get ahead in the organized world of today. For that matter, this principle will hold true for as long as human society continues. In *Megatrends,* which looks at major trends reshaping the character of American society, Naisbitt declared that Americans are calling for more participative democracy.

Assignment: List all the groups to which you belong. Be sure to include family groups, friendship and other social groups, activity groups, committees, work teams, athletic teams, classroom groups, study groups, political action groups, interest groups, and every other type of small group to which you belong (see figure 1.1).

Nuclear family of 5 people
Three roses friendship group
Evening crew at Wendy's No. 2
Membership committee of Public Relations Student Society of America
Dance arrangements committee of church singles' group
Discussion section 12 of Psychology 102
Backgammon players in Jones Hall
Young Republicans Steering Committee

Figure 1.1   Small groups I belong to.

"Citizens, workers, and consumers are demanding and getting a greater voice in government, business, and the marketplace. The guiding principle of this participatory democracy is that people must be part of the process of arriving at decisions that affect their lives."[2] Participatory democracy, such as that found in the Saturn plant, is largely achieved by working in small groups that provide information to large groups.

Groups in Your Life

The higher you go in any organization (government, service, manufacturing, education, communication, military, or whatever), the more time you will spend working as a member of small groups. Numerous studies have shown this. So, no matter what specific group you are in, you need to know how to behave in ways that are satisfying to you and other members, as well as productive for the larger organization of which your group is a part. If you don't work well in groups, you are more likely to be laid off or frozen at a low level job.

Even as a student, you may be surprised to discover how many groups you belong to that are important to you. Try listing them on paper and see if you find, like most of our students, that the list goes up to 8, 10, 15, or even 20 or more small groups.

We humans are social beings with powerful genetic *needs* to belong to small social groups. We need to affiliate with others of our kind, just as do many other mammals. The human infant is completely dependent on others for its care for a long time before it develops self-reliance. One lone adult cannot provide all a baby needs. This function is provided by small groups, often families with father and mother, but also groupings of the "Full House" sort, kibbutzim, or other child-care groups.

Groups as Problem Solvers

If you are alive, you are constantly solving problems: how to get food, where to sleep safely, how to keep body temperature within normal range while weather conditions are changing, and so on. Life can properly be called an unending series of problem-solving episodes. Solving any problem means coming up with some plan (even if it only takes a split second) and executing it. Planning solutions to problems used to be both the privilege and responsibility of high-status people we call generals, kings, dictators, managers and directors. Carrying out the solutions was usually the work of lower ranked people: secretaries, infantrymen, workers, and other subordinates. But things are changing. As you can see from the Saturn story, more and more planning is done by groups as problems become more complicated in a densely populated society. Even technological problems are not solved by lone rangers, but by groups of technical specialists.

In more democratic societies facing complex problems (AIDS, polluted oceans and beaches, deteriorating cities, and the like), increasing numbers of people are needed to plan workable solutions to problems. If you want to be someone other than a low-level functionary who carries out assignments planned by others, you will need to be able to work effectively in groups. Period!

Participating in Groups

This text emphasizes how groups can become better problem solvers, but that cannot be accomplished by focusing only on the rational side of human behavior. To understand how groups *really* operate, you must know something about human feelings and behavior. We believe that effective group problem solving depends on members understanding and managing such things as informational resources, how members feel about each other, how members feel about the task of the group, how skilled they are at expressing themselves and listening to others, and how well they collectively process the information they have to work with. Group members have a lot of work to do. They must make sure they have the materials (information, tangible resources, time, and so forth) to complete the task, but they also must learn to manage their interpersonal relationships effectively enough to complete the task well.

When groups solve complex problems, they usually go through two major stages: planning and working. The planning stage involves more discussion and interaction. This is the stage where all group members, with their differing viewpoints and opinions, must come to some overall conclusions if the group is to move successfully to the working stage, where the group's solutions are implemented. To be valued by your group, you must learn to become competent at the type of verbal interaction demanded in the group's planning stage. Later, you must demonstrate loyalty to the group by being willing to carry out what the group has planned. While *all* problem-solving groups will engage in planning, only some of them are also responsible for implementation.

There are always tensions among people who must coordinate their behaviors as group members. What to do, when to do it, how to do it must be decided and coordinated. Settling such issues among people with differing desires, beliefs, reasons, habits, and skills when resources are limited (and they always are) is the major source of tensions and stresses that affect *all* groups. Attitudes toward others and groups as a whole, communicative habits and skills, and ability to manage conflicts so the outcomes are satisfactory to all group members are the essence of working in groups.

Participation in a group always requires trade-offs. You give up the total freedom to do *what* you want *when* you want for the advantages of affiliating with others to produce the kind of work possible only when several persons coordinate their efforts. This is true in all small groups, from a tug-of-war team to a task force of engineers designing a rocket. Total submission to a group in violation of your core beliefs or needs is just as harmful as manipulating or forcing others to do your bidding against their desires. This is what *Communicating in Groups* is about: knowing what produces tensions in a group (both in the individuals and the group as a whole), and knowing how to manage the tensions so that the group's decisions are the best that can be made, the members gain from the group, and the organization that gave birth to the group is improved by the group's work.

"You take two of these at the first sign of the onset of boardroom turbulence."

Many organization members have come to dread participation in groups. (Drawing by D. Reilly; © 1985, The New Yorker Magazine, Inc.)

Groups versus Individuals as Problem Solvers

If tension is inevitable in group problem-solving discussions, why not have individuals plan the solutions to all problems? The benefits of having a group tackle a problem can (but not necessarily *will*) outweigh the costs in time and tensions, just as the benefits of marriage *can* outweigh the costs. Whereas in marriage the greatest rewards come from having your needs for belonging and affection met, in small problem-solving groups they come from the quality of the group's solution.

A long line of research into the effectiveness of solutions developed by small groups, compared to those planned by individuals acting alone, has shown that groups are far superior for solving many types of problems.[3] Groups tend to do much better than individuals when several alternative solutions are possible, none of which is known to be superior or "correct." This is the very sort of problem most groups and organizations face. For example: Which of several designs for a car is most likely to sell well? What benefit options should be available to employees? How can precision in machined bearings be improved? How can the destruction of the ozone layer be reduced?

The following actual story illustrates how a group's greater resources can help the problem-solving process. One of us recently participated on a steering committee to establish a new church. Other members of the committee included a lawyer, the widow of a minister, a retired business executive, a health practitioner, and another university faculty member. The lawyer's expertise helped the group incorporate and receive tax-exempt status. The business executive used his knowledge of the business community and his negotiation skills to secure an affordable place to meet. The minister's widow helped the group understand and deal effectively with correspondence from the executives at the denomination's headquarters, who initially opposed the creation of the new church. One of the faculty members used her expertise to create and conduct a prayer circle, and the other helped coordinate the group meetings and record decisions. The health practitioner, who travelled throughout the state, used his contacts to locate effective speakers for the Sunday services until an interim minister could be hired. The steering committee guided the new church for over six months, until by-laws were approved, a board elected, and the church's denomination finally gave its blessing to the venture. None of the members alone could have accomplished this feat, but together they had the expertise, energy and time to devote to the task.

When a Group Is a Good Choice

For several reasons, groups working on problems with several solutions typically make higher quality decisions than do individuals (see table 1.1). Groups usually have a much larger number of possible solutions from which to choose. Group members can help each other think critically by correcting one another's misinformation, erroneous assumptions, and invalid reasoning. Several people can often think of issues to be handled in the process of solving a problem that might be overlooked by any one member. In addition, several people can conduct more thorough investigative research than one person working alone. Group members often counteract each other's tendencies to engage in self-defeating behavior.[4] A further advantage is that group members who are involved in planning a job or procedure usually understand the procedure better and work harder to implement it. In addition, people are more likely to accept a solution that they have had a hand in designing. These principles have resulted in such small group techniques as quality control circles, self-managed work groups, and other sorts of employee participation in classical management functions. No plan for dealing with a problem or performing a task is better than the willingness to make it work on the part of those who must do the work or live with the results. Satisfaction, loyalty, and commitment tend to be higher when people have a voice. This voice is the participative democracy of which Naisbitt wrote and is found at plants like Saturn.

Table 1.1 Why Groups Can Make Better Decisions Than Individuals

1. Groups have more information available about the problem and are less likely to omit something of importance.
2. Groups can get more investigative research and other work done.
3. Group members can correct each other's misinformation, erroneous assumptions, and invalid reasoning.
4. Groups can think of more suggestions, ideas, and alternatives from which to create or choose a solution.
5. Group participation fosters loyalty to the solution and makes implementation easier and faster.

When a Group Is Not a Good Choice

On the other hand, not all sorts of problems are suitable for groups. Nor is democratic participation in decision making by all affected people always a wise or productive use of time. When a problem has a best or correct solution (such as in an arithmetic or accounting task), a skilled person working alone will often exceed the output quality of a group of less knowledgeable people, even if the group includes the highly skilled person as a member. Coordinating work of several persons when conditions are changing rapidly (as in a weather disaster, battle, or ball game) may be done best by one person (a commander, chief, or coach). Likewise, in small groups with certain social, procedural, or personality-mix problems the output may be inferior, even though members may produce it with confidence and pleasure. Much of this book is about how to apply small group theory—based as much as possible on scientific research—to make sure that groups work on the kinds of problems for which they are best suited, and to do so in ways likely to produce a high quality solution (see table 1.2).

Thus far we have seen that small groups are commonly involved in problem solving, that many problems are too complex for even the most talented individuals, and that both the types of problems and how they are handled make a difference. We will now introduce you to the *types* of small groups that engage in problem solving and the situations that create them. To do that we will first define *small group communication* and related terms necessary for your understanding of group communication. As you know, words mean only what we choose to have them mean. For us as writers to communicate well with you as a reader, we must define key terms. It will be equally necessary for you to understand and use our definitions when you think and talk about small group terms while you read this book, discuss it with members of class groups, or write papers required for your study of small groups.

Table 1.2   Problems Appropriate for Groups vs. Individuals

Problems Suitable for a Group

1. The problem is complex; one person is not likely to have all relevant information.
2. There are several acceptable solutions, and one known *best* solution does not exist.
3. Acceptance of the solution by those who are affected is critical.
4. Sufficient time exists for a group to meet, discuss, and analyze the problem.

Problems Suitable for an Individual

1. There is a *best* solution and a member who is a recognized expert most qualified to determine that solution.
2. Conditions are changing rapidly (such as during a fire, natural disaster, or other crisis) and coordination is best done by one person.
3. Time is short and a decision must be made quickly.
4. Group members have personality, procedural, or social problems that make it difficult or impossible for them to work as a team on the solution.

Groups, Small Groups, and Small Group Theory

To understand the term *small group* you must first understand the more general concept, *group*. Similarly, you must grasp the idea of *communication* before you can understand what happens in small group communication. We define these terms here.

Group

Group has been defined or used by writers in a variety of ways. Your previous uses of the word *group* may confuse you when you use this book. We use the term in a very specific way. Being a **group** means that people have interdependent relationships and these relationships are the essence of being a group—no relationships among members, no group. In a group, members are bound together through some commonality of purpose or function. Marvin Shaw, one of the most important writers about small group theory, defines a human group in terms of interaction producing mutual influence: ". . . persons who are interacting with one another in such a manner that each person influences and is influenced by each other person."[5] We add to this notion that group members strive to achieve a common purpose.

Implied in this definition is that any human group has some sort of organization. A collection of people may or may not constitute a group by this definition. For instance, several persons waiting in the same shelter for a bus, but who are not talking to each other, are not a group. If two of them begin to talk about the possibility that the bus will be late, and all the others join in the discussion, a group has been formed, even if it is unimportant and short-lived. Reciprocal, or mutual, influence is the key concept here.

Groups can range in size from small (three) to very large. In this book, we are concerned only with small groups. The principles that pertain to small groups do not necessarily hold true for large ones, and vice versa. Techniques appropriate for groups of from three to seven members may be disastrous if tried in groups of 30, 70, or more. Likewise, communication techniques and procedures appropriate in large group meetings may be harmful to the effective functioning of small groups. For instance, you may have met with a small committee in which a member insisted on following rules of order and precedence developed for large group meetings (e.g., *Robert's Rules of Order*). If you felt irritated and confused by these rules, it may have been because these rules do not fit the size of the group. Likewise if you have been in a large group meeting where there seemed to be no formal procedure for ensuring fairness and equal opportunity, then you have seen why something like *Robert's Rules* is needed for a large group when communication occurs face to face.

Small Group

Small is a relative term: a small elephant is large compared to a huge flea. *Small* as used for human groups has usually been defined either by some arbitrary number or in terms of human perception. We prefer to define it in terms of psychological perception: *We use the term* **small group** *to refer to a group in which individual members perceive each other and are aware of each other as individuals when they interact.* This definition is precise only for a given point in time. A committee of five new members may be perceptually *large* until after each member has had a chance to speak repeatedly, but a seminar of 15 people may be perceptually *small* after several meetings. At that point, each member could name or describe every other, could say who was and who was not at a meeting without taking formal attendance, and could say something about what each contributed to the discussion and meeting. *That* is the idea of *small group* as we use it.

More practically, small groups will usually consist of three to seven members, occasionally more. This seems to be the ideal range, with five as an ideal number if members possess sufficient knowledge and skills to do the job facing the group and have a diversity of perspectives and values relevant to the task. The more members, the more likely there is to be inequity and communication overload for some members. We intentionally exclude the dyad (two-person group) from our definition of *small group* because of overwhelming evidence that dyads function differently. For example, dyads do not form networks or leadership hierarchies. You are most likely to study dyadic communication in a book and/or course about interpersonal or marriage communication.

We are most concerned with *continuing* small groups, the members of which ". . . meet more or less regularly in face-to-face interaction, who possess a common identity or exclusiveness of purpose, and who share a set of standards governing their activity."[6] Such groups have definable stages or phases in their life histories, just as do individuals. Task forces, work crews, sport teams, committees, quality circles, and military squads are examples of such groups. One-meeting groups in which members have a sense of shared purpose, interact face-to-face, share at least some standards and procedures for governing their interaction, and have a sense of each other as group members also qualify as small groups by our definition.

Small groups are real phenomena. They are a life form, though of a different level from that of cells, organs, people, large organizations, and societies. Functional humans cannot exist apart from small groups of their kind. Understanding how they form, develop, and function can increase the satisfaction and joy we experience in life.

Group Dynamics

Like all life forms, small groups function lawfully. That is, certain principles have been observed to hold for all small groups, just as other principles hold for all individual humans and other life forms. The study of ways in which groups form and behave is known as **group dynamics.** Some people have used this term to refer to sets of techniques, rules, or a part of what was called the *human potential movement.* Like others who study small groups, we use it to refer to that ". . . field of inquiry dedicated to advancing knowledge about the nature of groups, the laws of their development, and their interrelations with individuals, other groups, and larger institutions."[7] Much of this book applies findings from the broad research field of group dynamics to the particular small task and problem-solving groups in which you are certain to be involved.

Communication

Communication refers to the perception and response of people to signals produced by other people. We develop this concept in detail in chapter 3, but we introduce it here so you can start to observe how communication functions in a small group setting. The definition states that group members send verbal and nonverbal messages—words, gestures, facial expressions, and so forth—and that the other group members observe and respond to these messages. This implies that members of a group pay attention to each other and coordinate their communication behavior in order to accomplish the group's assignment. We spoke earlier of the interdependence necessary for individuals to become a group. It is the members' communication with each other—their perceiving and responding to one another's signals—that creates this interdependence.

Small Group Communication

Small group communication refers to the part of the field of group dynamics that focuses on the *process* of influence among group members by the exchange of verbal and nonverbal information. Small group communication requires *interacting*. As members create verbal and nonverbal signals that become messages, perceive these messages, interpret them, and respond, they are engaging in small group communication. This is different from public speaking to large groups (audiences), participating in a large assembly (i.e., a legislature or convention), communicating in a more-or-less intimate dyad, or talking with one other person in assigned roles such as *waiter* and *customer*. While basic communication principles are common no matter what the communication setting, our emphasis in *Communicating in Groups* is communication that occurs within the group.

We differentiate small group communication from other communication contexts in a variety of ways. Organizational communication deals with the communication occurring in large structured groups (organizations), whether this communication involves the organization as a whole or occurs between small groups that are parts of the organization. Interpersonal communication is focused on communication between or among individuals as unique persons, not necessarily as members of small groups. Of course, understanding interpersonal communication is essential to functioning optimally in small groups, especially those groups that meet social, affection, and affiliation needs. Intrapersonal communication occurs *within* an individual human being; it includes thinking and the self-communicating that occurs among sensors, organs, nerves, muscles, and so on. All small group communication involves intrapersonal communication within group members.

Classifying Groups by Their Major Purpose

How a specific small group functions will in part reflect general laws of group dynamics, but will also reflect the purpose for which the group exists. We have classified small groups according to the reasons they exist.

Primary or Secondary Groups

Many small group writers accept the theory, proposed by psychologist Will C. Schutz, that three major forces motivate human interaction. These are the needs for inclusion, affection, and control. The first two concern needs for belonging and caring from other people. The third, control, refers to the need for power or

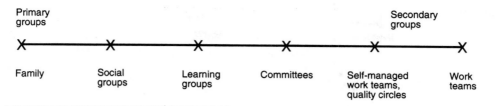

Figure 1.2 Types of primary and secondary groups.

control over the world in which we exist, including the people we encounter.[8] A group is classified by sociologists as *primary* or *secondary* depending upon which of these needs is the major reason it exists (see figure 1.2).

Primary Groups

Primary groups form to meet the first two types of needs, inclusion and affection. They may accomplish work, but that is not their primary objective. Love, caring, avoiding feelings of loneliness, sharing, feeling cared about—these are the motives for which we willingly give up some freedom as individuals to be members of primary groups. We are all familiar with families, friendship groups, sororities and fraternities, drinking buddies (for example, the regulars in *Cheers*), cliques, gangs, and those many small groups that seem to form spontaneously to meet interpersonal needs for inclusion and affection.

Secondary Groups

Secondary groups exist mainly for control needs: solving all sorts of problems. They are task groups. A secondary group may create or implement some plan (solution) to provide control. Control, in this sense, may include supplying physical needs for food and water, preventing or controlling disease, coping with insects and other vermin, or even more mundane matters like fixing a flat tire or designing a computer program to organize recipes. This book is mostly about secondary groups. Task forces, committees, work crews, quality circles, and learning groups are all secondary when classified by major purpose.

No group is purely primary or secondary in its functioning. Primary groups encounter and solve problems. Secondary groups supply members with some sense of inclusion and often with affection. Sometimes members of secondary groups lose their perspective and act as if group membership and loyalty are the only important things; however, this is a distortion of the main purpose of a secondary group.

Types of Secondary Groups

Secondary groups tackle a wide range of tasks. They may be formed for one specific job or a variety of related tasks. Included are learning groups, organizational groups (such as committees, work teams, self-managed work teams, and quality control circles), and activity groups.

Learning Groups

Learning groups of many sorts exist to help members with their personal needs to understand or to control events in their lives and the world around them. Your class is a learning group (probably a large one) which may be further organized into several small learning groups. Learning groups of people from preschool age to residents of retirement homes discuss all sorts of interests. Study, therapy, support, and personal growth groups are all learning groups. They do not exist to solve a problem as a group or to produce some item, though they often help members in solving personal problems. This book is not focused on such groups. Rather, it emphasizes problem-solving groups, most of which exist within larger organizations to solve either specific or general problems that face the organization. Certainly *learning* about the problem does occur in other types of secondary groups, but learning is normally just the first step in a long process. With learning groups, learning is an end in itself.

Organizational Groups

Organizations such as corporations, schools, agencies, legislatures, bureaus, large departments, hospitals, and even social clubs create problem-solving groups to serve them. **Organizational groups** include any such problem-solving group formed within the context of a larger organization.

There are two major types of organizational groups, planning and work groups, which are not mutually exclusive. Any person can be a member of many such groups in one organization, such as a committee, a quality control circle, and a self-managed work team.

Committees Most **committees** are created by larger organizations to perform some service for the organization. The organization *commits* a problem or duty to the small group (committee) created for that purpose. For example, a fact-finding committee may be asked to investigate the scope and effect of cheating on intercollegiate athletic rules, then report its conclusions. An advisory committee may be formed to determine the nature of problems with health care availability in the U.S., consider possible solutions, and recommend one or more to the President. Another type of committee may be authorized to write a job description, search for applicants, receive and evaluate credentials, and recommend someone to hire. Occasionally a special committee is empowered both to select a plan and execute it, though in most cases problem-solving committees do not go beyond recommending. Instead, they are usually advisory, reporting to an executive or board that has final authority and responsibility for deciding. However, wise administrators usually follow the advice given by such a special committee, or present a good reason for not doing so. A different committee is sometimes created with power to carry out the chosen plan, or an individual or work team may be assigned to execute the solution. Committees in organizations may be *standing* or *ad hoc*. Another special kind of committee is the *conference* committee.

A *standing* committee is generally a permanent committee required by the bylaws of an organization. The bylaws should include a procedure for creating it as well as a description of its purpose and area of freedom to act. For example, a *membership committee* may be responsible for recruiting new members and for screening the qualifications of applicants. A *legislative affairs* committee is often given responsibility for screening proposed laws that would affect the organization and reporting about them to the organization. Such a committee might also be authorized to propose new legislation or to lobby at the city, state, or national level.

As the name implies, standing committees continue indefinitely. However, the membership is usually changed by election or appointment on a periodic basis. Usually, some members continue from one year into the next while others are replaced. A typical term of office for a standing committee member is three years.

Ad hoc committees are created to perform one special assignment, then go out of existence. The end product might be a report of findings, or a recommended solution—e.g., evaluations of several sites for a new plant, or suggestions for new products to manufacture. This end product is often a report delivered in writing and orally to the person(s) who created the special committee.

Today such groups are often called *task forces*, with members selected because their knowledge and skills are thought necessary to do the group's work. Presidents have created many task forces to investigate and make recommendations on such national concerns as illegal drug traffic, acid rain, the condition of national parks, the effects of pornography, waste in government expenditures, disease epidemics, and many more. Innovative production and service corporations are constantly being reorganized into special task forces as their markets, technologies, and competitors change. Anyone above the lowest levels in any private or public organization is likely to serve on many task forces during a lifetime of work. Knowing how to get a task force organized and working smoothly as a unit is vital to corporate life. *Communicating in Groups* discusses this in particular.

Conference committees are composed of members who represent other groups that must find common ground in order to accomplish their work. For example, suppose both the U.S. Senate and the House of Representatives independently have written versions of a bill that will affect health care. The Senate and House versions of the bill will contain differences that must be resolved before it becomes law. A joint Senate-House conference committee will then be established, with senators and congresspeople as members, to iron out differences between the two versions of the bill. Conference committees do such things as coordinate efforts of law enforcement agencies in stopping drug traffic, achieve agreement between managers and workers on terms of employment and wages, or establish procedures for snow removal on highways passing through several cities. When members of a conference agree on a plan, they normally recommend it to their respective parent organizations, which must then decide whether or not to accept and enact the recommended plan. We will use the term *conference* to refer only to such groups of representatives, never as a synonym for *committee* or *task force*.

Quality Control Circles **Quality control circle** is a generic name for small groups of company employees who volunteer to tackle any issue that may affect job performance. Such groups may have different names in different organizations, but in all cases they are concerned with the quality and quantity of their work output, and attempt to improve their competitiveness with other organizations. Quality circles resulted from a collaboration between W. Edwards Deming and Dr. Joseph Juran, Americans, and Dr. Kaoru Ishikawa, a Japanese professor.[9] After World War II, Japan had to rebuild most of its industry and was notorious for low-quality products. In a relatively short time, Japan became the most productive industrialized society, famous for high-quality cars, optics, electronic equipment, tools, and so forth. Much of this success has been attributed to the quality control circle movement. The quality circle idea meshes well with Japanese culture, which is much more group-oriented and less individualistic than that of the United States.

After taking a terrible beating in the marketplace, American manufacturers began to study the quality circle idea, even sending many people to Japan for first-hand study. Now hundreds of major and minor companies, service agencies, government bureaus, and other institutions have developed some version of the quality control circle.

Each circle consists of a small number of people from a department or division who meet regularly during work hours to solve production problems that either they or managers identify. The leader may be elected or appointed. Managers must consider seriously and respond in a timely way to all changes proposed by the employees. The rewards of a change that is adopted must be shared by all people, and should not just benefit managers and stockholders. Some sort of profit sharing and job security is essential for this small group problem-solving form of consultative management to work. Needless to say, it has not worked in settings where employees are treated as expendable production tools.

Self-Managed Work Teams Self-managed work teams (sometimes called autonomous work groups) combine features of both planning and work groups. These are often assembly crews given considerable freedom to plan their work procedures and individual assignments. A self-managed work team elects its leader instead of having an appointed first-line supervisor. The work of a number of SWTs is coordinated by a middle manager. With fewer managers and greater authority to establish work procedures and control quality, more person-time is spent actually producing. Studies of such decision making by workers have indicated large increases in morale and cohesiveness (i.e., loyalty) in addition to better work.

(The Saturn Corporation is a good example of this.) Again, everyone must benefit from any productivity increases if this relatively democratic small group procedure is to work well.

The **work team** is a type of self-managed group that performs operations to build, operate, or otherwise implement some sort of plan that another group or individual has devised. The committees and quality circles described earlier spend more time in planning, whereas work teams spend more time executing plans. A work team may be a surgical team in a hospital, the night custodial staff in a school building, a crew assembling boat trailers, a restaurant staff, or firefighters battling a blaze. Probably many of you, like ourselves, have served as members of work teams in fast-food restaurants, on play production committees, and on summer construction crews.

Efforts of work team members are usually directed by a supervisor. Supervision of work teams is only one function of what is called *management*. Managers frequently are involved in the planning stages of problem solving, after which they give the plans to a work team to carry out, under the supervision of a manager.

The Participant-Observer Perspective

Earlier, we suggested that you make a list of all the groups to which you belong. Even as you learn about the principles of communicating in groups from reading this book, you will continue to be a member of these groups. You may find yourself wanting to use some of the principles and techniques you learn to improve the functioning of your groups. This means that you will be in the role of a **participant-observer,** someone who is a regular member of the group but who at the same time actively observes the group and adapts to its processes and procedures. Most group members have not been trained to be effective group participants. This makes it especially important for us who *do* know something about small group communication to monitor the group's discussions and help our groups perform as well as possible. A skilled participant-observer can help a group by supplying information, procedural suggestions, and interpersonal communication skills needed by the group. This is an important focus of this book— to help you become a more valuable group member as you sharpen your skills in observing small group processes.

The balance between participant and observer may vary; for example, the participant-observer may be primarily a participant who occasionally makes pertinent observations regarding the observation of the group, or may be primarily an observer who sometimes participates in the group's discussion. Some groups establish an *observer* role for the group, then elect an individual (or rotate the job) to watch the group's process and provide a periodic assessment of how well the group is performing.

We encourage you to become a participant-observer for the groups you are in. As you read the information in this book, try to think of examples from your own group experiences that illustrate the principles described in the text. Start paying attention in a conscious way to the processes of small group communication. As you learn more about communicating effectively in groups, you will feel more comfortable making suggestions to serve the groups to which you belong. We provide additional information about the participant-observer and other types of observers in chapter 12.

Summary

Humans inherit needs to form small groups, but they do not instinctively function well in them. Indeed, many people dislike working in small groups, perhaps because so many groups operate badly. The need for any person to understand the dynamics of a wide range of small groups and to be able to function well as a member of them is steadily increasing. Group skills are imperative for anyone today who wants to rise above the bottom ranks of any organization in American society.

Being a group member will mean experiencing tensions because the thinking and work of several people must be coordinated. Knowing how to manage these tensions so that small groups can succeed as problem solvers is the focus of *Communicating in Groups*. Groups surpass individuals in solving complex problems where many solutions are possible and no one solution is clearly better. This superiority results from many sources: groups can generate more potential solutions than can individuals, they can do more exhaustive investigations than individuals, they can think of more issues that need to be considered before making a decision, and members can counteract each other's self-defeating thinking and actions. Also, group members show more acceptance of the solution, as well as more loyalty and dedication to the organization, when they participate in making a decision than when a plan is imposed on them.

Small applied to groups of people is a relative perceptual term. A *small group* is one in which every member has some awareness of every other member as a unique person. Most small task groups range from three to seven members, but they can be as large as 15 or more when members have had enough time to become well acquainted with each other. *Small group communication* is the exchange of verbal and nonverbal signals by which members of a group mutually influence each other. To study this field, one must use with precision such terms as: *communication, group, small group, learning group, committee, task force, conference, quality control circle,* and *self-managed work teams.* Readers are encouraged to adopt the participant-observer perspective as they learn about the principles of small group communication.

Review Questions

1. What indicates that humans have inherent tendencies to form small groups? Why does every educated person need to understand and be able to function well in small groups?
2. Of the two major stages in problem solving, which is likely to involve the most small group discussion? Why?
3. On what kinds of problems do small groups tend to surpass even *expert* individuals as problem solvers? Why?
4. Explain the idea that a small group is a perceptual phenomenon. Give at least three examples each of small and large groups, then explain how a large group of 15 might become a small group without losing any members.
5. Is a task force an ad hoc or standing committee? Would a conference be classified as a committee? Is a committee a conference group?
6. What organizational conditions help quality control circles and self-managed work teams produce more and better work?
7. What is a participant-observer and how can a participant-observer help a group?

Bibliography

Brilhart, John K., and Galanes, Gloria J. *Effective Group Discussion.* 7th ed. Dubuque, IA: Wm. C. Brown, 1992.

Ruch, William V. *Corporate Communications: A Comparison of Japanese and American Practices.* Westport, CT: Quorum Books, 1984: 205–222.

Shaw, Marvin E. *Group Dynamics: The Psychology of Small Group Behavior.* 3d ed. New York: McGraw-Hill, 1981.

References

1. Information for the following story about General Motors is compiled from the following articles: William B. Cook, "Ringing in Saturn," *U.S. News & World Report* (October 22, 1990): 51–54; S. C. Gwynne, "The Right Stuff," *Time* (October 29, 1990): 74–77, 81, 84; "Road Test," *Consumer Reports* (April, 1992): 266, (July, 1992): 427; James B. Treece, "Here Comes GM's Saturn," *Business Week* (April 9, 1990): 56–62; and Douglas Williams, "Shop Floor Democracy," *Automotive Industries* (June, 1989): 48–49.
2. John Naisbitt, *Megatrends: Ten New Directions Transforming Our Lives* (New York: Warner Books, 1984): 75.
3. This line of research began in 1928 and continues to the present. For a concise summary of the research up to 1980, see Marvin E. Shaw, *Group Dynamics,* 3d ed. (New York: McGraw-Hill, 1981): 57–64.

4. Dennis S. Gouran and Randy Y. Hirokawa, "Counteractive Functions of Communication in Effective Group Decision Making," in *Communication and Group Decision Making,* eds. Randy Y. Hirokawa and Marshall Scott Poole (Beverly Hills, CA: Sage, 1986): 81–90.

5. Shaw, *Group Dynamics:* 8.

6. Paul V. Crosby, ed., *Interaction in Small Groups* (New York: Macmillan, 1975): 7.

7. Dorwin Cartwright and Alvin Zander, *Group Dynamics: Research and Theory,* 3d ed. (New York: Harper & Row, 1968): 7.

8. William C. Schutz, *FIRO: A Three-Dimensional Theory of Interpersonal Behavior* (New York: Rinehart, 1958).

9. William V. Ruch, *Corporate Communications: A Comparison of Japanese and American Practices* (Westport, CT: Quorum Books, 1984): 205.

CHAPTER TWO

Groups as Structured Open Systems

CHAPTER OUTLINE

Overview of General Systems Theory
The Small Group as a System
Definition of a System
Concepts Vital to Understanding Systems
Inputs
Throughput Processes
Outputs
Environment
Characteristics of Systems
Open and Closed Systems
Interdependence
Feedback
Multiple Causes, Multiple Paths
Life Cycles in the System
Organizations as Systems of Groups

KEY TERMS AND CONCEPTS

Closed System	Life Cycle
Environment	Multiple Causes
Feedback	Multiple Paths
Input	Open System
Interaction	Output
Interdependence	System
	Throughput Processes

STUDY QUESTIONS

1. Why is *system* such a useful perspective for studying small groups?
2. Why are egalitarianism and responsibility vital characteristics of group members?
3. What are inputs, throughput processes, and outputs of a system?
4. How do open and closed systems differ?
5. What does *interdependence* mean in the functioning of a small group system?
6. What does *feedback* refer to?
7. How do the terms *multiple causes* and *multiple paths* relate to small group systems?
8. What are the stages in the life cycle of a small group system?
9. In what ways are modern organizations composed of networks of groups?

When "Slammer" Rogers graduated, all the Rocky Ridge Community College basketball fans were worried about whether the team could keep its high standing in the conference without its star player. The team had relied heavily on his slam-dunking ability. The other players knew that when they passed the ball to him, Slammer would score six times out of ten. The coaches had spent a lot of their time scouting high school players and gathering as much information about possible replacements as they could. However, potential recruits were afraid to commit themselves because they believed that the team's success depended on Slammer, and without him the team was bound to fail. When the coaches were not able to recruit anyone with his slam-dunking skill, morale on the team fell.

In desperation, the coaches decided to place a player nicknamed "Speedy" in Slammer's starting position. While Speedy didn't have the height to dunk the ball, he was lightning-fast and almost impossible to catch. In addition, he was outgoing, always "up," and his enthusiasm was infectious. The coaches changed their game strategy to adapt to the new team conditions. Rather than relying on one powerhouse player, the activity on the court was now spread among all the players. As the team continued its winning streak, morale among players and fans began to rise, spurring the whole team on to even greater success and first place in its conference. As an added benefit, the coaches found that recruiting became easier as increasing numbers of high school players wanted to play on a winning team.

This story illustrates several important aspects of systems theory, the focus of this chapter. We will return to the story later to provide examples of what we mean. First, we will give you an overview of general systems theory and show you why we think it furnishes a useful framework for examining small group communication.

Overview of General Systems Theory

General systems theory was developed by a biologist, Ludwig von Bertalanffy, as a way to examine and explain complex, living organisms. Because living organisms are constantly changing, it is difficult to study them. When a biologist describes an organism, the description is out of date as soon as it is written. Only basic processes and relationships display any constancy. Think for a moment about your own body, one of the most complex of all organisms. Although it seems to operate as a single unit, in reality it is composed of many smaller units that work interdependently to sustain your life. When you walk across the room, for example, your muscles, skeletal, nervous, circulatory and respiratory systems all cooperate in moving you to your destination. Even if you are sitting still, your body is involved in constant activity—your eyelids are blinking, your heart is beating, you are breathing automatically, and so forth. Even your individual cells are engaged in taking in nourishment through the blood, restoring themselves, and excreting waste through the cell walls. A unit involved in such complicated, continuous activity is hard to study. Fortunately, Bertalanffy's work with systems theory provides us with a way of looking at how a system's parts are related to each other, even while they are changing.

For example, consider what happens to the various parts of your body if some event frightens you. Imagine you are walking along the sidewalk when a snarling dog runs toward you. Automatically the sight of the dog, registered through your eyes to the brain, triggers a number of changes in your body. Your muscles begin to tense in a typical "fight-or-flight" response as adrenalin is released into your bloodstream. Your pulse quickens and your breathing becomes shallow. Your blood is diverted away from internal organs to your muscles, stopping temporarily unnecessary functions like digestion so you have the energy you need to run away. When the owner restrains the dog, your body may begin to shake in relief. Eventually, the various systems in your body—muscle, nerve, hormone, circulatory, and so on—return to normal as you relax again. The perspective of systems theory helps us look at all these individual systems separately, but reminds us that, because they operate together, they must be examined *together* if we are to understand the system as a whole.

Systems theory has helped social scientists by giving us a useful framework for looking at complex human groupings such as organizations, families, and other small groups. Small groups *are* complex. Many individual elements affect the operation of a group—the reason the group was formed, the personalities of the group members, the information members have, the type of leadership, how the group handles conflict, and how successful the group has been in accomplishing its assigned task, to name only a few. Systems theory concepts keep us from oversimplifying our description of group interaction. They help us remember that groups are constantly changing, so operational procedures cannot be fixed once-and-for-all, and then ignored. Also, systems theory encourages us to recognize that there are many reasons something happens in a group, not just one single cause. It also invites us to look for several outcomes or effects of each individual action. Systems theory reminds us that no elements of a group can be understood in isolation from the other elements. All parts interact to produce the entity we call a "small group."

The Small Group as a System

We will now present concepts and definitions of terms that are important to your understanding of a small group as a system. We will use the winning basketball team we presented at the beginning of the chapter as an example of a small group.

Definition of a System

A **system** (in the example, a small group called a "team") consists of a set of elements that function interdependently with each other. The system (group) also functions interdependently with the environment in which it operates as part of a larger system. This implies that a group is made up of several elements that influence one another, and that the group both affects and is affected by its surroundings.

Consider the basketball team described earlier (see also figure 2.1). Some of the elements whose interaction affected the team included: (1) the players themselves, with their various abilities; (2) the game plan (for example, whether one player was the "star" or whether the action was spread out among all the players); (3) the leadership within the team members (Speedy's ability to motivate the other players, for instance); and (4) the ability of the coaches to assess the players' abilities and devise appropriate plans. Notice also the interaction of the group with its surroundings. The attitudes of the fans served first to depress then later to inspire the players. In return, the team's success influenced the fans and the potential high school recruits. To acquire a more complete understanding of systems theory you need to understand certain concepts basic to all systems.

Concepts Vital to Understanding Systems

Four concepts are essential to your understanding of the specific elements of systems, particularly small group systems. Our explanations of these concepts is based on scholarly work by Katz and Kahn.[1]

Inputs

Elements involved in a group's life processes can be classified into three broad categories: inputs, throughputs, and outputs. The first of these categories, **inputs,** consists of all those factors—people, information, energies, and other resources—that are brought into the group from outside (see table 2.1). Inputs are the "raw materials" with which the group forms initially and which the members use to perform their work. For example, the abilities of the basketball players—whether they can slam dunk or not, whether they are relatively fast or slow, how well they can "read" the defenses of the other team—are all characteristics that the players bring with them to the group and influence how well the team performs on the court. Other inputs include the continuous stream of information the coaches gather about the strengths and weaknesses of opposing teams and the new techniques and strategies both players and coaches learn as they keep developing their skills.

Perhaps your class has been divided into groups to complete a group project of some kind. Examples of inputs to your project group include the group's purpose (beginning with the assignment your instructor gave you), the members'

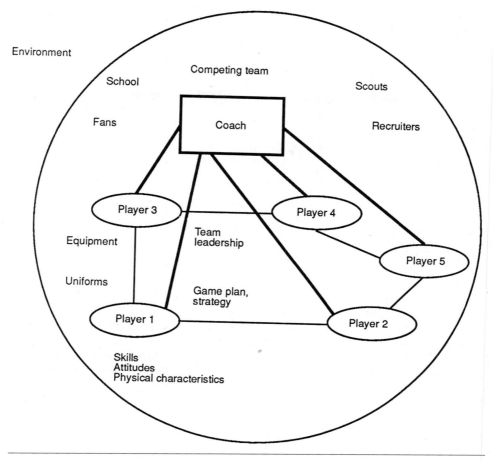

Figure 2.1 A basketball team as a small group system.

attitudes toward the project, the abilities and experiences of the members, the information members have or are able to find about the topic, and physical or social features of the environment that may affect the group, such as classroom noise that makes it hard to hear other members.

Because the attitudes and behavioral patterns of members are so vital to group processes, we discuss them here as an incentive for you to evaluate yourself as a potential group member. Will you be more of an asset or liability to groups of peers? The answer depends on your communication skills, your knowledge, and your attitudes toward information, other persons, and the group. We will explore the impact of attitudes toward information and communication skills in detail in later chapters. For this next section, think about your values and attitudes toward other members and the group.

Table 2.1 Examples of Small Group Inputs

Members

Personalities and characteristics (like age, gender)
Needs
Attitudes
Values
Abilities and skills

Resources

Information about the task
Knowledge and expertise
Time available for group work
Tangible resources (money, materials)

Environmental Factors

Physical surroundings
Degree of support from parent group or organization

Egalitarianism is vital if people are to work as co-equal team members instead of in superior-inferior relationships (such as boss/subordinate). "Egalitarianism" refers to the belief that all people should have the same rights as group members. Do leaders have the right to give orders as they see fit, or only to coordinate the behavior of members by exercising just those controls that group members authorize? How you answer that question shows whether you are predominantly egalitarian or authoritarian in your view of leader-follower relations. *Authoritarian* committee members tend to be bossy when they are in charge, but are subservient to chairpersons, even when a chair asks for unethical behavior. Select an authoritarian as chair and you have a petty dictator who assigns tasks to members regardless of their interests and makes major decisions for the group. Fortunately, being aware of a tendency to act in an authoritarian manner helps most people resist such conduct in both themselves and others. The more educated people become, the more likely they are to be egalitarian.

A strong sense of *personal responsibility* for the success of a group is typical of members who make major contributions to group achievement. In an ideal group, every member exerts the effort and time required to accomplish group goals such as winning a hard-fought basketball game in the closing minutes, completing an important written report, or producing an outstanding show. Such results depend on every person acting as if success depends totally on him or her, and it does. In small groups **everyone** is needed—there is no room for freeloaders. Everyone in a class project group must chip in to compile a complete bibliography and read all the references it contains, interview experts, make observations, conduct tests, and so forth. Any member not making such contributions is likely to be deeply resented, regardless of his or her excuses.

Responsible members are highly involved in the activity of the group. They communicate willingly, expressing what they think and hope. And they support group outcomes by doing follow-up work and speaking highly of the group to nonmembers. For example, one of the authors participated in a musical production by a group of highly responsible and cohesive members. The members built all the scenery, made their own costumes, sold tickets, and afterwards even struck the set and cleaned the theatre. After the production, they met to socialize and plan a subsequent production, speaking often of how "terrific it was to work with such a great, supportive bunch of people."

In most small group communication classes, we have found that one or two project groups are plagued with irresponsible members who want credit for the work but are unwilling to do an equal share. They fail to show for meetings, they miss deadlines for reports, they disappear with essential data, or they are absent for rehearsals. Irresponsible members seem to us to be the greatest single source of bad feelings among group members and of poor quality projects. In the business world such deadwood is weeded out of self-managing work teams and task forces, or the organization is bankrupted.

Throughput Processes

The **throughput processes** of the group are the activities within the group as it goes about its work (see table 2.2). These include processes like the development of roles, rules, and leadership; how members handle conflict; and how members evaluate the information they receive. Throughput processes are the "how" of the group, including all the verbal and nonverbal behaviors that occur within the group. In our basketball team example, the coaches' use of a new strategy that distributed the court action among *all* the players is an example of a throughput process. The informal leadership of Speedy, whose enthusiasm motivated the other members, is also part of the team's throughput processes.

In another example, members of your classroom group may have developed the habit of examining critically all the information they bring to meetings and arguing openly before they reach any decision. This style of handling conflict is an example of a throughput process. You can probably see that its effect on the group's decisions will differ from the effects on decisions of another group whose members uncritically accept any and all information.

The heart of the group's throughput process is **interaction,** or the mutual influence that occurs when people communicate with each other. You may be accustomed to thinking of *interaction* as any talk that occurs within the group, but it actually involves more than that. Interaction includes all the verbal and nonverbal behavior in the group, and implies that members of the group are open to each other's persuasive attempts. Interaction assumes that members are aware of one another, are simultaneously sending and receiving messages designed to influence, and are affected by one another.

Table 2.2   Examples of Small Group Throughput Processes

Members' Behaviors

Degree of encouragement for presenting ideas
Demonstration of members' willingness to work
Dogmatic or otherwise stifling behaviors
Methods of expressing and resolving disagreements
Degree to which cohesiveness is expressed

Group Norms

Support for using critical thinking skills to test ideas versus uncritical acceptance of ideas
Support for open disagreement versus suppression of conflict
Support for relative equality among members versus a strict hierarchy

Communication Networks

Extent to which each member talks to each other member
Extent to which participation is distributed evenly

Status Relationships

Type of leadership
Degree to which power and influence are shared

Procedures

Communication
Decision making and problem solving
Method for implementing solutions

Outputs

Outputs are the "results," the products of the group's throughput processes (see table 2.3). They include obvious outcomes, such as decisions the group has made and written reports. However, they also include less obvious results like cohesiveness, member satisfaction, personal growth of individual members, and changes in the structure of the group. In our basketball example, a clear result of the coaches' new strategy was a winning season, but outputs also included the increased morale experienced by the players and their new skills, since the modified game plan called for all players to participate more actively in the game.

Although we hope that the outputs of a small group's interaction are positive and helpful, some outputs are destructive to both the group itself and the organization that established the group. Hasty decisions that have not been carefully made, dissatisfaction of group members, and shoddy products are examples of destructive outputs. Harmful outputs are like toxic wastes, dangerous to everyone involved. For example, a committee that produces an inaccurate report may cause the organization accepting the report to take actions that reduce profits and eliminate jobs. A work group where members hate each other can produce an atmosphere of tension and mistrust that poisons the entire organization. An uncontrolled athletic program can weaken the academic quality of a college or university.

Table 2.3   Examples of Small Group Outputs

Tangible Outcomes

Reports
Recommendations
Solutions and decisions
Physical objects (e.g., table decorations, assembled cars)

Intangible Outcomes

Feelings among members (cohesiveness, trust; disharmony, dislike)
Personal growth of members
Personal satisfaction of members
Modifications in throughput procedures (such as alterations in the status relationships, use of different
   conflict resolution strategies, etc.)

Environment

A group does not exist apart from its surroundings or **environment,** which consists of everything outside the group that affects the group. In our example, the fans influenced the team's morale and the enthusiasm of the players. Notice also that the team affected its environment as well. When the public realized that the team could continue to win without its former star player, high school students, reassured by its success, now wanted to play for the team.

As another example, your classroom group's immediate environment is the classroom. The group is affected by whether the classroom is pleasant or ugly, noisy or quiet. In addition, what your friends in other classes say or do may cause your group to change a procedure, a topic, an approach, and so forth. These friends and their classes are part of your group's environment, too.

Characteristics of Systems

The concepts that follow describe several important characteristics of living systems. These characteristics help explain how a system functions, both internally and within the surrounding environment.

Open and Closed Systems

Whether a system is *open* or *closed* is determined by the amount of interaction a group has with its environment. A **closed system** (we know of *no* completely closed human system) has little interaction with its environment, whereas an **open system** has a great deal (see figure 2.2). As we discussed earlier, our basketball team had a moderate amount of interaction with its surroundings. The team was affected by the fans' reactions, and the fans and general public were influenced by the team's successes as well.

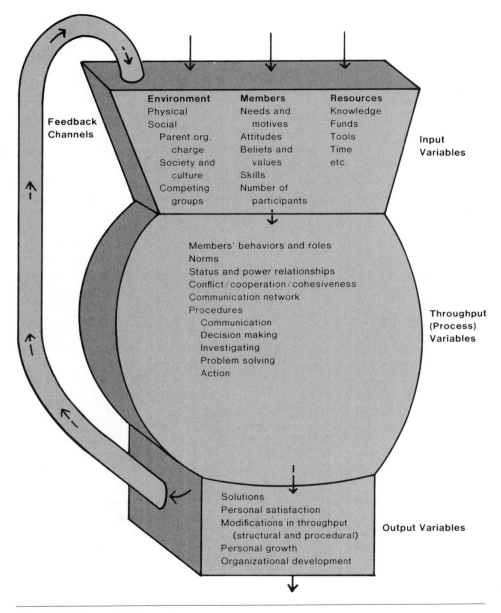

Figure 2.2 A model of a small group as an open system.

In a more familiar example, the United States is a relatively open human system. There is a free interchange of ideas, information, and people flowing between the U.S. and other countries. China, on the other hand, has been a relatively closed society. Travel into and out of China is carefully monitored and restricted, and ideas that contrast with official government positions are censored.

Each position has advantages and disadvantages. The United States is finding it hard to control the influx of drugs into the U.S. from other countries because its borders are so open. On the other hand, some restrictive countries experience a shortage of basic goods and technology that are developed outside their territories. Some American companies, resisting the changes brought by "outsiders," prefer to stay as closed to outside influence as possible. This enables managers to maintain more control over what happens internally, but it also cuts the company off from what could be helpful information that might improve its operation and profits.

It is a distinct advantage for most groups to maintain openness and free interchange with the environment. For example, the groups in Ford Motor Company that were responsible for the design of Ford's successful Taurus automobile made a point of seeking input (information, ideas, suggestions) from the factory workers who would build the Taurus and many of whom could be expected to buy it. The workers supplied numerous suggestions which were adopted. If the Taurus engineering group had remained closed to opinions from workers and others outside their immediate group, the Taurus might not have been so well designed and sought after by the car-buying public.

Interdependence

Interdependence refers to the fact that each element of a system influences and is influenced by the other elements. Just as the system as a whole is affected by its environment, so are the system's individual components affected by each other. Have you ever set up a row of dominoes, then tipped over the first one and watched the others fall in turn? That's interdependence. So it is within small groups, as one element, idea, behavior, or person can change the functioning of the entire group. For example, appointing a strong, controlling leader may mean that conflict in a group is suppressed, that information and input is not actively sought, that member satisfaction with the group is low, and that eventually the group disbands for lack of member participation. In our basketball story, we saw how the players' abilities determined, in part, the coaches' strategy, and how the personality of individual players like Speedy could spur a team to greater effort, which in turn increases the likelihood of team success. Each of these separate elements affect each other.

There is another characteristic of interdependence among elements of a small group: the interdependent goal toward which all group members work. The members of the group rely on each other as they strive to reach their objective; one member cannot reach the objective alone. As with the basketball team, group members win and lose as a group. It is impossible for sports teams to have one member win and the rest of the team lose. So it is with most small groups as they work to accomplish a task as a group. If *one* member is to achieve the goal, then *all* members must achieve it. For example, if your project group is to give a presentation to the rest of the class, the goal is reached for *all* members when the presentation is completed.

Feedback

One valuable feature of human systems is that they are able to adapt to changing conditions and circumstances. In part they can do this through the use of **feedback,** or part of the system's outputs that are returned to the system in the form of inputs. Feedback enables the system to monitor its progress toward the goal and make corrections when needed.

A useful example to illustrate this concept occurs when you drive a car. If the car veers to the left on a straight road, you know that you must steer it to the right to get it back on course. Seeing the car veer left is a type of visual feedback, based on the car's performance (output), that is given back to you in the form of information (input) showing you the car isn't traveling straight. In our basketball story, the coaches saw that their new strategy was successful. This feedback indicated that what they were doing *was* working, so they didn't need to change strategy again.

Assume for a moment that your classroom group is given the assignment of writing a group research paper on small group communication, and that it must submit a written outline to the instructor for comments before the final paper is written. The outline represents part of the group's output, which is sent out into the group's environment (in this case, the instructor). Let's say the group receives a *D* grade on its outline. The poor grade is feedback, information from the teacher showing that the group needs to correct something if it is to reach its goal of producing a successful group paper and receiving a good grade.

Multiple Causes, Multiple Paths

One feature of all living systems, including small groups, is complexity. Usually, many factors combine to produce a single outcome, indicated by the concept of **multiple causes.** As an example of multiple causes, the Rocky Ridge basketball team had high morale at the end of its winning season. This was due probably to the fact that the team was successful, that the fans supported the team, that the team had a leader who was well liked and effective, that all the members contributed to the team's success, and to other factors that are not readily apparent. Too often, individuals try to pinpoint a single cause for a group outcome. For example, you may have heard someone say, "We would have come up with an excellent proposal if our chair had listened to our suggestions. As it was, everybody hated the group." Well, the behavior of the group's chair definitely contributed to the group's low morale, but other factors probably had an impact as well. Perhaps members did not like each other, the task was not an interesting one, or the group did not have sufficient time or information to do its best. At any rate, all of these factors interacted to produce the outcome of dissatisfaction.

A related principle of groups is that there is usually more than one appropriate way to reach a particular objective. This principle is indicated by the concept of **multiple paths.** For example, there are a number of ways to plan a fun party, and a variety of ways to develop a respectable undergraduate curriculum for communication majors. Rocky Ridge's basketball team had two winning seasons—one where a single slam-dunk player was used as the central figure, and the other where the action was spread among all team members. Which was the "right" way? Both were right—the most effective approach depended upon the characteristics of the members. Also, the concept of multiple paths implies that two or more groups could come up with similar solutions to a problem, even though each group had members with different abilities and areas of expertise, leadership styles, and ways of resolving differences of opinion. Like "multiple causes," the concept of "multiple paths" encourages us to recognize the complexity of small groups.

Life Cycles in the System

A living system's primary objective is survival, but at some point this may be difficult or impossible. Even a casual look at nature tells us that the natural **life cycle** for any living system includes conception and birth, growth and development, maturity, decline, and finally death (see figure 2.3). Living organisms constantly adapt to changing environmental conditions as they fight off their eventual deaths as long as possible. For example, human beings take in food and drink to ensure that their bodies have available to them the nutrients they need to live. In the same way, human groups and organizations usually do everything in their power to help ensure their own continuation. The coaches of Rocky Ridge's basketball team did not abandon their goal of having a winning season after they lost their star player. Instead, they worked hard to find replacements—in other words, to find new inputs to replace lost outputs. Speedy eventually replaced Slammer in a new style of play developed to accommodate and capitalize on Speedy's quickness and his charismatic personality.

When members first come together as a new group, they must sort out a variety of factors before they can become a fully functional group. For example, they must get to know each other's strengths and weaknesses. For the group to be successful, a stable leadership structure must emerge and a set of rules and norms be established that all members agree to follow. When this has happened, the group can begin to mature and become productive. Individual members may leave and be replaced by new members, but the group can continue indefinitely as a functioning, successful unit. However, as with any living organism, our small

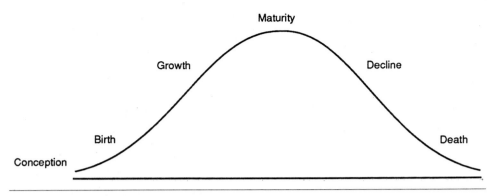

Figure 2.3   Life cycles of a small group system.

group system will eventually decline and disband, perhaps when it no longer has a purpose, when no new members replace those who leave, or when a competing group destroys it. At this point, the group has completed its usefulness and is appropriately laid to rest.

We hope that you see from this discussion that groups, like all other living organisms, are complex, dynamic, ever-changing systems that conform to the natural order of the universe. Although the complexity of small groups makes it difficult to study them, systems theory provides a framework for doing so. It also supplies a perspective for examining how groups exchange inputs and outputs with the environment as well as how several small group systems link to form a complex network.

Organizations as Systems of Groups

Much of the work of both corporate and nonprofit America is done in and by small groups. Most organizations are interlocking systems of groups (see figure 2.4). Think for a moment of how the automobile companies design, build, and market their cars. Although many individual engineers are involved in the design of specific car parts, there is an engineering *team* typically responsible for seeing that the individual parts come together into a car that works the way it was designed. Decades ago a single manager could oversee production of cars, but today a manufacturing *team* will have that responsibility. Marketing, too, is a complex activity that usually involves a *team* of researchers, artists, copy writers, photographers, and other specialists.

In a company like Saturn, subunits of self-managing work teams create major components such as engines and transmissions, while other teams assemble the units into completed cars. In addition, quality control circles and special project teams are composed of individuals from numerous departments and divisions.

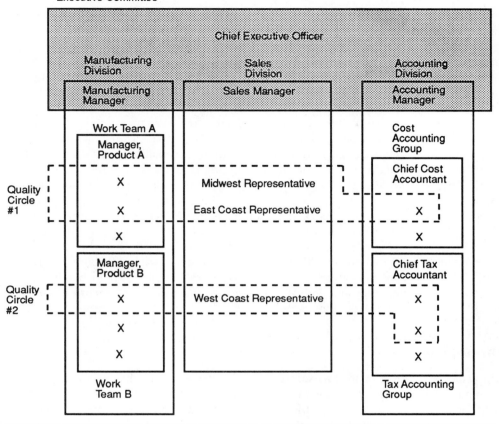

Figure 2.4 An organization as a system of interlocking group subsystems.

Many products other than automobiles cannot be manufactured and many types of services cannot be offered without the functioning of large systems composed of interdependent small groups. Any technical institute, college, or university is an example of interdependent subsystems making up a larger system.

Consider the typical approval process for a college faculty member who wants to teach a new course. Usually, the instructor must secure the approval of a departmental committee, which verifies that the teacher has the necessary expertise to teach the class. Then, a college committee must determine that the course does not duplicate other offerings or invade the turf of another department, and ensure that the quality and instructional level of the course meets the college's standards. Still more committees at successively higher levels may have to approve the course. Finally, the school's board of trustees must be satisfied that the course is consistent with the college's educational mission and resources. At each of these steps, small groups (i.e., committees) of faculty members, administrators, and trustees make decisions that affect the individual faculty member and possibly hundreds of students.

You can see from these examples that complex organizations have small groups as primary components. The principle of larger systems being composed of many subsystems (progressively smaller groups) has many important implications. First, knowing something about how groups function and how to be an effective group member is essential if you hope to survive and prosper in modern society. Second, because there are so many parts to a system, careful coordination and extensive communication among the parts is essential. The individual groups within an organization must find ways of sharing information with each other in order not to duplicate effort or allow important matters to "fall through the cracks." This spotlights the central position of communication, both within each individual group as well as among groups, to the effective functioning of modern organizations and society. Finally, the usefulness of the systems perspective should be clear. We can use that perspective to help us identify and describe the individual components of groups, so long as we always remember that each part functions in relationship to all the other parts of the system; what affects one part will necessarily affect all the other parts. This is true whether the system being studied is a person, a single group with several members, or a large organization composed of numerous interlocking groups.

Summary

This chapter opened with an example of a basketball team that illustrated several important concepts of the systems perspective. Developed by von Bertalanffy to help provide a perspective for the study of complex living systems, general systems theory offers the framework best suited to the study of complex human systems such as groups. Small groups are composed of elements that operate in relationship to each other and to the environment of the group. Inputs are elements such as people, tangible resources, or information that come into the group from outside the group. Egalitarian, responsible persons work well as team members and produce optimal outputs. Throughput processes include all the behaviors and interactions occurring within the group. They operate on the group's inputs to develop such things as the group's roles, rules, leadership structure, and outputs. Outputs are what the group produces, including tangible things like decisions, reports, and products, as well as intangible ones like morale, cohesiveness, and waste. Open systems freely exchange people, information, and resources with their environments, whereas closed systems do not. All the elements that are part of the group are interdependent and continuously affect each other. Feedback is information that enables a group to monitor its performance toward its goal and modify its behavior when necessary.

Groups are complex; usually there are multiple reasons why something occurs in a group as well as multiple paths to the same goal. As with any living system, groups have a life cycle that includes conception and birth, growth and development, maturity, decline, and death. A group prolongs its life by adapting to its environment and continuing to secure the inputs it needs to survive. Finally, both profit and nonprofit organizations are systems composed of subsystems of interdependent small groups, such as self-managing work teams, quality circles, and task forces. Today, all citizens need to know how groups operate and how to communicate well as team members and as subunits of large organizations.

Review Questions

1. Give at last three examples each of small group inputs, throughput processes, and outputs.
2. Use two or more examples to explain how the various elements of a small group are interdependent. Can you think of anything that would affect only one part of a group and not the other parts?
3. Create scales, each with polar extremes, to represent personal characteristics of the most and least productive group members. For example:

High sense of personal responsibility for group   No sense of personal responsibility for group

4. Give some examples of feedback that a classroom project group might receive. What could be the value of such feedback?
5. Think of a group you know that has developed an outstanding solution to a pressing problem. What are some of the reasons (causes) that may have contributed to the group's good work?
6. How do highly authoritarian and highly egalitarian people behave as leaders and as members of groups?
7. Why is it important for each member of a small group to have a personal sense of responsibility for the group's outcomes? How do members reveal their personal levels of responsibility?
8. What kinds of subsystems exist within your college or place of employment? How do these groups interact with each other? What, if anything, seems to be missing in such an interaction? How does interaction, or lack of it, seem to affect the organization?

Bibliography

Katz, Daniel, and Kahn, Robert. *The Social Psychology of Organizations.* 2d ed. New York: Wiley, 1978.

Von Bertalanffy, Ludwig. *General Systems Theory: Foundations, Development, Applications.* New York: Braziller, 1968.

Reference

1. Daniel Katz and Robert Kahn. *The Social Psychology of Organizations,* 2d ed. (New York: Wiley, 1978).

PART TWO

Foundations of Small Group Communicating

In order for groups to function effectively, they must have a solid foundation that supports members' efforts. How effectively the group's throughput processes function depends on how carefully this foundation is established. The cornerstone of this foundation is explored in Part Two, which focuses on the communication process itself and the critical thinking necessary to promote effective decision making. Chapter 3 presents the basic principles of interpersonal communication that members should understand if they are to be effective, and chapter 4 focuses on the verbal and nonverbal messages members send. Chapter 5 shows how using critical thinking skills can improve group decision making and explains how conscientious group members can improve their ability to think critically. Although chapters 3 and 4 may be a review for some of you, we recommend that you study them anyway so you will understand the terms as we intend to use them.

CHAPTER THREE

Interpersonal Communication Principles for Group Members

Chapter Outline

Communication: What's That?

Myths about Communicating

Listening: Receiving, Interpreting, and Responding to Messages from Other Group Members

Listening Defined

The Effects of Culture on the
    Communication Process

Habits of Poor Listeners

Listening Actively

Focused Listening

Study Questions

1. What is *communication* and what are the major implications of the communication process?
2. What are five common myths about communication?
3. What is *listening* and what are seven poor listening habits?
4. What is *culture* and how do the three dimensions of culture affect the interpretation process?
5. What is *active listening*? *Focused listening*?

Key Terms and Concepts

Active Listening

Assuming Meaning

Communication

Culture

Defensive Responding

Ethnocentric

Focused Listening

Focusing on Irrelevancies

Intercultural Communication

Listening

Mind Raping

Pseudolistening

Sidetracking

Sign

Silent Arguing

Symbol

The Lake Area Wellness Council is a nonprofit organization of people who are interested in natural healing methods as alternatives to traditional western medicine. Each month, the Council sponsors a seminar, open to everyone, where the featured speaker is a practitioner of some form of alternative medicine. The Council operates with a small budget and usually relies on volunteers to present the seminars; volunteers are given a token gift, such as a T-shirt with the Council's logo, but are generally not paid an honorarium. The Council's executive committee is responsible for scheduling and publicizing speakers. At one meeting, committee member Rhea suggested that the group schedule Chief Robert, a Cherokee medicine man, to speak, and furthermore suggested that the group buy Chief Robert a piece of equipment he needed as compensation for giving the seminar. Members agreed that Chief Robert, a prominent local healer, deserved a substantial gift, but the equipment was expensive ($200) and paying him would set a precedent for future speakers, which the Council could not afford. Norm, the chair of the executive committee, said, "I don't know how we'll be able to afford something like that, though I agree that he's certainly worth the money!" whereupon Rhea said, "Okay, that sounds good to me." The council went on to discuss other matters and Chief Robert was forgotten. At the next Council meeting, Sonya reported that publicity for Chief Robert's seminar was proceeding well, and the upcoming Sunday paper was planning a feature story on him and the seminar. Rhea noted how pleased she was that the Council had agreed to buy the chief his equipment, and especially how grateful he was for their generosity. At that point the meeting exploded into cries of "What? What do you mean 'pay him'? We didn't agree to pay him!" Committee members had misunderstood each other, and as a result, Rhea had obligated them to a $200 gift that would come close to wiping out their savings. However, at this point, members felt they couldn't back out. It took the committee members several meetings to overcome their anger and hurt feelings and to begin to trust each other again.

Real scenes like this one occur every day and illustrate what can happen when people fail to understand each other. To function effectively as a team, members must learn to put their thoughts and feelings into signals that other members can interpret and respond to. However, glitches can (and often do) occur in this *creating-sending-receiving-interpreting-responding* cycle we call *communication*. In our example, Norm said ". . . he's certainly worth the money." He *meant*, "It would be great to pay him and all of our speakers, they do such a wonderful job, but there's no way our budget can handle it, so let's stick to T-shirts." Rhea heard his words, but *interpreted* them to mean, "We don't have money to pay all our speakers, and it will be hard to come up with that amount for Chief Robert, but of all the speakers we've had, he is certainly worth the expense, so we'll figure out some way to pay him." She said, "Okay . . .," meaning "Great, I'll tell him we'll make an exception in his case." Norm heard her, but interpreted her meaning as, "I see what you mean about the expense, and I agree with you." These collective failures in sending and receiving messages, and failing to clarify potentially ambiguous interpretations, caused the Lake Area Wellness Council time, money, and energy. Unfortunately, this is not an unusual instance of misunderstanding within a small group.

The purpose of chapter 3 is to help you understand the communication process and to think analytically and critically about communication as it occurs in your groups. A secondary purpose is to help you improve your *personal role* in that communication. To function effectively as a team, members must put their thoughts and feelings into signals that can be perceived and interpreted by other members as intended. They must also perceive, interpret, and respond to the signals of other members. However, many factors can interfere with this process. Communicating effectively takes conscious thought and hard work. In this chapter and the next, we focus both on the process and on how you as a group member can communicate more effectively.

These chapters may be review for some readers. But we recommend that you study them carefully anyway so you, your classmates, and your instructor will be using terms in the same way. Additionally, these chapters provide a common vocabulary for you to discuss communication in groups.

Communication: What's That?

If you are thinking, "Gloria and Jack, what do you mean by *communication?*" you are asking the right question. This word has been used in dozens of slightly different ways by different writers. We use *communication* to refer to the process of humans creating, sending, receiving, and interpreting signals. To answer the question heading this section: **Communication** *is the perception, interpretation, and response of people to signals produced by other people.* This seemingly simple definition has five major implications:

1. **Communication is a process, not a thing or state.** Like life, it goes on with no clearly marked beginning or ending. Signals from a person start as feelings or thoughts, and no one can say when their impact on others ends. Messages, such as statements and memos, can be repeated and preserved relatively unchanged. But the human experiences from which they emerged and responses they evoke *can't* be duplicated or repeated exactly. You can't step into the same river twice, for the river has flowed, however imperceptibly, into something different. It is the same way with the flow among people who are communicating.

   Communication is an extremely complex process involving human senses, feelings, meanings, and cultural experiences, not just a simple matter of nouns and verbs. During the process, one person experiences a perception or feeling and expresses this experience by putting it consciously into words and/or nonverbal signals. The expression is sent out as energy pulses into the air, or other media, where others can perceive and respond to it. We diagram this process in figure 3.1. The energy pulses undergo

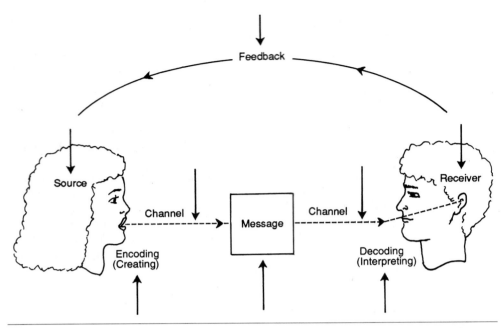

Figure 3.1 The communication process. (Arrows indicate places where mistakes can occur.)

many changes in form during an exchange between two people. We won't try to explain all that happens, partly because not all of it is yet understood. However, a great many sources of distortion and error can creep into the signal circuits linking a small group of humans. Talking about communication as if it were a simple signal-response event, with nothing likely to go wrong, is naive. It is more complex than any computer circuitry.

2. **Human communication is essentially a *receiver* phenomenon.** If you do not have a receiver, you do not have communication. If you are talking while no one is listening, no communication has occurred. If you want to be a better communicator in small groups, you should give more attention to how you *listen* and *interpret* than to how you talk. It is our joint judgment that far more of the communication problems we see in small groups come from bad listening and interpreting rather than speaking habits, as we saw with Rhea and Norm.

3. **Communication is symbolic; this implies both benefits and liabilities.** There are two major categories of signals from people: signs and symbols. **Signs** are natural events that are automatically related to what they represent. For example, a blush is a sign of personal tension we call *embarrassment,* and a rabbit track in the snow is a sign that a rabbit has passed. All signs have direct, inherent connections with what they represent.

An object represented by a variety of symbols (words). (Reprinted by permission of Johnny Hart and Creators Syndicate, Inc.)

A **symbol,** in contrast to a sign, is a type of signal created by a human that arbitrarily represents something with which it has no natural or direct relationship. For instance, there's no natural reason why we call something we sit on a *chair* instead of a *pig,* a *snorkel,* or *le chaise.* In addition, a symbol may stand for something that has no tangible form, like a relationship, an abstract concept like *love,* or an idea that cannot be observed, like *democracy.* All words are symbols.

There is no inherent relationship between any word and what it represents. If you have read any other language than English you know that different words can be used to represent the same object or concept. Even within a single language like English the same food might be called *dinner, supper,* or *the evening meal* by different people. New symbols are constantly being created to represent new things or ideas. For example, *black hole* was created by theoretical physicists to represent a state of all energy collapse and incredible density. Computer specialists have added all sorts of new terms to our everyday speech: *software, interface,* and *user-friendly.*

Symbols are convenient for thinking and communicating because we do not need to have the items present to represent them to other people. In addition, we can invent new items or concepts, or encode great amounts of information in small packages of signals. There is no limit to how many symbols we can invent and use to communicate. Further, symbols allow us to communicate through space and time.

Symbols can take a variety of forms. Words are the most common type in small group communication, but we also use numbers, pictographs (such as the international signs for cars and rest rooms), Morse code, magnetic charges such as those used in computer disks and tapes, and gestures like those we use for *OK*.

As convenient and helpful as symbols are, they also have liabilities. Dangers come from misuse and misunderstanding about symbols. Because symbols are arbitrary, their meaning must be *interpreted*. Two people can use a symbol to represent different concepts and, therefore, misinterpret each other without knowing it, as Rhea and Norm did. For example, when you say "I love you," do you mean the same thing as your boyfriend or girlfriend does? A person may believe that there is some relationship between symbols and observable events when none exists. A symbol can evoke different responses than the speaker intended. Liars can manipulate us even more easily with symbols than with signs. The point is, *misunderstanding is quite likely whenever we use symbols in small groups unless we continuously guard against it.*

4. **Face-to-face communicating is a transactional process.** *Transactional* has two major meanings relevant to face-to-face communication among members of a small group. First, it implies that communicating is a simultaneous, multidirectional process. That is, regardless of who is speaking at any given moment, *every* member is simultaneously sending signals that every other member (including the speaker) could potentially receive and interpret. Most of these signals are unspoken (nonverbal), and most of them are signs (for instance, the automatic face you may make when you don't

like an idea the speaker is presenting). The implication is clear: to be most effective as a group member, you must be aware of signals from all members, even when you are speaking. Communication is not a linear, one-way process, but occurs among all members simultaneously.

Secondly, as discussed in chapter 2, all elements of a system influence each other. There is no way to be a member of a group and *not* have influence on the group as well as on each member. You cannot "just be quiet" and have no effect. For example, a speaker may notice from facial expressions that group members are reacting negatively to her suggestions, and this in turn may cause her to modify her ideas *as she speaks*. This illustrates the complex, transactional nature of communication.

5. **Making communication productive is the responsibility of every member.** There is a great tendency to blame another person when some statement is not heard, misunderstood, forgotten, or ignored. "If he had just listened to me!" or "If she wasn't so (boring, arrogant, dominating, nasty, prejudiced, ignorant, etc.) I'd have paid more attention," and "She didn't speak in words I understand" are typical statements of group members placing blame for miscommunicating on others and rationalizing away any responsibility for what went wrong. But communication is a group-wide activity, as the example of the Lake Area Wellness Council illustrates. The responsibility for errors and glitches is not one person's alone. If you don't understand, you can (and should) say so. If you believe what someone else is saying is irrelevant to the group's purpose, you have both a right and a responsibility to say so. If you can't hear, you can ask the others to talk louder. If you failed to make note of some assignment for which you are responsible (such as the date when you are supposed to report on your research to your project group), you have the obligation to ask. You do *not* have the right to expect others to read your mind and supply you with information you are missing. In short, everyone must constantly monitor how the communication process is working, and correct problems as needed. This is a direct application of the definition of communication as transactional, complex, and symbolic. Remember, *if something can go wrong with communication it probably will.*

Myths about Communicating

We attempted to counter several commonly believed myths about communication when we explained the five implications of our definition of human communication. One myth is that *communication means creating messages, so the way to improve it is to improve the quality of the messages we send.* This false belief overlooks the transactional nature of communicating, especially the importance of how a person receives and interprets signals. A second myth is that *words have meaning.* Words have only the meanings people, both speakers and listeners, give

Table 3.1 Five Common Myths about Communication

Communication means "creating messages"; to improve communication you should concentrate on improving the quality of the messages you send. (Ignores the importance of the receiver.)

Words have meaning. (Meanings are what *people* give the words.)

Communication is a one-way-at-a-time process of source→message→channel→receiver→feedback. (Ignores the fact that both sender and receiver are *simultaneously* sending and receiving messages.)

Disagreement or conflict is a sign of communication breakdown. (Ignores the possibility that people can understand each other very well, but have differing values and beliefs about an issue.)

The purpose of communication is to achieve perfect understanding between people. (Perfect understanding is impossible because "meanings are in people, not in words." A primary goal of communication in small groups is the efficient and effective coordination of member efforts toward a common objective.)

them. In current wisdom, *meanings are in people, not in words.* A third myth is that *communication is a one-way process of source—message—channel—receiver—response* (response is also called *feedback*). Instead, communication is a multidirectional transactional process. In addition, there are two more myths that affect how people act in small groups. You need to understand them and watch for behavior based on these myths so you can prevent some otherwise unnoticed miscommunication.

A fourth myth is that *disagreement or conflict is a sign of breakdown in communicating.* This is not so. A breakdown may result when a message is not received, perhaps due to lost mail, or when a speaker's voice is too soft to be heard over background noise. *Real* disagreements do not come from either breakdowns or misunderstandings, but result from having different information about a problem, different goals, personal objectives at odds with group goals, different beliefs and values, etc. (We elaborate on several of these in chapter 10.) If the disagreeing individuals understand each other's positions well enough to explain them to each other's satisfaction, no breakdown or misunderstanding has occurred. Instead, there is a conflict whose satisfactory resolution calls for the skill and goodwill of all the members.

The other myth proposes that *good communicators achieve perfect understanding of each other.* Since we have different words in our vocabularies, and different experiences with words, we inevitably will have some differences in what we associate with the words we use and the signs we perceive. Hence, some degree of difference in meaning *always* exists between two or more people responding to each other's messages. If we can communicate well enough to coordinate our behavior toward a goal all members of the group can accept, we are communicating well enough for group success. All five myths are summarized in table 3.1.

Now that we have defined the concept *communication* as we use it to refer to members of small groups, we turn to the most important stage in the process of small group communication: receiving, interpreting, and responding to the messages of other group members—*listening*.

Listening: Receiving, Interpreting, and Responding to Messages from Other Group Members

Coordinating the efforts of group members in a functioning system is far more dependent on good listening than on good speaking skills. Doubtless you have seen groups of several eloquent people talking past each other, creating many vivid statements but little shared understanding. Everyone was talking well but listening poorly. Members switched subjects abruptly. They did not respond to others' suggestions. They forgot information vital to the group's progress. A beneficial group member must be able to synthesize group sentiments and summarize a discussion cogently. But that is not possible if the speaker was not listening well enough to recall the gist of what others said or to think carefully about what they mean. So for better communication within small groups we urge you to pay special attention to how you and other members listen and make whatever corrections are needed in your listening habits. Following this advice would have saved the Lake Area Wellness Council time and money.

Listening carefully produces an orderly discussion in which ideas are understood and the group progresses efficiently toward its goal. A recent national survey of one thousand personnel managers identified *listening* as the second most important skill that influences their hiring decisions.[1] Before examining what goes wrong and what to do about it, we need to have a shared understanding of the concept *good listening*.

Listening Defined

Many people use *hearing* and *listening* as if they were synonyms. But for people who have studied what happens when a person listens, these are different concepts. For example, Barker defines listening as a "selective process of attending to, hearing, understanding and remembering aural (and at times visual) symbols."[2] Steil, Barker, and Watson present listening as a four-stage process beginning with sensing (hearing), followed by interpreting, evaluating, and responding.[3] For them the act of listening has not been finished until some overt response has been given by the receiver so the speaker can judge the success of his or her sending. We, too, believe that **listening** is a process that begins with perceiving a message, interpreting it, deciding what it means, and finally responding to it. You can see that such listening is not passive; it requires *activity*. Listening is behavior over which we can exert considerable control.

We have found that the majority of participants in discussions we observed could not list the ideas proposed as possible solutions or the major issues discussed and decisions reached during a half-hour discussion. When we ask students to paraphrase previous speakers' ideas over half the time they cannot do so (and we expect that college students are not much worse at such listening than are other people!). In short, most of the time we listen rather badly. We misunderstand a speaker's statement, we fail to confirm a speaker's idea, and we forget promptly what a speaker said. As respondents, we often give the speaker little or no overt feedback. This gives the speaker little opportunity to assess whether the receiver understood the message as intended. This also sends the message that what the speaker said wasn't worth a response. This is as bad as saying "You don't matter, kid. You just don't exist so far as I'm concerned."[4]

Effective listening requires that the listener *hear* what the speaker said, interpret it accurately, and respond appropriately. Usually, hearing what the speaker said presents little problem. Group members are accustomed to asking a member to repeat a statement they weren't able to hear, for example. However, the interpretation and response steps can be tricky because of the nature of symbolic communication that we discussed earlier. Different people mean different things with the same words and actions. A major factor that influences what words and actions mean to us is our culture.

Although understanding the effects of culture on interpersonal communication is not the focus of this book, we believe that some understanding of the influence of culture is important for you to have. We also believe that in the future, as more companies become multinational and intercultural, this information about culture will be even more important. For this reason, we include here some very basic information about the effects of culture on the communication process, especially regarding interpretation.

The Effects of Culture on the Communication Process

As you have discovered by now, there is little that is automatic about communication. From the time we are born, we are taught rules for how to communicate, at first by those closest to us (usually our families) and later by others outside the family, such as teachers, playmates, colleagues, and so forth.

Culture refers to the system of beliefs, values, symbols, rules, and so forth, that are shared by a group of people. For example, people talk about the culture of the United States, which values individualism, hard work, direct communication, and so forth. However, even within a fairly broad culture such as that of the U.S., there is considerable diversity in which many smaller cultures, called *subcultures*, exist with their own identifiable patterns. For instance, the college professors in our department have a culture of their own, as do small farmers in rural Arkansas, as do Italians living in New York City. Even individual families create cultures with acceptable patterns of beliefs and behaviors.

Culture is important in the communication process because it is your culture that teaches you what words to use, when to use them, what to say and do in which circumstances—in short, what the rules for communication are. For example, in some families, children are to be seen and not heard unless an adult addresses them directly, but in other families children are encouraged to participate freely in conversations with adults. In some cultures, communication in groups occurs in an orderly process, with someone speaking only when the other has completed his sentence. In other cultures, free-for-all conversation and frequent interruptions are the norms. If you are talking with someone who is a member of the same culture as you, you will probably experience few problems interpreting what that person means and responding appropriately. However, if you are in conversation with someone from a very different culture, you may have a difficult time understanding each other, even if both of you are speaking the same language. **Intercultural communication,** which is communication between people of different cultures, complicates the listening process considerably; the more different the cultures, the more chances for misinterpretation and misunderstanding.

Even when we know that someone is from a different culture and may have different rules for communicating, we still tend to behave in an **ethnocentric** way, interpreting and evaluating that person by the rules of our culture rather than his. The rules our culture has taught us are so ingrained and automatic that they are, for all practical purposes, invisible to us unless something extraordinary happens, such as a major misunderstanding, to cause us to examine them. For example, a group of students one of us observed included a young woman from Taiwan. According to the rules of her culture, she sat quietly in the group and contributed to the conversation only when the others asked her a direct question. She made ambiguous statements when she was forced to express her opinion. According to the rules of her culture, she was being polite and fostering the harmony of the group. But the American students, who did not understand and had not considered the rules of her culture, interpreted her behavior ethnocentrically according to what is appropriate for *American* students, and gave her a negative evaluation. They concluded that she didn't care much about the group, was probably stupid, and was too wishy-washy to be relied on. Their ultimate response was to exclude her from the group. This might have been an appropriate response for an *American* student displaying "I'm not interested in this group" behaviors, but that was not the message she intended to send. Neither she nor the Americans realized that differences in their respective rules were causing the problems. Neither set of rules was inherently right or wrong—they were just different. Because both she and the Americans lacked cultural sensitivity, the interpretation and response steps in the listening process produced misunderstandings, harming the group's effectiveness.

A number of dimensions of interpersonal relations differ from culture to culture. Among the most important are the effects of individualism, power distance, and context. Principles of these dimensions are described in table 3.2. The

Table 3.2   Three Important Dimensions of Culture

	Individualism/Collectivism
High individualism	Values independence, autonomy, and privacy; encourages dissent; encourages people to "do their own thing".
High collectivism	Values harmony, conformity, and loyalty to the group; discourages dissent.
	Power Distance
High power distance	Maximizes status differences between people; values hierarchical structure, strong (authoritarian) leadership.
Low power distance	Minimizes status differences; values sharing power, participatory decision making, democratic leadership.
	Context
High context	The situation, or context, carries most of the meaning; communication is indirect; nonverbal signals are especially important to understanding a message.
Low context	Primary meaning of a message conveyed by the verbal (the words themselves); values direct, unambiguous communication.

individualism-collectivism dimension refers to whether a particular culture considers the needs of the individual person or the needs of the group more important.[5] As mentioned earlier, the United States is an individualistic country. People here are encouraged to stand out from the crowd. We have an elaborate system of court precedents that protect individual rights when they clash with those of the group. In individualistic cultures, members are encouraged to state their opinions regardless of whether others support these opinions or not. Individual initiative and achievement are rewarded. We admire people who succeed by marching to their own drumbeats. In contrast, collectivist countries consider the needs of the group to be more important. People who disagree with what the group wants to do are encouraged to suppress their disagreement. Standing out from the crowd is discouraged, as is direct confrontation. The Taiwanese woman described earlier was from a collectivist culture so she tried to blend her views with the views of the group, but the individualistic Americans were trying to get her to stand out from the crowd and take an individual stance.

Power distance refers to the distribution of power—whether it should be distributed equally or not.[6] In cultures with a low power distance, such as Israel and Denmark, people believe in minimizing status differences between individuals and in sharing power. In countries with a high power distance, such as India, Mexico, and all Arabic countries, status differences are very important and communication serves to emphasize those differences. Lustig and Cassotta note that cultures with high power distances prefer more autocratic group leadership than cultures with low power distances, which prefer democratic leadership and participatory decision making.[7] In addition, conformity is valued more highly in cultures with high power distance. A group leader from the U.S., a moderately low power distance culture, who asks Mexican members of his group to call him by his first name and encourages them to participate in group decision making is likely to confuse the Mexicans. They will interpret his behavior as proof that he is an incompetent leader, just as he is likely to interpret their reluctance to participate as lack of interest on their part. They may be "hearing" each other, but neither is listening or interpreting very accurately.

A third important dimension of culture is *context,* or the degree to which meaning is conveyed by words or by features of the situation.[8] In low context cultures, such as that of the United States, the meaning of the message is conveyed primarily by the words. Such cultures value direct, clear, unambiguous communication where there is little room for doubt. The American students mentioned earlier were trying to force the Taiwanese student to speak in such clear and direct terms. However, high context cultures, such as most Asian cultures, value indirect communication. In such cultures, which are often collectivist as well, stating a direct opinion might insult others in the group or hurt their feelings. Thus, opinions are expressed indirectly, with lots of room for doubt, and group consensus is built slowly. Someone who is not a native of such cultures may have a difficult time understanding the meaning. For example, a Japanese who disagrees with you won't say, "I really hate that idea." Instead, he is likely to say something like, "That sounds very interesting. Perhaps we should examine it further." Unless you are able to "read" the often subtle cues in the situation (or context) you will misinterpret the favorable statement as an expression of agreement, when in fact it is not that. You will be hearing well but listening poorly!

Although many of the examples of culture we have provided are examples that compared different countries, there are various cultures *within* countries as well. You may not have many opportunities to participate in a group with people from Japan, Mexico, or Greece, but you are likely to be in groups composed of whites, blacks, Hispanics, Native Americans, people from cities, people from rural areas, Italian-Americans, blue-collar workers, professionals, and so forth. Each of these groups represents a type of culture with its own rules for communicating. Even though some of these cultures may have much in common, there still will be subtle differences in the rules that may make interpretation difficult.

Important influences of culture that you cannot escape are the rules about gender. Many communication researchers now believe that men and women are taught different rules about what is appropriate. For example, men and women tend to use questions differently. Men use questions to acquire information, whereas women use questions as a way to keep the conversation going. Thus, "Do you think we should accept the first or the second option?" from a man is probably asking for a short answer, perhaps with some reasoning to support the answer. The same question from a woman is probably intended more as an invitation to discuss the topic than a request for information. The problem comes when men and women misinterpret each other. For instance, a man answering "The first option" to the woman's question, and stopping at that, will wonder why she is frustrated with him, and she will wonder why he's giving such curt, un-friendly answers. A wife may come home and say, "I'm really having a problem at work," and proceed to tell her husband about it. When he gives her advice about how to handle the problem, she gets angry and accuses him of treating her like a two-year-old who can't handle her own life. What happened? She wanted to feel close to him by having a conversation about work, but he assumed she needed information and advice about how to handle her problem. Again, they are hearing each other, but misinterpreting, thus not listening well.

A number of differences between the communication rules of men and women in the U.S. have been observed. Men tend to be direct, oriented toward the task, and to display more signs of power. Women use more references to emotions, appear more cooperative, and display more signs of liking. Women seem to work harder to keep a conversation going. They initiate more topics, partly because men often respond minimally ("Uh-huh" or "Mm-hmm" without elaboration) and often don't follow up on the topics women initiate.

It is difficult to generalize about the differences between the communication rules for men and women. This is true in part because the social rules are chang-ing so quickly, and what is considered appropriate behavior now may have changed from thirty or even as recently as ten years ago. Many of the differences observed between men and women occur in their nonverbal behavior; we elabo-rate more on these differences in the nonverbal communication section of the next chapter.

Our intent here has not been to teach you everything there is to know about cultural differences. Rather, our purpose has been to alert you to some common causes of misinterpretations in the listening process. Remember that cultural rules are not automatic; they are taught. Remember also that cultural differences are not a matter of right or wrong, and that you have absorbed the rules of your culture so completely that they are invisible to you until you start to examine them or to interact with people from a very different culture. We hope we have helped you become more sensitive to such issues so you will be a more conscientious and effective listener.

At this point you may be wondering what you can do to make yourself a more competent listener in small groups. In the next sections, we describe several of the bad habits of poor listeners as well as provide suggestions for improving your listening behavior. These bad habits are summarized in table 3.3.

Habits of Poor Listeners

Pseudolistening occurs when a listener fakes active listening by giving the speaker many of the signs that good listeners give, while actually thinking about something else. The pseudolistener nods, smiles, murmurs, and often looks the speaker in the eye. However, he or she may be daydreaming, thinking up some argument instead of trying to understand the speaker's perspective, or working on

Table 3.3 Habits of Poor Listeners

Pseudolistening: Pretending to listen while thinking about something else or while daydreaming.
Silent arguing: Failing to understand what a speaker is saying, then mentally rehearsing objections to the *misunderstood* notion of the speaker's idea.
Assuming meaning: Interpreting the speaker's behavior by using the cultural rules appropriate for the listener.
Mind raping: Insistence by poor listeners that they understand better than the speaker what the speaker meant, even though the speaker protests.
Focusing on irrelevancies: Becoming distracted from a speaker's message by unimportant details like dress, accent, physical appearance, or environmental distractions.
Sidetracking: Changing the topic because you weren't paying attention to the speaker: not connecting remarks to statements of the previous speaker.
Defensive responding: Failing to listen or failing to try to understand what a speaker is saying because poor listeners feel psychologically threatened by something the speaker said or did; responding with "chips on their shoulders."

a personal problem. Pseudolisteners often defend their phony behavior as "politeness" to a "boring" speaker. In truth, such behavior is demeaning to the speaker. Better to say you are uninterested than to pretend interest. Often pseudolistening is accompanied by other bad habits.

Silent arguing means the listener forms a quick judgment about the speaker's idea, rejects it without listening to the rest of what the speaker says, and then begins a silent mental search for arguments about what is wrong with the misunderstood idea. We tend to listen to that which supports our previous beliefs and to ignore or tune out what contradicts them. It is impossible to listen well while engaging in silent argument. The third bad listening habit is akin to silent arguing, but worse.

Assuming meaning often stems from the ethnocentrism we discussed earlier. This occurs when the receiver interprets what the sender said or did through the filter of the *receiver's* culture, and proceeds to make a judgement about the sender. For example, a Native American may answer a question from a white, middle-class American without looking the questioner in the eye; the white concludes that the Native American is hiding something or lying. However, looking down is a sign of respect in many Native American cultures. The white's conclusion is in error because it is based on what *white, middle-class Americans* do when answering questions. In other words, the Native American's behavior is being interpreted by the wrong set of rules, and a serious misunderstanding has occurred.

Mind raping, a stronger form of assuming meaning, is insisting that a speaker meant what the listener would have meant by a statement, and continuing to insist on this meaning despite protests from the speaker. For example, "I know what you *really* mean. You don't think our professor will object to our topic. You just want to do something else!" assumes that the listener knows better than the speaker what the speaker meant. This sort of behavior was named by George Bach, a counselor especially concerned with helping intimate couples.[9] Sometimes this behavior comes from the mistaken belief that words have only one meaning, but it may represent a form of domination and rejection of another. Regardless, it is the opposite of good listening, the first goal of which is to understand another as that person wants to be understood, and only then to judge the other's ideas and motives.

Focusing on irrelevancies occurs when a listener pays attention to something other than what the speaker is saying, and this produces failure to understand the speaker. Some people pay so much attention to dress, word choices, grammar, face or body details, accent or dialect, or things in the environment that they have little energy to give to the ideas of a speaker. For example, one of our students mispronounced a word during a group presentation. A faculty member smirked and rolled her eyes. She didn't listen to another word the student said, even though the information was valuable, because she had focused on the encoding mistake the student had made. If you are guilty of this bad habit, you will need to guard against it by constantly reminding yourself to concentrate on understanding the speaker well enough to summarize what was said to that person's satisfaction.

Sidetracking takes several forms, all of which result in going off on a tangent, either in the listener's mind or in what is being discussed. A group member mentions something that starts a reverie on the part of a listener, who may continue on this daydream while several discussion points have passed, all of which the "listener" has failed to hear or understand. Or, the listener makes a statement that is not connected to what was previously said, thus sidetracking the discussion by starting a new topic. Berg found that in the student discussions he analyzed the topic was switched on the average about every minute.[10] This sidetracking by switching issues—giving irrelevant responses to previous remarks—is a serious fault in listening. For example:

Pete: Professor Burke says we need to keep detailed diaries about our group meetings. I think it might be a good idea if we exchanged diaries periodically. We could learn a lot by reading each other's observations about our meetings.

Jean: That sounds like a helpful idea, but it might inhibit what I write if I know other people in the group will see it.

Mike (a sidetrack): What did you guys think of the old man's latest assignment, to write a detailed account of the development of norms in our group? What a dumb idea!

Defensive responding is likely to occur when someone feels some threat from another's remark. For instance, a listener may feel that the other member is trying to dominate or give orders inappropriately, devalue the listener's self-concept, or reject an idea proposed by the listener. Even an open, honest disagreement is enough to put insecure people into a defensive posture. Highly emotive words may evoke a defensive response, or they may inadvertently push someone's "hot button." For example, you may be sensitive to attempts of others to control or dominate what you do, so when another says "Get me a Pepsi while you are at the machine," you reply "Get your own blankety-blank drink!" When a person listens and responds defensively, he or she usually quits trying to understand the other's point of view and thus may miss important qualifications or statements that clarify the speaker's meaning. For example, someone calls your proposal for employee ownership of a company *socialistic* and you get ready to reply angrily without listening to his explanation that he believes this form of socialism is beneficial to the employees. It is especially important to guard against defensive responses when highly emotive words such as *abortion, right to life, gun control, welfare state,* and *do-gooder* are used. When you feel yourself getting tense and emotionally aroused, sit back, take a deep breath, and try to paraphrase what the other meant before you express either support or opposition. That will keep you from listening or responding defensively.

You probably noticed that in all the previous seven bad listening habits the listener was not focusing attention on the ideas of the speaker but on something else—a physical characteristic, a habit of speech, a personal belief, a different topic, a personal definition of some symbol, a private relationship with the speaker, or a personally held value. Where to focus attention and how to do so is a consistent problem for many of us, including those of us who are generally good listeners.

Listening Actively

Listening is *active* behavior, not passive. Listening requires as much concentration as speaking does. When a person is paying close attention in an effort to understand what another means, the heart speeds up as the rate of metabolism rises. In contrast, heart rates of passive listeners who take no personal responsibility for understanding another slow down. Active listening is partly a matter of *choosing* to focus on the other and of selecting what parts of a message to focus on and try to recall.

A good test for **active listening** is to paraphrase (*put in your own words*) what you think the other person meant. Merely repeating another's words does not demonstrate comprehension. Any tape recorder can repeat word for word. An accurate paraphrase requires the listener to process the information cognitively. When you paraphrase what you thought the speaker said, you give the speaker a basis for deciding whether or not you understood the original message adequately, or whether you missed or distorted parts of it. The original speaker should then listen to the paraphrase, accept it if it is accurate or correct the parts that were distorted or omitted, then ask you to try paraphrasing again. Only when the original speaker is completely satisfied that you have understood adequately should the discussion proceed with any expression of agreement, disagreement, elaboration, or a new topic. Here is a bit of dialogue that illustrates active listening:

Karla: Medical costs are incredibly high. Why, on the average, it costs about $1500 per day in the hospital. No wonder 37 percent of our citizens lack hospital insurance! Too many people are making too much money off the illnesses of others. We gotta stop that!

Jeannie: You're saying that the reason so many people lack hospital insurance is that hospital costs are high, and they are so high because a lot of people are paid too much in the health care business. Is that right? (Jeannie's attempt to paraphrase Karla's statement to understand what Karla meant, especially to clarify her reasoning.)

Karla: Well, basically, but I really don't mean people don't have insurance because the hospital costs so much, but because they can't afford it. That may be partly because it costs a lot for the insurance—like $300 a month for a young husband and wife with no kids—and partly because the insurance companies have to pay such high hospital and other medical bills. (Karla corrects the paraphrase and clarifies her own reasoning.)

Jeannie: Now let's see if I understand your thinking: 37 percent of our citizens lack hospital insurance because they feel they can't afford it. Part of the reason they can't afford it is because high medical costs have made premiums very high, like $150 a month for a young person. And a lot of people are making more money than you think they should out of the illnesses of others. (Jeannie's second attempt at paraphrasing Karla's statements.)

Karla: Right. (Karla's confirmation of second paraphrase as accurate.)

Jeannie: I partly agree and partly disagree. I think . . . (The paraphrase accepted, Jeannie now begins to explain her position on the issue about why so many persons lack hospital insurance.)

Every opinion bearing on a major decision by a group needs to be evaluated, but only AFTER it has been understood as intended. For example, in the Lake Area Wellness Council, Rhea failed to confirm her understanding of Norm's statement, and the rest of the members failed to confirm their understanding of her statement, "Okay, that sounds good to me." Active listeners confirm their understanding BEFORE they state evaluations. Then, confident of what the speaker meant, active listeners evaluate what they have understood. The response may be a statement of agreement or disagreement, that the idea is irrelevant to the issue being discussed, that it is logically unsound, that there is no evidence to support it, and so on.

One effect of active listening is that the discussion slows down. Most of us are our *own* best listeners—we like to talk, and given half a chance, we will. So we may become impatient, not taking time to paraphrase even when we should. We may sit poised like a heron waiting to strike at a small fish. At the first chance we burst into a conversation with *our* ideas, *our* examples, *our* positions. Correcting this habit takes self-discipline. Group members can remind one another to make sure they understand before they take positions on what someone else has said. We think you should listen actively all the time, but paraphrase only part of the time—when a controversial issue is being discussed, when you can see some possibility that the speaker has a different meaning from what you think, when you are confused by what the speaker has said, and when there has been a lot of topic switching or misunderstanding. We urge you to be on guard against pseudolistening. If you realize you didn't really listen, apologize and ask for a restatement.

Developing a habit of listening and responding actively takes self-controlled practice. The climate of mutual understanding that it helps foster is well worth the price.

Focused Listening

In a sense, focused listening is a part of active listening. Focusing involves comprehending all the statements made during a discussion, evaluating them, then giving special attention to selected ones so they can be recalled. Remember, many studies show that most listeners remember only half of new information immediately after a lecture. In a couple of days people have forgotten at least half of what they remembered at first. So the question is, "How can you learn to recall selectively?"

Focused listening means listening so you can select the main points you want to recall later and let the nonessential points go. In a meeting, it may entail choosing notes you will write down so you can later recall what occurred. Recall is needed because problem solving can go on over a long time. For example, a group of scientists trying to improve procedures for detecting AIDS infections would need many meetings to report and interpret their continuing research. Students working on a group project usually need many meetings to plan their work, find relevant information, conduct whatever observations are required, compile and analyze their findings, write a final report, and present that report to their class members. But even in single-meeting discussions we have found that many participants cannot summarize the issues raised, the important information presented, all decisions reached, and assignments made. When problem solving lasts over several meetings, most members forget important information. This lack of functional group memory produces arguments, needless repetition, and wasted time.

There are two things that can improve a group's memory, and thereby its functioning. The first is focused listening, the second is carefully maintained reports (i.e., minutes) of all group meetings. Focused listening means you focus on and try to remember the major points of the discussion, but not all the details of examples, stories, statistics, and comparisons. A discussion contains a sort of structure. The skilled listener keeps the major issue of the moment in mind, notes and points out when someone gets off the issue, and can readily summarize the major arguments or positions on the issue. Once the issue has been settled, this listener can state the decision and the reasons for it—*that* is what the listener will remember, not all the specific facts, anecdotes, or positions taken by various individuals as they worked toward agreement. A focused listener is highly selective. It pays to jot down brief notes about all of the points you want to recall, and to run brief mental summaries, such as:

> Let's see, now. We decided that there are likely to be more and more injuries of pedestrians in front of campus unless something is done to prevent them. An unacceptably high accident rate has been going on for years. We considered four options: added crosswalks, underground crossing, overhead crossing, and overhead crossing with pedestrian barriers in the median. We decided that an overhead crossing with barriers would be effective, affordable, and acceptable both to campus and city officials.

Practicing such mental summaries during a lull in discussion will greatly sharpen your skill in focused listening. So will volunteering to write your group's reports and minutes. An added benefit may be your ability to detect irrelevancies and subject switches at once and to avoid these sidetracks yourself.

Summary

This chapter presented basic information about how humans communicate with each other and then focused on helping you understand the communication process and improve your listening behaviors. Communication was defined as the process by which humans create, receive, interpret, and respond to signals from other humans. This definition implies that communication is an ongoing, transactional, *receiver*-oriented phenomenon that is the responsibility of every member of a group. During the communication process, people send signals to each other that consist of signs and symbols. Signs have a natural connection with what they represent (e.g., a blush indicates embarrassment). Symbols do not have this natural connection (e.g., there are many different words that stand for "something you sit on"). The arbitrary nature of symbols often creates problems in the communication process.

Most people believe several myths about communication. These include the mistaken beliefs that the best way to improve communication is to improve the quality of the *sender's* skill, that words themselves have meaning, that communication is a one-way process flowing from sender to receiver, that conflict is a sign of communication breakdown, and that good communicators can achieve perfect understanding with each other. We believe the best way to improve the communication process among people is to improve each person's listening skills, especially their interpretation skills. *Listening* implies that the signals sent by one individual are both heard and interpreted cognitively by another. The interpretation part of listening can pose numerous problems for group members because so many factors influence how we interpret what others intend to say. Among the most important of these is culture. The "rules" for how we should communicate are transmitted by our culture, starting with the culture of our families. Cultures vary on several interpersonal dimensions, including the relative importance of individualism/collectivism, power distance, and context. Because different cultures have different rules about what signals mean, the possibilities for misinterpretation are endless. Too often, many of us do not listen well. Instead, we fall into seven bad habits exhibited by poor listeners: pseudolistening, silent arguing, assuming meaning, mind raping, focusing on irrelevancies, sidetracking, and defensive responding. We recommend that members of a group listen actively by paraphrasing what they believe the speaker is saying, thereby giving the speaker a chance to correct misperceptions or clarify misunderstandings. In addition, we advise group members to focus their listening so they can remember and summarize the main points of the discussion.

Review Questions

1. Describe five major implications of the communication process and give an example of how each may occur in a small group.
2. Explain why each of the five common beliefs about communication is a myth.
3. What is the difference between a *sign* and a *symbol,* and what implications does this have for small group communication?
4. Explain the difference between *hearing* and *listening.* Why is it important to *listen* to fellow members of a small group?
5. Describe three dimensions of culture presented in chapter 3 and explain how these affect communication between people.
6. What is *active listening* and why was it recommended in small group discussions?

Bibliography

Brilhart, John K., and Galanes, Gloria J. *Effective Group Discussion.* 7th ed. Dubuque, IA: Wm. C. Brown, 1992, chapters 5 and 7.
Cathcart, Robert S., and Samovar, Larry A. (eds.). *Small Group Communication: A Reader.* 6th ed. Dubuque, IA: Wm. C. Brown, 1992, sections 5 and 6.

Gudykunst, William B. *Bridging Differences: Effective Intergroup Communication.* Newbury Park, CA: Sage, 1991.

King, Stephen W. "The Nature of Communication." In Robert S. Cathcart and Larry A. Samovar, (eds.), *Small Group Communication: A Reader.* 5th ed. Dubuque, IA: Wm. C. Brown, 1988.

Steil, Lyman K., and Barker, Larry. *Effective Listening: Key to Your Success.* Reading, MA: Addison-Wesley, 1983.

References

1. Dan B. Curtis, Jerry L. Windsor, and R. D. Stephens, "National Preferences in Business and Communication Education," *Communication Education* 38 (1989): 6–14.

2. Larry L. Barker, *Listening Behavior* (Englewood Cliffs, NJ: Prentice-Hall, 1971): 17.

3. Lyman K. Steil, Larry L. Barker, and Kittie W. Watson, *Effective Listening: Key to Your Success* (Reading, MA: Addison-Wesley, 1983): 21–22.

4. Kenneth N. Leone Cissna and Evelyn Sieburg, "Patterns of Intentional Confirmation and Disconfirmation," in *Bridges Not Walls,* 4th ed., ed. John Stewart (New York: Random House, 1986): 231–239.

5. William B. Gudykunst and Stella Ting-Toomey, *Culture and Interpersonal Communication* (Newbury Park, CA: Sage, 1988): 40–43.

6. Hofstede, G., *Culture's Consequences: International Differences in Work-Related Values* (Beverly Hills, CA: Sage, 1984).

7. Myron W. Lustig and Laura L. Cassotta, "Comparing Group Communication Across Cultures: Leadership, Conformity, and Discussion Processes," in *Small Group Communication: A Reader.* 6th ed., eds. Robert S. Cathcart and Larry A. Samovar (Dubuque, IA: Wm. C. Brown, 1992): 393–404.

8. William B. Gudykunst and Stella Ting-Toomey, *Culture and Interpersonal Communication,* 40–43.

9. George R. Bach and Peter Wyden, *The Intimate Enemy* (New York: Avon Press, 1968).

10. David M. Berg, "A Descriptive Analysis of the Distribution and Duration of Themes Discussed by Task-Oriented Small Groups," *Speech Monographs* 34 (1967): 172–175.

The blackboard reads:

Aristotle's parts
of Dramatic Action
1. Character
2. Music
3. Spectacle
4. Dialogue
   Idea
   Structure

CHAPTER FOUR

Verbal and Nonverbal Messages

CHAPTER OUTLINE

Creating Messages in a Small Group
Levels of Meaning
Using Language to Help the Group
**   Progress**
Follow the Rules
Adjust to the Symbolic Nature of Language
Use Emotive Words Cautiously
Organize Remarks
Make Sure the Discussion Question is Clear
    and Appropriate
Nonverbal Signals in Small Group
**   Communication**
Principles of Nonverbal Communication
Functions of Nonverbal Signals
Categories of Nonverbal Signals
*   Appearance*
*   Space and Seating*
*   Facial Expressions and Eye Contact*
*   Movements*
*   Voice*
*   Timing*

KEY TERMS AND CONCEPTS

Discussion Question
Emotive Words
Message
Nonverbal Signals

STUDY QUESTIONS

1. Describe the three levels of meaning
   contained in most messages.
2. What five suggestions should group
   members follow to improve their verbal
   communication?
3. What is nonverbal communication, what
   are its main functions, and what
   categories of nonverbal communication
   have major implications for small group
   communication?

On a recent trip to Greece, Gloria and her friend Noah were having dinner with several members of Gloria's family. Aunt Tula placed a beautiful tomato and cucumber salad on the table in front of Cousin George. Noah was just about to help himself to some salad when George, holding both hands out to encompass the salad bowl, said, in English, "Ah—these are mine!" Noah assumed that Aunt Tula had prepared the salad especially for George. Not wanting to offend anyone, Noah put his fork down and had none of the salad. The next day, when George talked about his wonderful garden and explained that he kept the family supplied with vegetables, Noah and Gloria both realized that his statement "These are mine" meant "I grew these in my garden," not "This salad is especially for me." The whole family, Gloria and Noah included, laughed at the incident, which became the running joke for the rest of the vacation.

This story, amusing as it was at the time, illustrates several important points about verbal and nonverbal communication, which are the topics of this chapter. First, it demonstrates that a group of words—a sentence—can have several different meanings, each of which is perfectly plausible. "These are mine" could reasonably be understood in more than one way. Second, it shows how nonverbal communication, in this case the encompassing gesture that took in the whole salad bowl, contributes to our interpretation of what words mean. The gesture together with the words led Noah to believe the salad was George's, not anyone else's. Third, it illustrates how important *context* is to determining what someone means. Someone more accustomed than Noah and Gloria to the culture of Greece would not have misinterpreted George's statement. In that context—a family gathering to honor guests from far away—no Greek would have insulted guests by bringing something to the table that the guests weren't welcome to enjoy.

The salad misunderstanding created no big problems—other than Noah missing out on a tasty salad—but similar misunderstandings *do* create major problems for many secondary groups. In this chapter, we will focus on messages group members exchange and the verbal and nonverbal components of these messages. As with the previous chapter, this information may be a review for you. Even so, we urge you to read it so you can improve your sending and interpreting of messages in a group.

Creating Messages in a Small Group

Message refers to any set of signals that is interpreted as a whole by some receiver or receivers.[1] During discussions messages may be entirely nonverbal or a mixture of verbal and nonverbal signs. For instance, a nod of the head may be interpreted by a perceiver as a message of agreement or disagreement. If a member speaks for a long time expressing her doubts about a proposal while she simultaneously frowns, gestures, and begins to speak louder and faster, others will probably see these behaviors, collectively, as disagreement.

Verbal and nonverbal signals are the components of messages the group members send. First we will look at the levels of meaning in messages, then we will look at the specific words people use. Finally, we will examine nonverbal signals and their contribution to the process of communication in the small group. In this chapter we concentrate on the face-to-face transactions that occur during a group's discussions. In chapter 8 we discuss how to keep accurate and complete written records, or minutes, of a group's meetings.

Levels of Meaning

In most messages there are three levels of meaning expressed by the sender: content, affect, and relationship. *Content* refers to what the message is about, such as a fact, an opinion, or a personal feeling the speaker is describing. *Affect* refers to how the sender feels about the content: Positive–negative, strong–weak, important–unimportant. A person who expresses a message with signs of strong feeling ("I DON'T LIKE that idea!") will command more attention and have greater impact than a speaker who seems unconcerned or uninvolved ("I don't like that idea."). *Relationship* refers to how the sender perceives the relationship between him- or herself and a listener. Generally, this will be one of three types: as equal to equal, superior to inferior, or inferior to superior. Ideas and beliefs are primarily encoded in words, whereas personal affect (feeling) and relationship messages are signaled primarily nonverbally. For example, one of us recently attended a lecture where the speaker addressed the audience as though the listeners were inferior. She stood with her hand on her hip, constantly shook her finger at the audience, and said things like, "Look, people, when are you going to figure out that. . . ." As you can imagine, even though audience members agreed with her *content,* they reacted negatively to her implied relationship message. In our experience, it is the relationship part of the message that causes many of the problems in groups.

Humans communicate ideas through language, the symbolic component of messages. Without words we could not express such ideas as "Twenty-eight pedestrians were injured by automobiles on National Avenue during the last three years" or "Both Republican and Democratic political leaders have contributed to the American economic problems indicated by the increasing national deficit."

All human progress depends on symbolic communication by which we pass on to others the information gleaned from our own experiences. We still use the ideas of Euclid, written about 2300 years ago in his book, *The Elements.* That is potent verbal communication. It could not be done without symbols.

Using Language to Help the Group Progress

Language, as we have already explained, is symbolic. A language for human exchange consists of symbols, both verbal and nonverbal, and rules for using them.

Table 4.1   Use Language Appropriately to Help the Group Progress

Follow the Rules of Standard English

1. Use standard sentence structure and vocabulary.
2. Use correct grammar.
3. Avoid jargon, excess slang, and profanity.

Adjust to the Symbolic Nature of Language

1. Guard against *bypassing.*
2. Be as precise and concrete as possible (e.g., *an adjustable crescent wrench* instead of a *tool*).
3. Give specific examples of what you mean when you have to use an abstract term, or use synonyms.

Use Emotive Words Cautiously

1. Recognize words that are likely to trigger strong emotional responses in others (e.g., *broad, honky*) and substitute with neutral words (e.g., *woman, Caucasian*).
2. *Never* use name-calling.

Organize Your Remarks and the Group's Discussion Process

1. Relate your statement to the preceding statement.
2. Make one point at a time, not a multi-point speech.
3. State your case directly and concisely.
4. Keep yourself and other members on the topic.

Be Sure the Discussion Question Is Clear and Appropriate

1. Use open-ended questions instead of either-or ones.
2. Word questions clearly and concretely.
3. Don't give the answer in the question.
4. Make sure all group members know what question or issue is being discussed.

In print, the nonverbal elements are things like punctuation marks, underlining, CAPITALIZATION, **boldfacing,** and s p a c i n g. The verbal code is the *vocabulary,* the set of words available to the person who uses the language. The *rules* are the spoken and unspoken guidelines for arranging words: what to capitalize, how to space, how to structure sentences, where to place punctuation marks, etc. Collectively we call these the rules of syntax and grammar. Both the codes and rules vary according to social contexts, such as during a male bull session, a formal meeting of a city council, or a church building committee. Suggestions for using language effectively are detailed in the following section and summarized in table 4.1. The suggestions in the table and the discussion that follows are appropriate for most organizational groups in the U.S. As we noted in chapter 3, different rules will apply in different cultures.

Follow the Rules

As we noted in chapter 3, different groups and cultures have different rules for communicating. You will increase your chances of both being accepted and being understood if you follow the rules for the groups you are in. For example, some academic groups are formal: members address each other by title (e.g., Dr. Smith or Ms. Jones) and use many abstract words with a complex sentence structure. However, these rules would be inappropriate in a self-managed work team responsible for producing a car with zero defects. In the work team, concrete language with a clear and concise sentence structure will be more effective. Flowery language would be expected in a cultural group that included members from Mexico or Brazil, but would be looked upon with suspicion by a group of Austrians. In some groups, using *ain't* and *he don't* might be acceptable; in others, it would not. Try to be aware of and conform to appropriate standards of behavior *for the particular group.*

Even as we advise this, however, we note that many of the secondary groups you participate in will take place in the mainstream of the U.S. business and educational communities. In such cases, you are well advised to conform to the vocabulary and grammar rules of standard English. This will help other people understand you and increase your influence because numerous studies have shown that nonstandard dialects lower the credibility of speakers with a variety of listeners. Avoid gross mispronunciations and misuses (ain't), mix-ups in agreement between subject and verb (they isn't . . .), and excess slang (it's really neat, gross, awesome, etc.) when precise language is possible. Also, avoid profanity in almost all task groups. Jack remembers a university dean who spoke in the most elevated of language in large group meetings but then swore profusely in conferences with only two or three other males present. Several times a person leaving the meeting would express shock and dismay at the language because it had seriously interfered with listening to ideas and had lowered the dean's credibility.

Adjust to the Symbolic Nature of Language

People who use language effectively in group discussions are keenly aware of its symbolic nature. They realize that words do not have meanings in and of themselves, so they strive to express their ideas in words likely to evoke similar meanings in listeners.

As listeners, they try to interpret accurately by asking themselves, "What does the speaker mean?" rather than "What do those words mean?" or "What would I mean if I said that?" They are on guard against *bypassing,* where two or more people have different meanings for a word but do not realize it, which leads either to a false agreement or the perception that a disagreement exists when it really doesn't. For example, members of a student group agreed to meet in the "Thayer Room." However, there were two different places on campus called "The Thayer Room," and part of the group showed up in each place. Members of each subgroup began to call the ones who weren't present "irresponsible." No one had bothered to ask "Do you mean the Thayer Room in the library or the one in Hill

Hall?" Finally someone thought of that, and went from Hill to find the other members in the library. The words had been the same, but the meanings the members gave to the words were different.

Efficient communicators are keenly aware that many words, especially abstract ones, are likely to be interpreted differently by different people. Words vary from highly concrete to highly abstract. The most concrete forms are those that refer to one and only one thing: *Dr. Brilhart's desk, John Brown of the Harper's Ferry raid,* or *Standard Poodle number PD736251.* However, words and phrases like *social scientist, flora, cosmos, democracy,* and *love* are highly abstract and likely to be understood quite differently by different participants in a group discussion. The terms in the following list become more abstract (more vague) as you proceed down the list; therefore, the likelihood increases that other members of your group will understand the term differently.

Mario Cuomo, Governor of New York

governors

elected officials

public servants

humans

mammals

life

energy

The level of abstractness matters a lot during discussions. With concrete terms, little misunderstanding will occur, but confusion can be rampant when highly abstract words are used. Leathers found that highly abstract statements (such as "Don't you think this is a matter of historical dialecticism?") consistently disrupted discussions among college students, and that the amount of confusion and disarray increased as the statements were made more abstract.[2]

We are not saying never use abstract language during discussion; that would be impossible. Many of the ideas group members discuss must be in fairly abstract words such as *criteria, equal opportunity, cost effective,* and *fair.* But you can do a lot to prevent misunderstanding when these terms *are* used. First, speak as concretely as possible to express what you mean. People who want to confuse or show off their learning often use *doublespeak* or jargon. You can improve mutual understanding by referring to "an adjustable crescent wrench" instead of to a "tool," or to "Word Perfect 5.1" instead of "a word processing program."

Second, whenever you use a highly abstract term that may be ambiguous to many people, use concrete examples of what you mean. For example, "He was a really domineering chair (abstract concept) who decided alone when the group would meet, what would and would not be on the agenda, who could and could not speak at the meetings, and what the recommendations of the committee would be to the president of the fraternity" (concrete examples of the abstract idea of *domineering*).

Third, you can frequently define highly abstract terms by using synonyms, descriptive terms, or explaining some operation the term refers to. Thus you might define *democracy* as "a government in which the people making laws are elected by popular vote of all adult citizens, and in which candidates from two or more competing parties run for all national offices." In another example, *drunk driving* in many states is defined as "having a level of .10 percent alcohol in the blood as measured, immediately after driving, by a machine called a breathalyzer." This definition combines both a procedure and precise quantification for the term *drunk*.

Fourth, you should quantify when possible. Frequently groups use relative terms for comparisons when precise quantification is possible. For instance, instead of saying "the chances of developing lung cancer are *higher* (a relative term) if you smoke a pack of cigarettes a day than if you don't smoke," you now are able to state quite precisely what the increase in percentage of people developing lung cancer will be. In analyzing risks of some actions, a statistical probability of failure can often be computed. Instead of saying "a convicted rapist has a low probability of repeating his crime if paroled," state the actual percentage, *then* decide whether the risk is worth the advantages of parole over prison.

As a listener, you can ask speakers who use highly abstract language to quantify, give examples, or define their terms with less abstract language. You can paraphrase in more concrete terms, then ask the speaker to accept or revise your paraphrase. This will help you interpret the speaker's meaning more accurately.

Use Emotive Words Cautiously

Emotive words are terms associated with either highly pleasant or highly unpleasant experiences and images. Often these are called *trigger* words because they evoke almost instantaneous emotional responses that interfere with good listening.

For instance, for some people *male chauvinist* conjures up an image of a man with little regard for women as individuals, one who wants to keep women subservient because he considers them inferior. Among the worst trigger words are sexist terms and racial epithets (such as *nigger, spic, honky, WASP*). During the 1988 presidential race *liberal* was often used as an emotive term to cast scorn on Michael Dukakis.

You can improve the quality of thinking during group discussions by avoiding such words yourself and suggesting alternatives when someone uses one of them. Consider the following two lists. The first has negative emotive terms, the second, neutral ones that denote the same things.

"Can you cut it a little finer, Mergeson, than 'umpteen'?"

Quantify precisely whenever you can. (Drawing by Donald Reilly; © 1985 The New Yorker Magazine, Inc.)

Negative	Neutral or Positive
Broad	Woman
Jock	Athlete
Ay-rab	Arab
Jew them down	Negotiate or haggle
Ree-tard	Down's syndrome
Hillbilly	Native of the Ozarks
Bonehead	Remedial

So if someone were to say "He's nothing but a hillbilly jock taking bonehead English; why should I vote for him for student body president?" you could paraphrase as follows: "So you think the fact that he is an athlete, a native of the Ozarks, and enrolled in remedial English disqualifies him as student body president?" This will help defuse the trigger words, enforce norms of appropriate language, and begin an objective evaluation of the person's qualifications.

"Sorry, Chief, but of course I didn't mean 'bimbo' in the pejorative sense."

Don't use trigger words that may offend others. (Drawing by Lorenz; © 1987 The New Yorker Magazine, Inc.)

Organize Remarks

Organization of the discussion in general and of your own remarks in particular are both affected by what you say and how you say it. Frequently discussions jump almost aimlessly from topic to topic. No one seems to be responding to prior comments. All too often it is hard to tell exactly what issue or question a speaker is addressing, or even what the point is of some remarks. Good organization can do a lot to overcome these communication problems. Consider the following excerpt:

Nom: What do you guys think is the central message of the chapter we're supposed to discuss today?

Nemia: I'm hung up on the word *consensus*. I can't see how it differs from *majority* or *unanimous*.

Jane: Well, it's about problem solving, I mean, like what problems are and how to go about solving them, and stuff like that.

Marcos: I think maybe, uh, problem solving is more effective if the group ·follows some procedure, like an outline of steps in the discussion, beginning with a very complete description of the problem. At least that's what I think.

Laura: I really don't think that's true. You know, some of the greatest solutions to big problems came as sudden insights like when an apple fell on Newton's head and he figured out gravity, or when Archimedes took a bath and solved his problem of how to tell if the king's crown was pure gold by noticing how much water ran out of his tub when he got in.

Let's re-do that bit of discussion to make it organized as a *group* process by organizing the remarks of the individual participants.

Nom: What do you guys think is the central message of chapter 12? (No big change here, but more specific and with slightly improved syntax. As before, Nom has asked a question that could be the issue for considerable discussion, or else the group could decide not to discuss that question at this time.)

Nemia: Before we discuss that, Nom, I'd like to get help in defining the term *consensus*. I wasn't ready yet to end our discussion of the definitions we didn't understand. Soon as we do that, I'll be glad to talk about the central message of chapter 12. Okay? (Nemia now responds directly to Nom's question, and suggests an alternate procedure.)

Nom: Okay by me. Group, what do we understand *consensus* to mean? (With this direct response to Nemia, Nom revises his suggestion, which had overlooked Nemia's need to define another term before moving to the next item on the group's agenda.)

Dave: *Consensus*—I understand that means an agreement by all members that a proposed solution is acceptable to them, one they can live with and support, though not necessarily the one they most prefer, like if they unanimously vote for one solution as the best. Consensus is a sort of compromise, but there are no winners and losers, no trade-offs in a consensus. In a majority vote, there are winners and losers. (Dave responds directly to Nemia's question.)

Others: Yes, Uh-huh. That's it. (These signals indicate agreement with Dave's prior statement.)

Nemia: Thanks, got it. Okay, now I'm ready to talk about the central message. (This responds directly to Dave and the group, and returns to the issue Nom suggested earlier as the next agenda item. The discussion is kept coherent and organized.)

Jane: Um, I can't say exactly what the central idea is, Nemia, but I know the chapter is about problem solving. Can anyone summarize the chapter as a central message? (She acknowledges that she is not addressing the issue fully, but wants to test her understanding of the topic.)

Marcos:	I'll try, Jane. I think this chapter is saying that problem-solving outcomes are likely to be better when a group follows an outlined, step-by-step procedure that begins with a thorough description of the problem, moves to a period of creating as many alternatives as possible, then goes into critical thinking about all proposals until consensus is reached about the best one, and finally ends with a definite plan to act. How do the rest of you summarize chapter 12? (Marcos responds directly to Jane's question and Nom's original one, gives his answer concisely at as low a level of abstraction as is feasible, then invites others to respond to the same issue. This keeps the discussion organized on the same topic.)
Laura:	Marcos, I think you did a great job of stating the central message. However, I'd like to add one thing I think is also part of the central message: problem solving means finding a way to get from some unacceptable situation to a desired one, a goal.
Group:	Good. I agree. That's it.
Nom:	Guess we are ready to move on. Right? First, let me see if I can combine what Marcos and Laura said: . . .
Group:	Nods, comments of acceptance, *thumbs up* sign.

In the second version (not what was actually said but what would have been more productive) each comment begins with some confirmation of the prior speaker, often by naming the person or responding directly to the prior statement. No one switches topics abruptly, though Nemia asks the *group* to do so for a definite time and reason. You will also notice that statements are right to the point, as unambiguous as possible. In almost all cases the speaker stays with *one* point. If the Lake Area Wellness Council mentioned in the previous chapter had used such an organized procedure, perhaps their misunderstanding would not have occurred. The following is a list of guidelines for speaking that will facilitate coherent, orderly, and clear discussion:

1. **Relate your statement to the preceding statement.** Sometime this will have to be done explicitly in a statement; sometimes it can be done with a word or phrase (e.g., Dave—"*Consensus*"; Nom—"Okay by me.")
2. **State one point, not a multi-point speech.** If you talk about two or more issues, the discussion is likely to go off track because no one can predict which issue the next speaker will pick up on even if she responds directly to your remarks. (There is one major exception to this rule in group meetings: when you present an initial description of a problem to a group or make a planned report of your research for the group, you may have more than one point to make. In fact, you will be making a brief multi-point speech to the group. In that case, we suggest you prepare a handout for everyone that includes details such as the main findings or facts, statistics, quotations, formulas, etc.)

3. **State the point directly, concretely, and concisely as possible.** Simple declarative sentences are preferable to flowery language and emotive terms in the dominant culture of the U.S. Phrases such as "My point is that . . ." and "This is the idea: . . ." may help a lot.

Make Sure the Discussion Question Is Clear and Appropriate

Verbal exchanges among members are about some question or issue. Issue here refers to a point that has not yet been settled or decided upon by the group. It may be a matter of controversy, or just a matter of information still under discussion. During effective discussions, all members should be able to state the **discussion question.**

Unfortunately, group members often cannot do this. A careful analysis of members' remarks will show that different members are attempting to answer different questions at the same time. For example, Mary is trying to evaluate a suggestion Thuy has proposed—to solve the lack of parking spaces on campus—while Sonya is explaining how student parking fees are being spent and LaShonda is presenting *her* proposal to solve the parking problem. This is certainly a sign of poor listening, as well as confusion about the group procedure. Far too many participants in small group discussions seem to be answering questions no one has asked. The result is the kind of confused topic switching we described earlier.

Establishing the right question is crucial and can determine whether the group produces a good or poor solution. For example, consider the following two discussion questions: *How can we raise money to build another classroom building?* versus *How can we relieve the overcrowding in classrooms?* The first question focuses on an already-decided solution, which may or may not be the best solution to solve the problem. The second focuses on the problem (overcrowding) without biasing the solution in advance. Building more classrooms may work, but perhaps the problems are due to poor scheduling of existing facilities. Maybe holding classes at off-campus locations like shopping centers, factories, and offices throughout the city would be more effective in reducing the overcrowding. However, these options would never be discovered if the group is determined to solve the problem by building more classrooms. So you see, how a group states its discussion question is important and influences the entire progress of the group's discussion. As an input, it has a far-reaching effect on the system's throughput process and its output. The types of discussion questions, with examples, are described in table 4.2.

Any time you feel confused about what is going on during small group meetings it will pay to ask yourself or the group what question is being discussed. Get an answer to that question before you proceed, and help the entire group become mutually oriented toward the same goal at the same moment. When you ask a question, be sure the *type* of answer you seek is clear from the phrasing of the question. Table 4.2 explains seven types of questions on the basis of the type

Table 4.2   Types of Discussion Questions

Information Questions

Ask for specific information or facts, but not interpretations or opinions.

Examples

1. Why was this meeting called?
2. How many thefts were reported on campus last year?
3. Where did you learn that?
4. What did Jim say was his reason for missing the meeting?

Interpretation Questions

Ask for personal opinions, interpretations, judgments; they invite discussion.

Examples

1. What might have caused this increase in the rate of theft?
2. What connection might there be between college grades and whether a student has a computer?
3. Do you think our presentation should emphasize the need to reduce the deficit or the need to keep down inflation?

Value Questions

Ask how good, how important, significant, or worthwhile something is in the opinion of the responder. A value question is a type of interpretation question.

Examples

1. How good a president do you think Ronald Reagan was?
2. Is this question important enough to take up the group's time?
3. What are the pros and cons of this alternative?
4. How good a case does the prosecuting attorney have against William Roberts?
5. Which of these suits do you think looks best?
6. How much do you like this painting?

Policy Questions

Ask what *should* be done about some issue or matter; key word is *should*. Usually, groups have discussed a number of information and interpretation questions before they begin to discuss and decide what policy to take.

Examples

1. What should the U.S. government do to reduce the federal deficit?
2. What should our school's attendance policy be?
3. What kinds of skills should be required of all "med tech" graduates?
4. What should the Washington, D.C. police do to reduce drug-related crimes?

Action Questions

Ask how to implement a decision or policy already decided by the group.

Examples

1. How will we make this recommendation to the student senate?
2. Now that we've decided what food to serve at the banquet, who will see to it that it is prepared and served?
3. How can we guarantee that all pilots know about this policy and follow it?

Procedure Questions

Ask how the group, or an individual member, does something; what procedure the group will use.

Examples

1. How shall we start compiling information about why talented young people leave town after high school graduation?
2. What would be the best way to present our proposal to our client?
3. What sequence should we use to organize our discussion of this issue?
4. How can we divide the work of the committee in a way that's fair to everybody?

Relationship Questions

Seek information about how members feel toward each other, the group, their responsibilities to the group, the relative status of members, and sometimes what members expect from each other.

Examples

1. Do we need some introductions, or does everybody know everybody else?
2. How do you all feel about our assignment to select an insurance carrier for our medical programs?
3. How did *you* get the authority to decide when we meet?
4. Paul, something seems to be bothering you. Is there something about how we've been treating you that's got you upset?

of response asked for and gives several examples of each type. When you reply to a question, be sure you are giving the *kind* of response sought by the questioner: (1) specific information; (2) an interpretation or opinion; (3) an evaluation or judgment of relative worth of the topic of the question; (4) a proposed policy or solution; (5) a course of action or way to implement a decision; (6) a group procedure; or (7) an expression of how you perceive your relationship to the group and/or another member. Here are a few guidelines to help you phrase questions that focus and facilitate group interaction.

1. **Unless the group has already narrowed a list of alternatives to two, avoid *either-or* questions.** Usually these grossly oversimplify the issue by treating questions of interpretation, value, or policy as if there were only two legitimate answers instead of a wide range. In the list that follows, the first question of each pair is poorly worded in *either-or* terms, the second version is worded as a matter of degree:

    Is this a fair way to treat our secretary? (Implied is a *yes* or *no* answer.)
    How fair will this be to the secretary?

    Should we make all illegal aliens citizens or deport them to their native countries? (This implies that there are only two options for dealing with illegal aliens.)
    How should we handle illegal aliens?

    Shall we ship this by truck or UPS?
    How shall we ship this package?

    Instead of either-or questions, make your questions for discussion open-ended. Leave room for any sort of appropriate response, not just a few responses like the kind supplied in multiple-choice tests.

2. **Word questions as concretely as possible.** A confusing practice is to ask a *double-barreled* question, one that combines two questions in one. For example, "What is wrong with Sol, and why is he acting that way?" is a double-barreled question. Listeners don't know which part of the question to respond to. Perhaps both issues need to be addressed, but if so, say that and then ask the first question. For example, we can restate our earlier question about Sol: "We are here to try to find out what Sol is doing that is making other members angry, and to try to determine why Sol might be acting in irritating ways. First, what actions have angered anyone here?"

3. **Avoid suggesting the answer in the question.** A question that suggests an answer is not an honest question but an indirect way to make a point. For instance, "Wouldn't it be a good idea to tell Sol we will expel him from the fraternity if he ever takes a brother's clothes without first asking for them?" suggests a solution.

4. **Apply skills of critical thinking to questions you ask.** Most important are the guidelines for evaluating information and detecting errors in reasoning. These skills are explained in chapter 5. Use them to evaluate and improve both the questions you and others ask during discussions. Logical errors in reasoning implied in questions are likely to be found in the answers as well.

Up to now we have been emphasizing the importance of words to the messages that are sent and received in small groups. However, no matter how skilled and sensitive you are with words, your communication will be inefficient if you overlook the kinds of nonverbal signals that carry much of the communication load in a group.

Table 4.3   Principles of Nonverbal Communication

Nonverbal signals are ambiguous	Nonverbal behaviors can be interpreted in a number of different ways. Both context and culture are important in determining what a particular nonverbal behavior means.
People cannot stop sending nonverbal signals	Group members cannot choose to stop communicating because they send nonverbal signals even when they aren't talking. You cannot *not* communicate.
Nonverbal signals are more believable than verbal signals	It is easier to control words than nonverbal behaviors. When there is a discrepancy between nonverbal and verbal signals, most people believe the nonverbal signals.

Nonverbal Signals in Small Group Communication

Nonverbal signals are all the signals contained in a message except the words themselves. These signals may be either signs or symbols and include such things as tone of voice, gestures, and appearance. They serve a number of purposes, especially helping us express how we feel and how we perceive our relationships to others. We will explain several important principles of communicating with nonverbal signals, examine key functions performed by nonverbal signals, and finally look at the categories of nonverbal behavior that have the most important influence on small group communication.

Principles of Nonverbal Communication

Most of the time in a small group, only one person speaks at a time. However, all the members are sending nonverbal signals all the time! Understanding something about nonverbal signals is crucial to understanding what is happening in your groups. However, interpretation of nonverbal signals can be trickier than interpreting verbal signals, because of the nature of communicating nonverbally. Principles of nonverbal communication are summarized in table 4.3.

1. **Nonverbal signals are ambiguous.** Do you think that a smile means someone is happy? Well, most of the time in our culture that will be the case, but in Japan someone who is feeling quite miserable may smile so as not to upset the person to whom he is speaking. Do you think that someone who has her arms folded across her chest is indicating that she is not interested in hearing what you say? Maybe. But maybe she is merely trying to keep warm. There is nothing absolute about interpreting nonverbal signals because too many factors influence their meaning, including cultural differences. Nonverbal signals should be considered in context and in conjunction with the words group members are using.

"That's bass with broccoli and mushrooms. Stop calling it animal, vegetable, and fungus."

What you call it *does* make a difference. (Drawing by W. Miller; © 1985 The New Yorker Magazine, Inc.)

2. **People cannot stop sending nonverbal signals, even when they are not talking.** As we mentioned earlier, only one person in a group usually speaks at a time, but all members continuously send and receive nonverbal signals. Even if you choose to be quiet in a group meeting, you will likely be leaking your feelings or thoughts nonverbally. For example, at a church board meeting a member who was unhappy with the way the church secretary was handling office business chose not to say anything when personnel matters were discussed because the other members seemed pleased with her performance. However, after the meeting the board chair asked him what was wrong and why he had seemed uninterested at the meeting. This example points out two features of nonverbal communication. First, even though the member chose not to say anything, he certainly was sending something nonverbally. Second, the emotion he was feeling was anger at the church secretary, but the board chair thought he was uninterested in the meeting. Nonverbal signals are often difficult to interpret, so we shouldn't jump to conclusions without first checking them out.

3. **When verbal and nonverbal messages clash, most people believe the nonverbal signals.** Let's suppose the committee member in the previous example says to the board chair, "No, there's nothing wrong." What is the chair likely to believe? Probably that there *was* in fact something wrong, but

the member didn't want to share it. In fact, when a person is trying to interpret what someone else means in a face-to-face interaction, the nonverbal part of the message counts almost twice as much as the verbal.[3] When the verbal and nonverbal signals don't fit, most people will trust the nonverbals because they are less subject to deliberate control. Many nonverbal behaviors, such as sweating, blushing, and shaking are controlled by primitive structures of the brain over which we have little or no conscious control. You can pick and choose your words more easily than you can your nonverbal behavior, which often gives you away! So when you clench your fists, turn red, and scream at another group member "NO, I'M NOT MAD!" no one will believe you.

Functions of Nonverbal Signals

Nonverbal signals perform a variety of functions, the most vital of which is to express how we feel. Likewise, we indicate how we perceive our relationships to other people mostly nonverbally. In addition to expressing affect and relationships, nonverbal signals modify the verbal component of messages exchanged among group members. They can *supplement* the words we utter by emphasizing them or in effect repeating them, just as underlined or **boldfaced** words in a text are emphasized. Thus nonverbals can call special attention to the words they accompany. For instance, a person may say "Look at the part of our income that comes from user fees" while pointing at a segment of a pie graph. Or one might say "The new cabinet is about *this* high" while holding the palm of one hand five feet from the floor. Nods, headshakes, leans, changes in pitch, stares, and other nonverbal signs give emphasis to supplement the symbols they accompany.

Nonverbal signals can *substitute* for spoken or written words. In this case, a gesture becomes a symbol, substituting for the more conventional words. For instance, a circled thumb and index finger can express "OK," or a beckoning finger can indicate you want someone to lean closer to you. Gloria's choir director gives a "thumbs up" signal when the choir performs well. A nod can express agreement, or a head shake can signal a vote of "no." Because only one person can be speaking during an orderly discussion, much of the communicating among members must be with unspoken substitutes for spoken words. If you aren't conscious of these signals and don't look for them, you will miss many important messages among group members and misinterpret other nonverbal messages. In a sense, you will be only half-listening.

Another major function of nonverbal messages is to *regulate* the flow of verbal interaction among members. The coordinator of a discussion group may use nods, eye contact, and hand signals to indicate who should speak next. Direct gaze from listeners indicates "continue" whereas looking away is a nonverbal way of saying "Shut up!" People who want to speak lean forward, slightly open their mouths, extend a hand or finger, and may even utter a sound such as "um."

Speakers who ignore such cues are judged inconsiderate and rude. One of us observed a group containing a blind person who obviously could not see such regulating cues. Other members began to judge this member as arrogant and self-centered for "talking out of turn." Some discussion of visible regulatory cues increased the members' sensitivity to the communicative problem experienced by their blind member and helped the group pull together.

Finally, as we noted earlier, nonverbal signs can *contradict* words we utter. A person who says "I agree" hesitatingly with a rising pitch at the end of the words may be perceived as having reservations, or even as disagreeing. A person who says "I heard you" but will not attempt a paraphrase has indicated nonverbally that he probably was not really listening. Signs of out-and-out lying often include nonverbal leaks such as wiggling feet, unusual inflections, or glancing away. When you observe nonverbal signals that seem to contradict what a person has just said, and it matters to you what the person really thinks, it will pay you to say "I heard you say . . . , but the way you said it bothers me." Then explain the apparent contradiction you perceived, and ask the person to clear it up for you.

Categories of Nonverbal Signals

Several categories of nonverbal behavior are especially important to your understanding of small group communication. Failure to attend to these aspects of nonverbal communication in a group may mean that you overlook or misunderstand important information or alienate other members of your group. Personal appearance, space, facial expression, eye contact and movement, gestures and body movement, voice, and time cues are among the major types of nonverbal signals most relevant to small groups. Sensitive group members are aware both of the nonverbal signals they send as well as those they receive.

Appearance

Accurate or not, members of a group form impressions of each other long before anyone says anything. Sex, race, attractiveness, height, build, dress, grooming, and other visible cues have been shown to influence the responses of other people. Violating societal norms about dress, grooming, makeup, and accessories can arouse suspicion or even mistrust. Dressing noticeably differently from other members will almost certainly be interpreted as a sign that you do not identify with them. Others may peg you as undependable and uncooperative, and you may have to prove yourself in other ways in order to be accepted.

When Gloria was in graduate school, she was in a study group with a fellow student who wore outlandish clothing, used heavy make-up, and had bright orange hair. She thought, "Can't count on that one for any help." She was wrong. This student was one of the brightest, most conscientious members of the group, but it took the other members a long time to reach that conclusion because they

Figure 4.1 The group's leader may sit apart from other members.

had to overcome their initial stereotypical impressions that she was a bimbo. It is unfair that appearance is regarded so importantly; therefore, we advise you to suspend judgment based on appearance until you have observed how that person behaves as a group member. Also, be aware of how your own appearance may be judged by others.

Space and Seating

Many scientists have examined how people use space to communicate. The amount of space people prefer between them depends on a variety of factors, including culture and gender. For example, in the U.S. most business transactions are conducted at what Hall calls *social distance,* which is between four and eight feet.[4] We are comfortable allowing only our intimate friends within a foot or two. However, four feet is much too far for someone from the Arab world or from Latin America. In these countries, people transact business at what we consider close personal distance, which often makes Americans very uneasy. In the dominant culture of the U.S., females tend to sit closer together than males, as do people of the same age and social status, and those who know each other well. In a group, sitting close together, especially if the room is large enough for members to spread out, indicates that members like each other and there is a sense of cohesiveness. A person who sits apart from the others may be signalling that he or she does not feel a part of the group.

Space, seating, and status are closely related. Dominant people often claim more than their fair share of space, and a group's leader usually is given more space by the other members than they claim, as is shown in figure 4.1. In addition, group leaders will generally sit in a central position, such as at the head of a rectangular table, where they can see as many of the other members as possible. Most of the long, rectangular, or boat-shaped conference tables found in many offices and businesses are not ideal for effective discussions. Such tables make it difficult for all members to see all other members and contribute to uneven verbal participation patterns. For instance, people who sit across from each other respond to each other more than people sitting side by side or on the edges of each other's vision. The ideal table for most small group discussions is a round table where all members have easy eye contact with each other. If that is not possible, group members are advised to position themselves around the table, whatever shape it is, in something close to a circle or oval.

Facial Expressions and Eye Contact

Sitting where you can see every other member of the group is important because it allows you to make eye contact with other members. Eye contact and facial expressions are among the most important nonverbal signals for group members. For Americans, making eye contact signals that the channel for communication is open. This is why many students look down at their notebooks when a teacher asks a question—they want to avoid eye contact so they won't be called upon to answer. Prolonged eye contact can signal cooperativeness or competitiveness, depending on the circumstances. Most Americans establish eye contact before speaking and continue it intermittently when talking to someone they like. However, people from other cultures are sometimes offended by Americans' direct gazes, while others prefer to maintain an intense, unbroken stare when conversing, which is uncomfortable for Americans. As with other nonverbals, there are numerous cultural factors that influence what a person considers to be appropriate eye contact. In groups that are unified and cohesive, members tend to look continuously at each other during a discussion. In hostile or tense groups, members will avoid eye contact.

Studies using photographs have shown that people can accurately determine the type of emotion someone is experiencing from looking just at the face and eyes.[5] Anger, sadness, happiness, support, disagreement, interest, liking—all are indicated by facial expressions. Some people have "poker" faces; their facial expressions change very little. They tend to be trusted less than those whose faces express their feelings more openly. Although most of us have learned to control our facial expressions, feelings still show through. Most of us monitor the facial expressions of others because they provide clues about what is going on in the group. Even if a group member isn't saying anything about your proposal, you can tell by her frown and grimace that she doesn't think much of it. That gives you information about what your next steps should be—drop the proposal, modify it, ask the other member directly what she thinks, or speak with her privately after the meeting.

Movements

Movements of the hands, arms, and even the body signal many feelings and attitudes. For example, Scheffler found that people turn directly toward others they like and away from those they dislike. Leaning toward each other indicates a sense of mutual inclusiveness, whereas leaning away signals rejection.[6] When group members feel a sense of unity with each other, they tend to imitate each other's posture and body movements. This takes place automatically, without conscious awareness. Mabry found that body orientation changes significantly from one meeting to another.[7] As group members get to know, like, and trust one another more, they show this by increasing their eye contact and angling their bodies more directly toward each other.

Both tension and status can be revealed with movements. Members who are swinging a foot, twisting a lock of hair, or tapping a pencil may be indicating tension. It may be hard for the other members to know whether the movements indicate frustration, impatience, or annoyance with the group's progress. It pays to be alert to such movements and what might be causing them. Attentiveness to movement can also indicate who has high status in the group. Members are more likely to imitate the movements of high status members than those of low status members.[8] High status workers tend to be the most relaxed, so they lean back and look around.[9]

Voice

Vocal cues include such factors as pitch, speed, fluency, loudness, and pauses. We rely on tone of voice to interpret someone's mood. Someone who says "Yeah, I could live with that" softly in a questioning tone of voice is not likely to be believed. In addition, listeners tend to judge the status, educational level, ethnicity, and attitudes of speakers on the basis of vocal cues.[10] People who speak in a monotone have less credibility and are less persuasive than those who speak in a more animated tone of voice. However, those who are extremely animated may appear to be irrational or hysterical.

Nonverbal *backchannel* sounds, such as the *mm-hmmm* and *uh-huh,* are sounds that people make to indicate interest and involvement when listening. Interestingly, there are cultural variations in the use of the backchannel. Most people from western European backgrounds use the backchannel less frequently than Blacks, Hispanics, or people with southern European backgrounds. These differences can cause misunderstandings in a group if members are not aware of them. For example, a Hispanic member who is used to receiving backchannel responses may believe the other members of the group are not interested in her ideas because they do not respond with encouraging *mm-hmmm* sounds like she is used to. The other members may in fact be interested, but they express their interest in other ways. Men and women seem to use the backchannel differently, too. Women use backchannel responses to mean "Keep talking, I'm paying attention." Men, on the other hand, use the backchannel to mean "I agree with you." Misinterpretations can easily occur. A male group member who has been receiving backchannel responses from a female member may conclude that she supports his suggestion. Later, he will be confused and probably angry to learn that she disagrees. Each was using the backchannel to mean something different.

Timing

Time cues are both culture-related and relational. In some other cultures and subcultures of this country, no one would expect to get right to work in a group meeting; first, one must get the feel of the other people. Most rural people tackle business at a slower pace than their urban counterparts. In the fast-paced business world, people who come late to meetings are judged inconsiderate, undisciplined, and selfish. Americans will allow only about a five-minute leeway before they expect an apology from someone who is late.[11] In the predominant culture of this country, by coming late and leaving early you indicate to fellow group members that you are more important than they, and that your time is precious but it's okay to waste theirs. We have had dozens of case studies of student groups in which one consistently late member was the subject of bitter complaints by the others.

Time is a vital commodity during meetings. People who talk little and those who talk excessively have little impact. Excessive talkers are considered rude and selfish. Although they did not protest at the time, many students have complained about fellow project group members who waste time by chattering at length about social matters or other topics irrelevant to the group's purpose. On the other hand, those who talk somewhat about average are judged favorably on leadership characteristics.[12] Likewise, people who structure the group's time so every item on an agenda can be discussed are appreciated. If you are insensitive to time cues in your group, you will have little influence and not be completely accepted by the others.

No type of nonverbal communication can be overlooked if you want to understand what is going on in a group. Remember also that you cannot state with confidence exactly what someone else is thinking or feeling from nonverbal cues alone. We hope the list of nonverbal signals presented here encourages you to increase your awareness and sensitivity, but you should not consider this list exhaustive.

Summary

Most messages people send have three levels of meaning. The content refers to what the message is about, the affect refers to the feeling the sender has, and the relationship level indicates what the sender believes is the type of relationship (equal, superior, inferior) between sender and receiver. Most of the affect and relationship messages are indicated nonverbally.

Since there are so many things, verbal and nonverbal, that can interfere with effective group discussion, several suggestions were presented for helping improve the verbal aspects of group communication. First, members are encouraged to follow the rules of standard English for most secondary groups. Second, whenever possible, members should adjust to the symbolic nature of language by using concrete rather than abstract and ambiguous language. Third, members should steer clear of emotive words that are likely to evoke strong feelings in others, especially any form of name-calling. Next, group members individually should organize their own remarks by addressing only one point at a time and making their remarks relevant to the topic of discussion. In addition, the group as a whole should make some effort to make sure that members stay on the topic and that each remark is relevant to the remark preceding it. Finally, group members can improve their discussions and prevent time-wasting by making sure the discussion question is clear and appropriate. Questions should be open-ended, worded concretely, and the answer should not be suggested by the way the question is worded.

The chapter concluded with a discussion of the importance of understanding and being sensitive to the nonverbal cues sent by members of a group. Group members constantly send out nonverbal signals, and they are more believable than the verbal signals, although they can be difficult to interpret. Nonverbal cues function to supplement the verbal, express feelings, regulate the back-and-forth flow of communication, and substitute for the verbal (such as the *thumbs up* gesture). Nonverbal signals can also contradict the verbal. Several categories of nonverbal behavior have special importance to small group communication. For example, a member's appearance can send a message that the member values the group and wishes to be part of it, or that the member couldn't care less about offending others. Use of space reveals how members feel about each other (members who like each other tend to sit closer together) and who are the most dominant members of the group. Nonverbal cues especially important to communication in small groups include facial expressions, eye contact, movements, vocal cues, and time cues. The group member who is insensitive to nonverbal cues in the group will be likely to make many mistakes in communication, thereby hurting the group's overall performance.

Now that you are aware of some fundamental concepts in communication, you can begin to focus on how these concepts appear within the small group. In the next chapter we discuss how members can use language to think critically about information and ideas.

Review Questions

1. From your own experience, give an example of each of the three levels of meaning contained in most messages.
2. For each of the five guidelines for improving verbal communication in a group, describe the guideline, explain why it is important, and indicate what you would do if a group member fails to follow the suggestion.
3. Describe each major function of nonverbal communication and give an example of each.
4. Describe the major categories of nonverbal communication most relevant to small group communication and give examples of behavior in each category that could cause problems in a group.

Bibliography

Anderson, Peter A. "Nonverbal Communication in the Small Group." In Robert S. Cathcart and Larry A. Samovar, (eds.), *Small Group Communication: A Reader*. 6th ed. Dubuque, IA: Wm. C. Brown, 1992: 272–286.

Brilhart, John K., and Galanes, Gloria J. *Effective Group Discussion*. 6th ed. Dubuque, IA: Wm. C. Brown, 1989, chapters 5, 6, and 7.

Burgoon, Judee K. "Spatial Relationships in Small Groups." In Robert S. Cathcart and Larry A. Samovar, (eds.), *Small Group Communication: A Reader*. 6th ed. Dubuque, IA: Wm. C. Brown, 1992: 287–300.

References

1. Joseph A. DeVito, *The Communication Handbook: A Dictionary* (Harper & Row, 1986).
2. Dale G. Leathers, "Process Disruption and Measurement: Small Group Communication," *Quarterly Journal of Speech* 55 (1969): 288–298.
3. Ray L. Birdwhistell, Lecture at Nebraska Psychiatric Institute, Omaha, Nebraska: May 11, 1972.
4. Edward T. Hall, *The Silent Language* (Garden City, NJ: Doubleday, 1959).
5. P. Eckman, P. Ellsworth, and W. V. Friesen, *Emotion in the Human Face: Guidelines for Research and an Integration of Findings* (New York: Pergamon Press, 1971).
6. A. E. Schefler, "Quasi-Courtship Behavior in Psychotherapy," *Psychiatry* 28 (1965): 245–256.
7. Edward A. Mabry, "Developmental Aspects of Nonverbal Behavior in Small Group Settings," *Small Group Behavior* 20 (1989): 190–202.
8. Judee K. Burgoon and Thomas Saine, *The Unknown Dialogue: An Introduction to Nonverbal Communication* (Boston: Houghton-Mifflin, 1978).
9. Martin Remland, "Developing Leadership Skills in Nonverbal Communication: A Situational Perspective," *Journal of Business Communication* 3 (1981): 17–29.
10. Joel D. Davitz and Lois Davitz, "Nonverbal Vocal Communication of Feelings," *Journal of Communication* 11 (1961): 81–86.
11. R. G. Harper, A .N. Weins, and J. D. Matarazzo, *Nonverbal Communication: The State of the Art* (New York: John Wiley, 1978).
12. E. T. Hall, *The Silent Language* (Garden City, NJ: Doubleday, 1959): 175–176.

CHAPTER FIVE

Critical Thinking in the Small Group

CHAPTER OUTLINE

What Makes Thinking "Critical"?
Attitudes
Gathering Information
Assessing Information Needs
Collecting Needed Resources
Direct Observation
Reading
Interviews
Other Sources
Evaluating Information
Determining the Meaning of What Is Being Said
Distinguishing Fact from Opinion and Inference
Identifying and Clarifying Ambiguous Terms
Evaluating Opinions by Determining the Credibility of the Source
Assessing the Accuracy and Worth of the Information
Checking for Errors in Reasoning
Overgeneralizing
Attacking a Person Instead of the Argument
Confusing Causal Relationships
Either-Or Thinking
Incomplete Comparisons
Asking Probing Questions
Behaviors Counterproductive to Critical Thinking
Impulsiveness
Overdependence on Authority Figures
Lack of Confidence
Dogmatic, Inflexible Behavior
Unwillingness to Make the Effort to Think Critically

KEY TERMS AND CONCEPTS

Ambiguous
Analogy
Argument
Critical Thinking
Dogmatic
Either-Or Thinking
Evidence
Fact
Fallacy
Open-mindedness
Opinion
Overgeneralization
Probes
Willingness to Communicate

STUDY QUESTIONS

1. What are the differences between critical and uncritical thinking?
2. What personal attitudes encourage critical thinking in a group?
3. How can group members prepare *before* they begin to search for information they need?
4. What methods can group members use to find the information they need?
5. What guidelines can help a group evaluate the available information?
6. What are five common reasoning errors and how can they be discovered?
7. What are the behaviors that make it difficult for other group members to use their best critical thinking skills?

On January 28, 1986, the space shuttle *Challenger* exploded shortly after take-off, killing all seven members of the crew. The Rogers Commission, charged with discovering the reasons for the disaster, identified the primary cause as a malfunction of the O-ring seals on one of the solid rocket boosters. The commission revealed that this was an avoidable accident. NASA officials and the manufacturers of the rocket boosters knew about potential problems with the O-rings in cold weather; therefore, the disaster was predictable. The real problem, according to the Rogers Commission, occurred in the procedures used to make the launch/no launch decision. This decision-making procedure involved many knowledgeable individuals and groups and should have produced the type of high-quality decision for which groups are noted, one that utilized all relevant available information. How could the experts have allowed such a poor decision to be made?

Communication scholars who analyzed the *Challenger* decision making concluded that the procedure was flawed in several ways.[1] Because the launch had been postponed three previous times, NASA officials were biased in favor of launching. In addition, a relatively rigid organizational structure, which specified who should report to whom, made individuals reluctant to step outside normal channels and demand that superiors pay attention to their concerns. Rather than asking the technical experts direct questions, several decision makers made incorrect assumptions. They failed to ask obvious questions whose answers could have led to a different decision. They discounted the relevance of pertinent technical data. Worse, they rejected an interpretation of the data by those people who disagreed. Serious consideration of those data would have cancelled the launch. Engineers used ambiguous language rather than stating their concerns simply and clearly. In short, the group of officials who decided to launch the *Challenger* failed to do the critical thinking that would have led them to delay the launch until warmer weather.

Although following critical thinking and communication guidelines cannot guarantee effective decision making, failure to follow those guidelines leads to poor decisions like the one to launch *Challenger*. Thinking is an important throughput process, the quality of which directly affects the quality of the group output. *Critical* thinking in a group requires both critical thinking and skilled communicating by members. In this chapter we explain what critical thinking involves, why it is important to small group decision making, and what you can do to help ensure that members of your groups think critically as they work toward collective goals.

What Makes Thinking "Critical"?

You can understand what *critical* thinking involves by understanding what its polar opposite, uncritical thinking, lacks. In an unabridged dictionary we found the following synonyms for "critical": "exercising or involving careful judgment or judicious evaluation," "discriminating," "careful," and "exact."[2] The other end of a

Figure 5.1 Essential elements of critical thinking.

critical-uncritical thinking scale was described as "lacking in discrimination," "not evaluating or judging," and "marked by a disregard for or improper use of critical standards or procedures."[3] So judging, standards, and procedures all play a part in thinking critically whether by individuals acting alone or as a group. Watson and Glaser, who devised one of the earliest and most well-researched tests to assess critical thinking skills, define **critical thinking** as follows:

> . . . critical thinking involves a persistent effort to examine any belief or supposed form of knowledge in the light of the evidence that supports it and the further conclusions to which it tends, as well as the ability to recognize problems, to weigh evidence, to comprehend and use language with accuracy and discrimination, to interpret data, to recognize the existence (or non-existence) of logical relationships between propositions, to draw warranted conclusions and generalizations and to test the conclusions by applying them to new situations to which they seem pertinent.[4]

In order for thinking to be *critical,* we must *examine the evidence systematically and logically, the statements should be supported by evidence and reasoning, and the reasoning used should be examined systematically and logically.* That is our definition of "critical thinking" (see figure 5.1).

Critical thinking involves backing up all assertions or conclusions both with tested evidence and a clear line of reasoning supporting claims included in the statements.[5] Thus critical thinking is differentiated from such uncritical thinking as hunches, intuition, gut feelings, impulses, prejudices, superstitions, and so forth by two principles: (1) the use of **evidence** (facts, data, opinions, and other information backing a claim or conclusion); and (2) logical **arguments** that speakers and writers make from that evidence to support what they believe are valid reasons to accept the claims and assertions they make. While productive decisions *may* be made on the basis of hunches and intuition, such decisions are not the product of

Table 5.1 Characteristics of Critical Thinkers

Curious and inquisitive
Willing to take responsibility for decisions
Aware of gaps in their supply of information
Systematic in their search for information
Open-minded; attempt to find information supporting a wide variety of opinions

critical thinking. For problem solving to involve *critical* thinking, the problem must be analyzed thoroughly, with as much relevant information as possible examined during that analysis. Then the solution must be developed on the basis of (1) *all* that information and (2) the best reasoning and logic that can be employed. Critical thinkers act *systematically,* not impulsively or instinctively, and they use definite standards to evaluate their conclusions.

Watson and Glaser note that individuals who use critical thinking skills are predisposed to examine problems thoughtfully, understand *how* to think and reason logically, and are skilled in applying reason to solve problems. You can see that critical thinking is not just *one* thing that people know or do. Rather, it involves a constellation of attitudes and behaviors that are based on habits of systematic, reasoned examination of issues and potential solutions of problems (see table 5.1). Major components of critical thinking include the attitudes of individuals toward information, the approach used in gathering information, the care taken in evaluating information, and skills in making reasoned judgments on the basis of that information. You will next examine each of these critical thinking factors.

Attitudes

The *desire* to make the best possible decision, based on reason, is necessary for critical thinking in groups. The importance of the group members' attitudes toward ideas and information, as well as toward each other, cannot be overstated (see table 5.2). Critical thinkers are open-minded. **Open-mindedness** is a general willingness, even a desire, to *understand* new information and ideas and to suggest new and different solutions, including concepts in sharp contradiction to what one has previously accepted as truth. Critical thinking by a group requires that members be open-minded while they retain an attitude of skeptical inquiry toward all questions of discussion and toward all information and ideas they encounter. Critical thinkers look for gaps in their supply of data about a problem. They insist on gathering as much relevant information as possible in preparation for making their decision. They are curious. They really *want* to know why something occurred, or why someone holds an opinion. They are systematic, not haphazard, in their

Table 5.2   Ideal Attitudes for a Critical Thinker

Desire to make the best possible decision
Show-me attitude that encourages testing of information, opinions, and data, even if this means
    confronting others
Active, not passive, in both gathering and testing information
Intellectually honest and unbiased regarding both people and information
Able to tolerate ambiguity and to suspend judgment until all the facts are in
Responsible and committed to the process of thinking critically

---

search for information. They tap into a wide variety of sources and attempt to find information that supports *all* sides of an issue. They are *pleased* when new information requires them to change an old belief.

The desire to be objective is important. For example, it appears that the NASA officials involved in making the *Challenger* launch decision were prejudiced in favor of the launch. This desire biased their search for information, so they did not work as hard to get information that opposed the launch as they did to get information that supported it. It also affected their evaluation so that they uncritically accepted pro-launch information, but were hypercritical of anti-launch data.

People who are good at critical thinking are aware of *when* it is necessary to take the extra time that critical thinking demands. For example, choosing between green and yellow pencils probably does not warrant taking time to make a critically thought-out decision. However, officials who participated in the decision to launch the *Challenger* should have been keenly aware of the need to follow systematic decision-making procedures on this issue. Indeed, NASA had attempted to create a decision-making procedure that minimized the chance for a disaster. The procedures at NASA involved several organizational layers in the decision-making process, with supposed fail-safe mechanisms at each step. But individuals' attitudes and uncritical behaviors undermined this systematic procedure.

Critical thinkers want to test pertinent information and opinions as well as the sources which supply such information. A certain amount of skepticism and a *show-me* attitude is healthy before you make an important decision. Critical thinkers do not assume that anything they read or hear is true. They think for themselves. They will not accept something as true just because a parent or friend or teacher "said so." They are willing to challenge any information presented by raising questions about it. They are willing to confront other group members about their opinions, beliefs, and feelings. They ask **probes,** which are inquiries to determine the adequacy and quality of evidence and reasoning supporting a claim or decision. Among probes typically asked by critical thinkers during problem solving discussions are questions like the following:

"What evidence do you have to suggest that statement is true?"

"Where did that evidence come from?"

"Does anyone have any evidence to contradict the statement we just heard?"

"What might the consequences be if we are wrong?"

"How much danger is there that we have reached the wrong conclusion?"

"How did you arrive at that conclusion?"

In contrast, officials of the company that manufactured the *Challenger* rockets avoided asking their engineers precisely what their opinions were about the safety of the launch. Instead, these managers were confident they knew what their subordinates were thinking, so they didn't ask directly. Successful critical thinkers engage in an *active* (rather than passive) process of testing information. Critical thinking demands hard work to find the information necessary to understand the problem and subject solutions to the most rigorous tests possible. Mentally lazy group members object to this hard work.

Critical thinkers are open-minded to others' opinions as well as to information. If you have your mind made up, as the NASA officials appeared to have done, then you cannot be honest in your search for and evaluation of information. *All* points of view, not just popularly accepted ones, must be considered and subjected to the same careful evaluation process. It is intellectual cheating to ignore some information or people because they do not fit your preconceived views. Instead, to protect yourself from inadvertent bias, you should suspend final judgment for as long as possible while the group is still gathering and evaluating information. You must be able to tolerate ambiguity, at least for a while, so that you don't reach a premature conclusion just to end a difficult decision-making process! Patience at this point allows the time needed to think critically, but impatience will not.

To review, the ideal group member is aware of the need to think critically, is willing to spend the time and work it takes to make a systematic decision, is open-minded and fair, but at the same time is a skeptic who asks probing questions. Such a person is interested in the opinions of others and the reasons for things, takes responsibility for finding information and reasoning, and evaluates them thoroughly with critical thinking skills. We next examine how critical thinkers gather information.

Gathering Information

One skill essential to critical thinking is the ability to organize ideas.[6] Thus, the first step for group members who are serious about employing critical thinking is to assess the information they have available at the start, identify gaps in the information, and then establish and implement a plan for plugging those gaps.

Table 5.3 Gathering Information in the Critical Thinking Process

Assessing Information Needs

Take stock of existing information.
Identify holes and weaknesses.
Make a master list of what information is needed and where it may be found.
Collect needed resources.
    Assign members specific responsibilities for finding needed information from the master list.
    Use all appropriate information-gathering techniques:
        Direct observation
        Reading
        Interviews (individual or group)
        Other sources (radio, television, casual conversation)

Assessing Information Needs

Before group members begin their research, they first need to take stock of the information they possess (see table 5.3). The quality of an output such as a plan or policy cannot be better than the information members possess or the way in which they share and process it. *Information* includes members' opinions and perceptions of the issue as well as factual data relevant to it. For example, a committee one of us chaired was charged with revising the curriculum for communication majors. The committee first pooled the information of the members, who were able to describe the current major requirements, relate the problems and issues from their own points of view, and provide information about what nearby colleges and universities required of communication majors.

You can begin to see, as the committee members did, that there were several important areas where information was needed before any adequate discussion of the problem could begin. The committee members decided they needed to discover the perceptions of current students, as well as alumni, about the strengths and weaknesses of the existing program. Likewise, the opinions of faculty in other departments were deemed important. So were those of administrators whose positive opinions of the recommended changes would be essential for approval and financing of the changes. In addition, prospective employers could provide information about graduates' and student interns' skills and deficiencies. Finally, committee members knew they must have information about current practices in the field of communication and what communication leaders and professionals were saying about the direction of the field.

You can see that the committee members would have been acting prematurely to try to establish a new curriculum during their first meetings. First, they pooled their data to place the issues into perspective. They discussed what they saw as the scope of the problem, what elements contributed to it, and what people would be affected by the eventual solution. Next, an inventory was made of the information members currently had. Then, members began to compile a master list of additional needed information and sources from which to obtain it. They continued to add to this list as more items occurred to them.

The act of making a list of needed information helps determine not only *what* information is missing but also *where* it may be found. The next step in the critical thinking process is the methodical gathering of accurate information. To get help in locating information, we cannot stress enough the importance of accuracy. Even the most careful reasoning will fail if it is based upon incorrect information. We strongly recommend that you participate in a guided tour of your school's library or learning resources center. We also suggest that you ask professional librarians to help you evaluate the credibility of your sources and the accuracy of your information.

Collecting Needed Resources

Group members should organize their information-gathering procedures before proceeding. First, members should make a master list of all information needed. Then they should assign themselves research responsibilities on the basis of their preferences, strengths, and time schedules. Finally, as members proceed with their research, they will discover additional information they need. This additional information should be added to the list and assigned to the appropriate group members.

As was illustrated by the example of the faculty curriculum committee described earlier, the information a group needs will rarely be found in one location. Usually, a variety of information is needed and will have to be gathered in various ways. Some of these are described briefly.

Direct Observation Sometimes information you need will come from first-hand observation. For example, assume the faculty curriculum committee decided that public relations majors should be able to create appropriate copy and artwork for a brochure designed for a specific audience. Direct observation by faculty members of students in classes could show whether public relations students were able to do this. In another example, a student committee observed pedestrian and vehicular traffic near campus before deciding what to recommend as a way to reduce injuries to students.

Reading A wealth of information can be found in many kinds of printed sources. Often, published material can save you considerable time and effort needed to gather information yourself. Useful information may be found in newspapers, books, magazines, scholarly and professional journals, technical and trade publications, government documents, and so forth. The sheer number of sources available can be intimidating. Your job will be simplified if you ask a reference librarian to help you. Librarians can save you hours of wasted effort by pointing you in helpful directions and steering you away from likely dead ends. Ask them for help—this is exactly what reference librarians are trained to provide.

In addition, there are a number of publications that can save you time and effort in locating printed information. Annotated bibliographies and abstracts provide a preview of the type of information in a publication so that you can decide whether or not it will be worth the search. Encyclopedias summarize vast amounts of information. Specialized indexes and abstracts frequently can help you save time locating relevant information. For example, the *Business Periodicals Index* summarizes articles from numerous business and trade journals.

Finally, if your school library has a computerized data base available it can be used to locate pertinent information rapidly. The librarian will help you enter key words that describe your topic and the computer will find titles of articles with these key words. In some cases you may receive a brief abstract or summary of the publication. This helps you sift through your list and concentrate your efforts on locating the sources that appear to be the most relevant.

Interviews You will recall some of the information the curriculum committee needed had to come directly from certain individuals. Members of your group may need to conduct several interviews. These may be face-to-face individual interviews, group interviews, or those conducted over the phone. For example, the curriculum committee members interviewed their colleagues in person, phoned colleagues at other schools, and called a sample of alumni to ask for their perceptions and opinions.

Depending on the time available and the type of information needed, interviewers may elect to ask open-ended or closed-ended questions. Open-ended questions are easier to construct and allow the people being interviewed the freedom to touch upon *whatever* they think is important. Closed-ended questions that are clear and unbiased are difficult to construct, but answers to them are easier to tabulate. Examples of each type of question are shown in table 5.4.

Other Sources Useful information may come when you least expect it. Radio, television, casual conversation with family or friends, stumbling onto relevant information in a magazine while you are waiting to get your hair cut—all are potential sources. Be prepared to take advantage of these sources by recording the information as soon as possible so you don't forget it or distort it. Once you have gathered the information you need, you must decide how useful it is to you. Critical thinkers *evaluate* the information they gather.

Evaluating Information

Group members must evaluate their information once they have gathered it. If a group bases its decision on inaccurate or outdated information, its decision will be flawed no matter how systematic the process of gathering has been. For example, the curriculum committee we described earlier recommended that communication majors take several writing courses offered by the English department. However, even though the recommended courses were listed in the school's current catalog,

Table 5.4 Open- and Closed-Ended Questions

Open-Ended Questions	Closed-Ended Questions
What do you think about the proposal to raise taxes?	Do you agree or disagree that taxes should be raised?
What is your opinion of the performance of the committee chair?	Has the committee chair done a good job?
How might we enhance our presentation audiovisually?	Should we use a skit or a videotape for our presentation?
How can we solve the parking problem on campus?	Where should we put the new parking garage?
How effective are your group's critical thinking skills?	Are your group's critical thinking skills: Very effective? Somewhat effective? Average? Somewhat ineffective? Very ineffective?

the English department had revised *its* curriculum. The course numbers, content, and in several cases the prerequisites had been changed. This mistake was not a disaster, but it would not have occurred if curriculum committee members had verified the catalog's accuracy in the first place.

How can you tell whether a particular piece of data is accurate and up-to-date, and whether a source is credible? Evaluation of available information is perhaps the most crucial step in the critical thinking process. We have found Browne and Keeley's second edition of *Asking the Right Questions: A Guide to Critical Thinking* to be an excellent summary of ways in which you can assess the value of information. Much of the information that follows is based upon this source.

Determining the Meaning of What Is Being Said

The first thing you must do is decide exactly what the speaker or writer means. This is not as easy as it may sound. Frequently, people bury the meaning of what they are saying among a jumble of opinions and irrelevant statements. It helps to take the statement or argument apart and examine each component separately. For example, first ask yourself what *conclusion* the author is drawing. What does he or she want us to do, think, or believe? Is there an action (such as voting for a particular candidate, writing letters to a television producer, or buying a particular product) that the author wants us to take? Next, determine what the main arguments are that the author provides in support of the conclusion or recommended

Table 5.5 Listing the Conclusion, Reasons, and Supporting Evidence of an Argument

---

Letter to the Parents' Excellence in Schools Committee

Argument:

Mary Alice Beasley is the best candidate we have running for the Central City school board. We need people like her who care about our kids. After all, she has lived in Central City all her life and now has three children of her own in the school system. She has been an active member of the P.T.A. for the past 6 years and was chair of the fund-raising committee for Westwood School. Her experience will be invaluable. In her second term as city councilwoman, she was the chief author of the plan to desegregate the city schools; as we all know, other cities have used this plan as the model for their own desegregation efforts. Mary Alice can represent the entire community well—she taught for 9 years herself before she ran for city council, and she has a Master's Degree in Education. Hers is exactly the kind of caring, experienced leadership we need on the school board. Mary Beasley deserves your endorsement.

Conclusion: Endorse Mary Alice Beasley for school board.
  Reason: She is experienced.
    Evidence: Served 2 terms on city council
                 Chaired Westwood School's fund-raising committee
  Reason: She cares about the schools.
    Evidence: Has three children in school now
                 Active in P.T.A. for 6 years
  Reason: She is competent.
    Evidence: Has a Master's in Education
                 Wrote the model plan to desegregate the city schools
  Reason: She understands many points of view.
    Evidence: Is a parent
                 Was a teacher for 9 years
                 Was a student in the same school system

---

action. For instance, does the author say that you should vote for Candidate Smith for school board because she is experienced, dedicated, and a strong supporter of education?

Now that you know that the candidate, in the opinion of the speaker or writer, is "experienced, dedicated, and a strong supporter of education" you are in a position to determine exactly what *reasons* (i.e., evidence) the author gives for describing Candidate Smith in these ways. Perhaps Smith's experience has come from serving previous terms on the school board and from being a parent with children in the schools. Perhaps the claim that she is a strong supporter of education is based on the fact that she voted twice to increase property taxes to provide more money for the schools. Keeping track of the arguments and evidence that supports them is easier if you outline the argument on paper. Write the main conclusion at the top, then list each argument beneath it with space after each one. In this space, list every piece of evidence the author or speaker offers in support of the claims (see table 5.5). This will simplify your later task of evaluating how good both the author's evidence and reasoning are, and how valid the conclusions are.

Distinguishing Fact from Opinion and Inference

It is important for you to recognize the difference between a statement of **fact,** and statements of opinion or inference based upon that fact. Facts are not arguable. They are truths that can be verified by observations. For example, we can verify that the population of Springfield, Missouri is 133,100 by counting all the people in Springfield or, more reasonably, by looking in any of several government publications that record population data. Facts are all equal because each *fact* given in support of an argument is a true statement (although some facts are more relevant to the argument than others). Of course, some statements presented as facts are not facts at all, but false statements. For example, the statement "Springfield, Missouri has 300,000 residents" is *not* true; therefore it is not a fact. You will need to determine whether statements presented as facts are true and up-to-date.

Opinions, on the other hand, are *not* all equal. Einstein's opinion about the way the universe operates should carry more weight than such opinions of the authors of this book, neither of whom is a theoretical physicist. Opinions and inferences go beyond what was observed directly. They imply some degree of probability or uncertainty. The value of an opinion depends on the evidence supporting the opinion and the quality of the reasoning that ties the evidence and opinion together. Determining an opinion's value is part of your job as a critical thinker. For example, someone might say "Springfield, Missouri is growing rapidly." That is not a fact; that is an opinion. It is your responsibility to determine the validity of the opinion by asking questions like the following: What was Springfield's population ten years ago? What is the average annual rate of growth? How does that rate compare with other cities in Missouri? With other areas of the United States? Thus, opinions *are* arguable and should be evaluated systematically during a group's deliberations.

Identifying and Clarifying Ambiguous Terms

Many times authors or speakers make the job of evaluating information difficult by using terminology that is **ambiguous** or unclear. For example, Candidate Smith was termed "dedicated." What does that mean? Does it mean she has a perfect attendance record at previous school board meetings? Does it mean she bakes brownies for every school bake sale? Does it mean she spends one day a week as a volunteer in the school's library? Each of these statements of fact supporting the claim that Smith is "dedicated" paints quite a different picture of the candidate. You can see that clarification of vague terms is very important in evaluating the worth of the information your group has. Furthermore, ambiguous statements often disrupt a group's discussion because they provoke confusion and tension among the members.[7]

Earlier in the chapter we discussed the decision made by NASA officials to launch the *Challenger*. In their analysis of the decision-making process, Gouran and his associates discovered that failure to clarify ambiguous terms contributed to that terrible decision. They explain that

> . . . no one went so far as to say, "We recommend that you do not launch." Instead, they claimed making such statements as, "we do not have the data base from which to draw any conclusions for this particular situation," "we did not have a sufficient data base to absolutely assure that nothing would strike the vehicle."[8]

This kind of *doublespeak* confuses issues because it leaves room for a variety of interpretations by permitting others to read their own favorite interpretations into the message. At NASA, no one asked explicitly for clarification of the ambiguous terms.

Evaluating Opinions by Determining the Credibility of the Source

We noted earlier that not all opinions are equal. How can you tell whether the author or speaker is someone whose opinions are worth your attention? You can ask yourself several key questions to help you decide how much trust to place in an opinion.

1. **Is there any reason to suspect the person(s) supplying the opinion of bias?** For example, if you find a source that tries to debunk the idea that smoking causes lung cancer, you should treat that information with suspicion if it comes from a publication of the American Tobacco Institute. On the other hand, if that statement appeared in the scientifically respected *New England Journal of Medicine,* you would have greater reason to expect objectivity.

2. **Is the individual, or other source, a recognized expert on the subject?** Is this someone whom other experts respect? Would you feel proud or silly quoting this person? We may feel comfortable citing Michael Jordan's opinions about basketball, but very uncomfortable citing Aunt Tilly's.

3. **Is the opinion consistent with others expressed by the same source?** People do change their minds for good reasons. Is there an acceptable reason for the change? If so, you can evaluate the evidence and reasoning offered to explain the change. If not, you should suspect some unknown bias.

Table 5.6   Evaluating Information in the Critical Thinking Process

Determining What the Speaker or Writer Is Saying

What is the conclusion?
What does the author want us to do?
What are the main arguments in support of the conclusion?

Distinguishing Fact from Opinion and Inference

What are the facts?
What are the opinions?

Identifying and Clarifying Ambiguous Terms

What are the ambiguous terms?
What do you think the author means by each term?
If you can't decide with confidence, what problems does this create?

Determining the Credibility of the Source

Who is the author or speaker; what are his/her credentials on this issue?
Is this a recognized expert?
Is this a biased source or one with something to gain by expressing this opinion?
Is the information consistent with other credible sources?

Assessing the Accuracy and Worth of the Information

What type of evidence is being offered in support of the author's arguments (i.e., personal experience,
   statistical support, opinions of experts)?
Is the evidence supported by other experts or authorities, or just this author?
Is the information based upon the scientific method?
If the information is based on interviews or questionnaires, was the sample large enough and
   representative enough? Were the questions clear and not biased, or loaded?

Assessing the Accuracy and Worth of the Information

Now that you have established a context for evaluating the information by determining exactly what is being said and how credible the source is, you are in a
position to evaluate how good that information is (see table 5.6). After all, it
could be *mis*information. There are a number of questions you should ask yourself about information before using it in group decision making.

1. **What types of evidence are being offered to support the argument?** Is
   it a personal experience? Statistical support? The combined opinions of a
   number of recognized experts? Although many people do so, it is unsafe to
   accept personal experience as the sole basis for supporting an opinion. For
   example, assume you were once in a group with a dominant leader who
   decided what everyone should do and delegated these tasks to other
   members. Perhaps your group produced a high quantity and quality of work
   and you were satisfied with the experience. Thus your personal experience
   may lead you to believe that groups work best under strong, controlling
   leaders. Someone else's experience might have been different. Perhaps a

fellow group member worked in a democratic group where there was no *one* leader but all members contributed to leadership based upon their areas of expertise. This member thinks that the only good group is a democratic one. Which of you is right? Each of you is right, for the particular circumstances of your experience. Neither of you should use personal experience *alone* as a basis for a general conclusion or as a criterion to guide your actions. One person's experience neither proves nor disproves a conclusion.

2. **Is the information based upon the testimony of a number of experts or authorities in the field?** If so, you can place greater trust in it, especially if these experts are widely recognized and accepted by their peers. Be sure to determine if other experts disagree and *why*. Be especially careful about accepting information from an expert in one field about another field. For example, movie stars frequently express strong opinions about the American political scene. While some may be well-informed, others are not. Don't let such a person be your sole source of information.

3. **Is the information based upon the scientific method and/or valid statistical reasoning?** You should ask how the information was gathered, how the questions were worded, whether the data came from a properly designed survey, and so forth. Information must follow strict guidelines before it can legitimately be termed "scientific." First, such information must be verifiable by others. Thus, although an experience that happens to someone may be *true,* it is not scientific unless the event is observed or can be recreated by other people. Second, scientific information must be obtained under controlled conditions by controlled observations. Having an informal conversation with your classmates about the death penalty and concluding that "American college students have the following attitudes toward capital punishment . . ." may be interesting but it is not scientific. On the other hand, if you surveyed a representative sample of students, asked each of them the same questions and systematically analyzed their answers, you could reasonably make a statement like this: "Students at my college believe the following about capital punishment . . ." Finally, scientific information must be expressed precisely. Another researcher, after reading an account of a scientifically controlled research, should be able to carry out a study in exactly the same way, using the same procedures, equipment, and statistical tests.

Information gathered by questionnaires or interviews poses additional questions regarding the individuals who were queried. Were there enough of them, and were they *representative* of some larger population? In most cases, some form of random sampling is most likely to ensure representativesness of response. For example, assume your committee is charged with making a set of recommendations regarding parking on your campus and you decide to poll students who drive to campus. If you survey only students who park in one particular lot between 7:00 and 8:00 A.M.

Table 5.7   Checking for Errors in Reasoning

Does the author overgeneralize?
Does the author attack a person instead of the issue?
Does the author argue that because two events are related, one caused the other?
Does the author present you with an either-or choice when other alternatives are possible?
Does the author present you with a comparison that is incomplete or invalid?

your results are not likely to reflect the views of the entire student population. On the other hand, your information will be much more representative if you systematically survey students from all campus lots at varying times during the day and evening. Likewise, make sure that survey data are based on samples of adequate size. For example, making parking recommendations that will affect thousands of students on the basis of responses from five students is irresponsible. Thus, when you evaluate scientific and statistical information, you should be alert to questions of clarity, representatives, number of respondents or cases, and so on.

Checking for Errors in Reasoning

Speakers and writers often make a variety of common reasoning errors, called **fallacies,** but critical thinkers working together in a small group should be able to spot each other's fallacies (see table 5.7). Some of the most prevalent of these are overgeneralizing, attacking a person instead of the argument, assuming that because two events are related one caused the other, arguing that a complicated activity like human behavior is caused by one thing, setting up a false either/or dilemma, or making an incomplete comparison. Fallacies like these tend to divert a listener's attention from the issue or side-track the discussion so that members of a group begin to debate something other than evidence and claims. The following is a discussion of these fallacies.

Overgeneralizing

Generalizations are made when information about one or more instances is said to apply to many or all instances of the same type. For example, someone may read in the newspaper that a certain number of college students have defaulted on their government-guaranteed student loans. If that person concludes from this that "college students are irresponsible borrowers," he or she has made a generalization. Even though it isn't stated that way, this implies that *all* college students are irresponsible borrowers. A generalization like this argues that because something is true (or false) about a few instances, it is true (or false) about most or all instances in the same category.

Generalizations are not automatically wrong. For instance, conclusions based upon carefully gathered data that were analyzed with appropriate statistical procedures are often highly accurate. Usually such generalizations are qualified and not stated as applying to *all* cases. The problem with generalization occurs when the conclusion is an *over*generalization. An **overgeneralization,** like the loan default example given above, is a conclusion that is not supported by enough data. Remember, for a generalization to be factual for *all* cases of some sort, someone would have to observe all of these cases.

We encounter overgeneralizations every day: *You can't trust politicians. Women are more emotional than men. College students are more interested in having a good time than in learning. It's not what you know but who you know that helps you get ahead.* It is easy to see how a single dramatic experience tempts us to believe that we have discovered a general truth about people or things. However, without systematically gathered, verifiable evidence, our conclusion is a weak opinion, not based on adequate facts.

To decide whether a generalization is a valid conclusion, there are a variety of questions you can ask:

1. Is the source asking us to accept only his or her personal experience to support the generalization, or are other forms of evidence offered?
2. Upon how many cases is this generalization based? Are there any exceptions?
3. Is this case representative of all cases of this sort?
4. Did the author or speaker sample a variety of individuals or sources, with varying points of view? If so, do the other sources support the generalization?
5. Is the sample biased in any way?
6. Is the generalization expressed as a probability, as a description limited to the cases actually cited, or in "allness" terms?

Attacking a Person Instead of the Argument

Attacking a person instead of the argument, even if subtly done, is a form of name-calling used to direct attention away from the evidence and logic (or lack thereof). Sometimes called *ad hominem* attacks, such arguments take this form: "Because So-and-So is a _____ (woman, black, white, Catholic, foreigner, intellectual snob, hillbilly, member of the Democratic Party, and so on) you can't believe his/her opinions about the topic." Although the argument may not be stated so explicitly, the effect of such an argument is to sidetrack the discussion of the opinion into a discussion of the merits of So-and-So. It diverts a group from a careful consideration of the facts and reasoning behind opinions. So-and-So may indeed be a "crackpot" about some things, but his/her views about the topic might be quite accurate. More information is needed before a critical thinker will make that judgment.

Confusing Causal Relationships

Another common reasoning error occurs when the speaker or writer mistakenly states what caused an event. Two forms of this error are observed frequently. Sometimes authors oversimplify by implying or stating that only *one* cause exists for an event. In other instances, they imply that, because two events are related by subject matter or in sequence, one causes the other. For example, we have heard students say that if a manager implements quality control circles in a company, the company's profits will increase. Such a statement implies that quality circles cause higher profits. We think you will recognize that a variety of factors is likely to contribute to, or cause, increased profits. For example, better employee training, lower costs of raw materials, increased prices for a company's products, improvements in technology, along with improved upward communication and morale produced by the quality circles—all of these factors may contribute to the increased profits. It is oversimplifying to assume that quality circles alone are the single cause.

Nor can we assume that just because two things are related in time one causes the other. It may be that both are caused by some third event or condition. For example, one of us recently overheard someone mention recent statistics indicating that female graduates of women's colleges were more likely to become members of the U.S. Congress and serve on the boards of Fortune 500 companies than graduates of coed schools. The person speaking was arguing that attendance at women's colleges *caused* this type of career achievement. However, many women's colleges are academically selective as well as expensive. Women attending such schools are often both exceptionally bright and come from families who own or are connected to Fortune 500 companies. It is plausible that these additional factors—ability and family connections—"cause" the attendance at women's colleges *and* the career achievement. The relationship between college attendance and later achievement is likely to be a complex one that does not lend itself well to simple causal descriptions. You may recall the discussion in chapter 2 that what happens to humans and other living systems usually stems from a variety of factors. It is dangerous to assume a single cause for any event or phenomenon.

Simple causal statements are rarely warranted. So whenever you hear someone claim a causal relationship between events, you should ask whether there are *other* factors that could have contributed to the observed events, and whether there might be some relationship other than causal between them.

Either-Or Thinking

Either-or thinking (sometimes called a false dilemma) says that you must choose one thing or another, and no other choices are possible. Seldom is this the case. For example, assume your group is preparing a panel discussion about sex education in the schools and you encounter the following statement: "Sex education is an important element of a young person's education. It is the parents' responsibility and privilege to teach their children about sex, and it should not be left up to the schools." Most people would readily agree with the first sentence. The second, however, reveals either-or thinking. The author is forcing the reader to accept the premise that *either* the parent will teach the child about sex, *or* the school will. In fact, other alternatives are possible. Perhaps churches could take on the job, or parents and school officials together could design a cooperative program. You do not have to accept the writer's original premise, which places you in an unnecessary either/or mental box. Just because a writer does not mention other alternatives should not blind you to their existence.

Incomplete Comparisons

Comparisons, especially **analogies,** help us understand issues more vividly. However, there are limitations to these kinds of comparisons. Because one thing bears a resemblance to another is no reason to accept that they are identical. At some point the resemblance will end because no two situations are identical in all their characteristics. An incomplete comparison (often called a *faulty analogy*) asks us to stretch a similarity too far. For example, let's say you are trying to sort through the opinions of students regarding how well the climate control major at your school prepares students to be heating and air conditioning professionals. One of the students you are interviewing says, "You really can't learn much about heating and air conditioning from school anyway. It's like trying to ride a bicycle by reading books about it, but never getting on an actual bicycle."

At first glance, this remark hits home with many of us who complain that school can't prepare us for the "real world." However, let's look more closely. Yes, there are professional climate control experiences that cannot be duplicated in school. But there are many activities that *will* help prepare students for professional practice. Analyzing the job, selecting the best systems for a particular building, selecting equipment, writing up specifications and a schematic drawing, planning installation procedures, and so forth, are all examples of typical activities climate control majors perform in school and which are also necessary on the job. Thus, whenever you see or hear someone make a comparison, first determine in what ways the two things being compared are similar, but especially look for ways they are *different*. Ask yourself if the analogy breaks down at any point. If so, where? How does this affect the reasoning you are being asked to accept?

The fallacies previously described are five of the most common ones. Being alert for them will help you become an effective critical thinker. The following advice will help you see through these and other fallacies: Ask the right questions about the ideas, opinions, interpretations, and conclusions someone is asking you to accept. Pay careful attention to the answers you receive (or don't receive). You will eventually arrive close enough to the truth to be able to make a decision.

"I still don't have all the answers, but I'm beginning to ask the right questions."

Asking the right question is at the heart of critical thinking. (Drawing by Lorenz; © 1989 The New Yorker Magazine, Inc.)

Asking Probing Questions

Asking the right questions is the most important thing you can do if you want to be a critical thinker. Do not accept information just because it sounds good, is presented in an entertaining way, because it supports what you already believe, or because the rest of the group accepts the information. Such a situation is called *groupthink,* where some group members go along with the opinions of the rest of the group unquestioningly. (*Groupthink* is explored in detail in chapter 10.) Question the accuracy of the information and the appropriateness of the reasoning you are being asked to accept.

According to Gouran et al., failure to ask probing questions at several steps during the decision-making process and groupthink were prime contributors to the *Challenger* disaster. The problem with the O-ring seals in cold temperatures had been observed for years before the launch, but no one asked the tough questions about what was being done to correct the flaw. The problem just kept getting ignored. One engineer who opposed the launch assumed that his objection was passed to superiors, but he did not ask specifically whether this was so. When representatives of North American Rockwell, the manufacturer of the shuttle, were

Table 5.8 Behaviors Counterproductive to Critical Thinking

Impulsiveness; Jumping to premature conclusions
Overdependence on authority figures; Waiting for someone else to tell you how to think, what to
  conclude, or what to do
Lack of confidence; Withdrawing if someone challenges your ideas
Dogmatic, inflexible behavior; Closing your mind and being afraid of change
Unwillingness to make the effort to think critically; Taking the easy way out

relaying their concerns about the launch in vague terms, no one asked specifically whether or not they were recommending the launch. All these isolated incidents, where no one *asked* the right questions, together contributed to the *Challenger* disaster. The single most important thing you can do to prevent this kind of disaster is to *ask probing questions,* even though this is not always easy or pleasant to do. If other group members call such questioning argumentative or quibbling, reassure them that the *purpose* of your questioning is not to argue or put anyone down, but to clear up any possible misunderstandings, oversights, or fallacies. State clearly that your intention is to *cooperate* in the search for the best possible decision.

Behaviors Counterproductive to Critical Thinking

Students sometimes have difficulty thinking critically, even when group work demands it. One primary reason for this is that many students oversimplify the thinking process.[9] For example, either-or thinkers believe that there is one right way to do something, and all other ways are wrong. Thus, if they are convinced that they have a solution to a problem, they cannot conceive that someone else may also have different solutions that are equally appropriate.

Critical thinking is characterized by a level of independence that many people never achieve. You need faith in your ability to think and reason to be willing to challenge beliefs and judgments of other people. You don't argue to try to prove someone wrong. Instead, you question and probe so that members of your group can collectively evaluate information and ideas for the ultimate good of the group. You do not accept others' opinions as gospel; rather, you test beliefs by holding them up against the best reasoning you can muster. If they hold up under careful scrutiny, then you accept them. When you can do this, you may call yourself an independent, mature, *critical* thinker, in contrast to an insecure, dependent, uncritical follower. You will be someone who prevents *groupthink.*

It will be beneficial for you to examine your own behavior and determine whether you are helping or hindering your group's critical thinking efforts (see table 5.8). The following behaviors are counterproductive to a group's critical thinking effort.[10] Do any of them apply to you?

Impulsiveness

Impulsive thinkers tend to leap before they look. These are people who do not wait until all the information has been gathered and evaluated before they jump to a conclusion. They often adopt the first proposed solution that comes along. We have seen students do this frequently in our classroom groups. For example, some groups quickly select a topic on which to do a major group project just to get the decision over with, only to realize later that the topic cannot be used. With a little patience, research, and time the group would have realized this and selected a different topic.

Overdependence on Authority Figures

Students, particularly freshmen, are often afraid of not doing what they think authority figures (especially teachers) want. Students in our classes frequently ask us to tell them not only how long an assigned paper should be but even how long we want the introduction to be, how many sources should be cited, how many sections the paper should include and how long each should be, what we want them to say in the conclusion, and so forth. Such overdependence stifles critical thinking. We want students to learn to think for themselves and organize their papers in ways appropriate for the topics they have chosen. Overly dependent students do not mature into independent thinkers capable of analyzing information when an authority is not present.

Lack of Confidence

Related to overdependence on authority figures is the lack of confidence in one's own abilities. Students and others who lack self-confidence often respond to questioning or criticism by withdrawing and refusing to volunteer information or opinions.

You can see that a **willingness to communicate** is vital to problem-solving discussions. Members who lack a strong urge to speak up whenever they possess relevant information or ideas are functionally useless to the group. Whether silence is a reflection of shyness, lack of self-confidence, reticence, or apprehension about what others may think is immaterial, information held back is useless to the group. Failing to express doubts or to challenge faulty conclusions during discussions withholds needed resources and results in faulty outputs.

Why might a member possessing vital information not speak up? Some answers can be found in studies about the level of willingness of individuals to speak up. Different scales to measure this characteristic have named it *communication apprehension* (James McCroskey), *reticence* (Gerald Phillips), *shyness* (Phillip Zimbardo), and *willingness to communicate* (Judee Burgoon). In general, research with such scales indicates that people who lack confidence in themselves and what they know tend to avoid speaking up in groups. Although a few people display this characteristic often, most people will only speak cautiously or will remain silent when they feel an authority figure (e.g., a teacher or boss) is evaluating them.

Chances are you know whether you are unwilling to speak up during discussions with peers, especially when others disagree with you. If so, there are steps you can take to increase your willingness to communicate during discussions. Of course we urge you to prepare thoroughly so you will have the confidence that comes from knowing you are well informed. Doing special research for a group, then making an organized report followed by answers to questions, may help. You can think about how much you might hurt the group by *not* speaking out. Your instructor may provide you with a scale to measure your willingness to communicate (or your communication apprehension), then recommend a program of special training. **Now** is the best time to practice new skills and develop new attitudes of willingness and readiness to speak, thereby freeing yourself from the handicaps of low self-confidence and shyness. Changing your attitude regarding speaking out will only get harder as you leave school and move into a career.

Dogmatic, Inflexible Behavior

Many groups suffer from self-appointed experts who act and speak as if they know everything. Such a member is acting in a closed-minded **dogmatic** way. Dogmatic people are unable or unwilling to listen or read carefully in order to understand information, values, and ideas different from those they already hold. They cannot engage in a search for the best possible solution to a problem faced by a group because they are convinced they have already found it. If two of them disagree about information and ideas bearing on an issue, they will never be able to reach an accord. You can observe dogmatic behavior when such persons discuss abortion laws, the nature of God, taxation, gun control, and other controversial topics with which they are personally involved. All of us tend to become somewhat closed-minded when the issue being discussed is central to our definition of self. Extreme dogmatics, however, act as if what they believe to be the truth is the *whole* truth and anyone who disagrees is misguided, wrong, stupid, or evil. Highly dogmatic persons argue not to test ideas or guarantee that they are fully understood, but to get everyone else to agree. They are not seekers; they can only support beliefs they have previously formed.

Dogmatic people express many ideas in absolute or two-valued terms (good **or** bad, black **or** white, true **or** false). As a result, they are inferior problem solvers unless the problem has a known best solution. They do poorly when faced with a challenge with new dimensions, unexpected twists, and unusual characteristics; they are much less creative than open-minded persons.[11]

Dogmatic people are not welcomed in most small groups, with the exception of groups of like-minded persons. A study by one of the authors found that discussants who spoke in dogmatic, rigid ways were chosen by fellow discussants much less often as future group members than were people who expressed opinions in ways that seemed to encourage different opinions. We have both observed that dogmatic students are rarely selected as group leaders in our classes.

Dogmatic people are often frightened by change and novelty. They cling to the security of doing something in a familiar way, even though there may be more productive ways to operate. They may resist new ideas because they are threatened by the unfamiliar. Such group members stifle the creativity of a group and block critical thinking, especially if the information or reasoning to be evaluated is something that is part of the "conventional wisdom" about how things *should* be done.

Unwillingness to Make the Effort to Think Critically

Perhaps one of the most damaging behaviors to a group's ability to think critically is one or more members' unwillingness to expend the effort. Thinking critically takes time, energy, and effort. Unfortunately, some group members are content to let other members tell them exactly what to do. While they may be perfectly willing to work hard for the group in other ways, they are unwilling to engage in independent thinking. This type of attitude can seriously harm a group's decisions because the group is deprived of the critical thinking skills of some members.

Critical thinking is not learned in one lesson. It takes time and commitment, but an individual's critical thinking skills *can* be improved through practice. Using these skills in a group is one of the best ways to observe them in others and learn them yourself. The commitment to learning and using critical thinking skills is worth the effort—remember what happened with the *Challenger*.

Summary

This chapter opened with a discussion of the ill-fated *Challenger* launch and the procedures by which the decision was made. Failure to do some needed critical thinking led to this tragic decision. Critical thinking involves concentrated effort to assess the value of ideas and conclusions by gathering relevant information, assessing that information carefully and judging the reasoning that supports the conclusions and decisions. Critical thinking in small groups requires certain attitudes of group members, a methodical search for information, thorough evaluation of the information, and careful assessment of the reasoning behind opinions and beliefs based on that information. Ideally, members are curious, willing to expend the effort to think critically, and skeptical of information and inferences. In gathering information, group members first should pool their knowledge and identify any gaps that are apparent. Then, they should fill those gaps by using appropriate research methods, including direct observation, reading, interviewing individuals or groups, and consulting other sources like television and radio. When members evaluate information they first should determine what is being said, which statements are facts and which are inferences or opinions, what terms are ambiguous, how believable the source is, and how accurate and valuable the information is. When they check for errors in reasoning, they should be especially alert to the common fallacies of overgeneralizing, attacking the person instead of the issue, assuming that because two events are related one caused the other, either-or thinking, and presenting an incomplete comparison. Behaviors that are counterproductive to critical thinking include impulsiveness, overdependence on authority figures, unwillingness to communicate, dogmatic, inflexible behavior, and unwillingness to make the effort required to think critically. Critical thinking consists primarily of asking the right questions, which can prevent harmful throughput processes like groupthink. This skill can be learned with diligent practice.

Review Questions

1. Give examples of instances from your own experience where you used critical thinking and where you did not. What specific critical thinking behaviors were hardest for you? How did each event turn out?
2. Think of groups to which you have belonged. What member attitudes and behaviors seemed to promote critical thinking? What attitudes seemed to suppress it?
3. What specific steps would you recommend a group take in the process of gathering information in preparation for making an important decision?
4. Give examples from your own experience of what you did to find information you needed for a project. What were the best sources of information for you? The worst?
5. Clip an editorial from your local paper. Outline the writer's conclusion, arguments, and supporting evidence. How well do you think the writer's argument holds up? How much faith would you place on the conclusions? Did you discover any reasoning errors in the editorial? What were they?
6. Look at the behaviors that are counterproductive to critical thinking in a group. Do you ever engage in any of them? Are any of them particularly troublesome for you when used by other group members? What can you do to combat the tendency many people have of falling into these behavior patterns?

Bibliography

Beyer, Barry K. *Practical Strategies for the Teaching of Thinking*. Boston: Allyn & Bacon, 1987.

Browne, M. Neil, and Keeley, Stuart M. *Asking the Right Questions: A Guide to Critical Thinking*. 2d ed. Englewood Cliffs, NJ: Prentice-Hall, 1986.

Campbell, Stephen K. *Flaws and Fallacies in Statistical Thinking*. Englewood Cliffs, NJ: Prentice-Hall, 1974.

Ehninger, Douglas, and Brockriede, Wayne. *Decision by Debate.* 2d ed. New York: Harper & Row, 1978.

Neimark, Edith D. *Adventures in Thinking.* San Diego: Harcourt, Brace Jovanovich, 1987.

Raths, Louis E., Wasserman, Selma, Jonas, Arthur, and Rothstein, Arnold. *Teaching for Thinking: Theory, Strategies, and Activities for the Classroom.* 2d ed. New York: Teachers College, Columbia University, 1986.

References

1. Dennis S. Gouran, Randy Y. Hirokawa, and Amy E. Martz, "A Critical Analysis of Factors Related to Decisional Processes Involved in the *Challenger* Disaster," *Central States Speech Journal* 37 (1986): 119–135.

2. *Webster's Third New International Dictionary of the English Language, Unabridged* (Chicago: Encyclopedia Britannica, Inc. 1966): 538.

3. *Webster's Third New International Dictionary . . .* : 2486.

4. Goodwin Watson and Edwin Glaser, *Manual of Directions for Discrimination of Arguments Test* (New York: World Book Co., 1939): 3.

5. Barry K. Beyer, *Practical Strategies for the Teaching of Thinking* (Boston: Allyn & Bacon, 1987).

6. Richard Huseman, Glenn Ware, and Charles Gruner, "Critical Thinking, Reflective Thinking, and the Ability to Organize Ideas: A Multivariate Approach," *Journal of the American Forensic Association* 9 (1972): 261–265.

7. Dale G. Leathers, "Process Disruption and Measurement in Small Group Communication," *Quarterly Journal of Speech* 55 (1969): 288–98.

8. Gouran et al.,: 130.

9. Chet Meyers, *Teaching Students to Think Critically* (San Francisco: Jossey-Bass Publishers, 1986).

10. Louis E. Raths, Selma Wasserman, Arthur Jonas, and Arnold Rothstein, *Teaching for Thinking: Theory, Strategies, and Activities for the Classroom,* 2d ed. (New York: Teachers College, Columbia University, 1986): 24–28.

11. Milton Rokeach, *The Open and Closed Mind* (New York: Basic Books, 1960).

PART THREE

Understanding and Improving Group Throughput Processes

The interaction that occurs among group members is the heart of small group communication. Part Three focuses on this interaction among members and describes in detail several important group throughput processes. Chapter 6 explains how a group develops from an initial collection of individuals into a team. Chapters 7 and 8 discuss small group leadership. Chapter 7 presents theoretical information that will serve as a foundation for your understanding of the practical information and suggestions presented in chapter 8. Chapter 9 focuses on group problem solving and how it can be improved. Chapter 10 describes why conflict occurs in a group and how it can be managed to benefit a group.

CHAPTER SIX

Becoming a Group

CHAPTER OUTLINE

Primary, Secondary, and Tertiary Tensions

Managing Tensions

Phases in the Development of a Group

Rules and Norms

Development of Group Norms

Enforcement of Group Norms

Dealing with Deviants

Changing a Group Norm

Group Roles

Types of Roles

Role Functions in a Small Group

Individual Roles and the Hidden Agenda

The Emergence of Roles in a Group

Development of the Group's Culture

Fantasy Themes

Group Climate

Trust

Cohesiveness

Supportiveness

STUDY QUESTIONS

1. Describe primary, secondary, and tertiary tensions and explain how a group can manage its tensions.
2. Describe the two major phases in the development of a group.
3. What is the difference between a rule and a norm? How do group norms develop? How can an unproductive norm be changed?
4. What kinds of norms are groups most likely to enforce, and how do groups handle members who deviate from group norms?
5. Describe the two general types of group roles and the three major functions of roles in a group. What is a hidden agenda?
6. How do roles emerge in a group? What is a role profile?
7. What is group culture and what are the two major contributors to group culture?

KEY TERMS AND CONCEPTS

Cohesiveness	Norms
Deviant	Primary Tension
Fantasy	Production Phase
Fantasy Chain	Roles
Fantasy Theme	Rules
Formation Phase	Secondary Tension
Group Climate	Tertiary Tension
Group Culture	Trust
Hidden Agenda	

In the movie *The Breakfast Club* five high school students must spend an entire Saturday in detention at their school. Claire, the prom queen, and Andy, the jock, are both "cool" kids who belong to the elite crowd. Brian, the scholar, is a studious nerd. Alison, the artsy misfit, wears heavy makeup, shapeless clothes, and doesn't say anything for a long time. Bender, the tough guy, is loaded with resentment against the others, whom he assumes have happy families. He has an instinct for finding people's vulnerable spots so he can goad them into losing their composure. A more varied collection of individuals is hard to imagine. Yet by the end of the movie these five students have developed into a cohesive group, if only for that one Saturday.

The teacher responsible for watching the students gives them an assignment: to complete an essay on "Who Am I?" by the end of the day. Bored with watching the kids, the teacher leaves for his own office. At first, only Claire and Andy think they have anything in common, so they form a loose alliance by smiling at each other, nonverbally showing their mutual support. One of the kids calls the teacher a "brownie hound." This establishes the first common ground the students recognize—their shared dislike of the teacher. When Bender closes the door to the room in violation of the teacher's order, the teacher demands to know who shut the door. The rest of the students, even though they dislike Bender, refuse to betray him to the "enemy."

Gradually, the kids realize that they have a lot of things in common. They all have problems with their parents, are worried they won't be accepted by their peers, are afraid they are different or weird in some way, and generally feel insecure about growing up. As *The Breakfast Club* students begin to share their feelings and find things to do together (sneaking out to the student lockers to smoke pot, for example), we see leadership, group norms, and cohesiveness develop. The antagonism between Claire and Bender fuels much of the group's conflict, but at the end of the movie, she gives him her earring and he accepts, thus demonstrating their mutual acceptance and respect.

Although *The Breakfast Club* is not about a task-oriented group, the movie shows much of the process through which collections of individuals develop into groups. Each group will create its own personality, but principles of group development apply equally to task and primary groups. In chapter 6 we seek to answer the question, "How does a bunch of *individuals* become a *group?*"

Primary, Secondary, and Tertiary Tensions

Whenever individuals come together some tension and conflict are inevitable. All groups must find ways to manage the three major types of tensions among members. **Primary tension** refers to the interpersonal tension that occurs when a group first begins to form into a unit.[1] It can be identified by the extreme politeness members show each other, stiffness, and perhaps long pauses in the conversation. You probably recall how you felt the first time you met with a new group.

If you are like most people, you worry about how the other members will perceive you, so you are careful not to say or do something that might alienate the others. You don't know, yet, what your contribution or that of the others will be. Who will become the group's most valued members, and will you be one of them? Will you be able to influence the group in a positive way? Will the other members appreciate your contributions? Just as *you* are thinking these things, so are the other members. Thus, early in the group's life, most members will avoid behavior that might offend other members. Rather than disagreeing directly, for example, members will express wishy-washy opinions. This contributes to that sticky-sweet, overly formal and polite atmosphere often observed in newly-formed groups.

Primary tension is obvious in *The Breakfast Club* as the students first begin to size each other up. Unlike the polite behavior usually displayed in new groups, Bender insults and teases the others. At first the others gently remind him that he does not know any of them, so his judgments are unfair. Once they have gotten to know each other better, they are not so tentative. For example, Claire calls Bender a "prick" for his cruel remarks.

Secondary tension usually occurs later in the group's life; it is work-related tension coming from differing opinions about substantive issues. For example, one committee member might favor recommending Candidate A to fill a vacant position, but another member prefers Candidate B. The disagreements may be mild or intense, members may be soft-spoken or loud as they disagree. Nevertheless, the group must somehow come to a conclusion *as a group* in resolving these secondary tensions that are a normal part of a group's development. To an observer, secondary tension looks different from primary tension. While primary tension frequently comes through to the group as uneasiness, fidgeting, or perhaps even boredom, secondary tension usually is unmistakable as members argue vehemently for their different positions.

Tertiary tension results from status or power struggles. Members disagree about *who* will decide the rules and procedures for the group. Conflict may occur over how to decide, how to resolve conflicts, who has the authority to determine what will happen in the group, who can make assignments and how, who is expert at what, what the rights and privileges of membership are, and so forth. Much of the tension we have observed in groups is not strictly primary or secondary. Instead, groups often become bogged down in arguments that seem to recycle over and over, but are never resolved. When we have observed the dynamics of such groups, we invariably discover that a power or status struggle exists over who will fit where in the system.

One of us attended a meeting of a classroom group that was experiencing such a struggle. The group's class assignment was to observe a task group and gather data, either through observation or by talking to the members. Mike insisted that the group use *his* questionnaire as one method of gathering data. Michelle demanded instead that the group use *her* questionnaire. This endless argument was a thinly masked power struggle. If this really had been only secondary tension, Mike and Michelle could easily have combined their questionnaires or settled on a compromise of some sort. Instead, each was demanding to be in charge of deciding the group's procedures. This tension—neither primary nor really secondary—is what we term tertiary tension, and it can be quite destructive to the development of an effective group.

In *The Breakfast Club,* the students escape their "prison" to wander the halls, but come close to being spotted by the teacher. Bender leads them down one set of hallways toward a dead end. Andy shouts, "We're through listening to you, we're going this way!" This argument takes place long past the point where primary tension inhibits the group members from expressing their opinions. It is an example of both secondary and tertiary tension. The students are trying to figure out the best way of returning to their detention room without being caught by the teacher, but there's a status struggle happening between Bender and Andy over who will lead the group out of its dilemma.

Managing Tensions

If a group is to do the best job it is capable of doing, all three types of tension must be managed appropriately. First, group members can move through the primary tension stage more quickly if they know each other. A get-acquainted period helps members do this. You should not hesitate to suggest this, even if your group's designated leader doesn't. The members will be able to accomplish their task much more effectively and quickly if they know the backgrounds of the other members, what they do on the job, and even what hobbies and outside interests they have. Joking, laughing, and having fun together prior to getting down to work help as well. Remember, time spent in getting acquainted at the beginning of a group's formation usually saves time in the long run.

Second, members can reduce both primary and secondary tension by sharing what they know about the problem at hand. For instance, if a committee is charged with recommending solutions to a campus parking problem, each member's perception of the scope and seriousness of the problem can be shared so that all will have at least some common understanding of the problem.

Third, secondary and tertiary tensions can be managed if group members demonstrate tolerance for disagreement. When group members believe that their opinions and ideas are appreciated, even if these opinions are contrary to the ideas of others, then they feel valued by the group. They also are less likely to demand high status if they already believe the group appreciates them. When members feel free to disagree and to express critical testing of ideas, they begin to trust in the cohesiveness of the group. It helps if members express this solidarity by saying things like "We'll be able to find an answer—we've done a good job so far," and other statements that acknowledge confidence that the group is a dependable system.

Table 6.1   Suggestions for Managing Group Tensions

Make sure members know each other as individuals.
  1. Include a get-acquainted period.
  2. Schedule an informal chat period before each meeting.
  3. Engage in group social activities.
Have members share information and feelings about the group's task so members arrive at a common understanding.
Make sure members display tolerance for disagreement.
  1. Use sensitivity in expressing disagreement; disagree without putting down the person with whom you disagree.
  2. Remind the group that disagreement can help achieve a superior outcome.
Confront inappropriate behavior by describing its effect on the group.
Use humor, joking, and shared laughter to lighten the mood.

Expressing appreciation to others for their critical thinking and reasoning is one way to help demonstrate tolerance for disagreement. One of us served on an important university committee with a distinguished meteorologist, with whom your coauthor was in frequent disagreement. One day, the meteorologist expressed how much he appreciated someone who intelligently and reasonably argued against his (and others') proposals when misgivings occurred. He believed such arguments caught flaws in his reasoning and exposed his biases and prejudices. Your coauthor had been feeling exactly the same way about the meteorologist and told him so. This mutual appreciation made it much easier to manage the secondary tension in the group.

Humor can be an effective way of handling secondary and tertiary tension in a group. A well-timed, lighthearted comment can move a group past an obstacle that seems insurmountable. Joking and laughing together increase the members' good feelings toward each other. This in turn helps members become more open toward each other, which can lead to resolution of their substantive and status differences. One of us belonged to a group where people shot baskets with paper wads, reminisced about fishing, and talked about ice cream. These topics established common ground and helped members relax with each other. *However, NEVER joke to change the topic or put someone in his or her place!* This can destroy whatever cohesiveness the group has developed.

Finally, tertiary tension in particular can be difficult to manage using indirect methods, and a group may have to address the problem directly by saying something to the offending members. Either a group's designated leader or one of the other members can politely but firmly confront the members involved in the status struggle by pointing out the negative effects the tension is having on the rest of the group. The suggestions given later in the chapter for changing ineffective group norms can also be used to address tertiary tension. A summary of all these suggestions for managing tensions may be found in table 6.1.

Phases in the Development of a Group

Groups go through predictable phases, just as people do, on their way to becoming mature. (These phases of the group's overall development are not the same as the phases groups experience during decision making. We will discuss decision-making phases in chapter 9.) A group will usually not function smoothly as a system at its first meeting. Just as a human baby must stand before walking, a group must resolve some of its internal business before it can concentrate its efforts on work. For example, when group members are dealing with primary tension, they are expending emotional and mental energy that is unavailable for productive work. On the other hand, when group members are concentrating fully on their assignment, they are paying less attention to each other's human needs. One of the great group theorists of our century, Robert F. Bales, calls this the *equilibrium problem*. A group's attention must shift between concentrating on the task and concentrating on the relationships among members.[2] Attention to both is necessary for a group to function well. First, the group must develop dependable, harmonious interpersonal relationships that will give it stability. Bales called this the group's *socioemotional* concern, wherein the group focuses on interpersonal relationships. Second, the group must concentrate on completing its assignment. Focusing on the work of the group is called the *task* concern, from which come secondary tensions. Neither can be ignored if the group is to be successful.

Task and socioemotional concerns predominate at predictable periods in the group's development. The first overall phase of the group's development from a collection of individuals into a system is the **formation phase,** where interpersonal/ socioemotional concerns predominate. In this phase, members focus on working out their relationships with each other. Ideally, members will agree on what their relationships are without recurring power struggles and tertiary tensions. Rules, roles, and a leadership structure emerge. Members assess their own and others' talents and weaknesses to create roles needed in the group. They identify who can be counted on to do what. For example, perhaps Lee is an excellent organizer but is not skilled at coming up with creative alternatives. Pat, on the other hand, is a great idea person but is unreliable on follow-through. As the group progresses through the formation stage, members begin to mesh themselves into a coordinated whole that can function as a unit. A division of labor that includes *all* needed behaviors emerges if the group is to produce excellent results.

The group moves gradually into the **production phase,** the stage where it is able to concentrate on its assigned task. Most groups do not have the luxury of getting to know each other well before they have to start working. Instead, they are resolving their primary tensions *at the same time* they are dealing with the task-oriented business of the group. Thus, instead of being separate, sequential phases, they partially overlap and run parallel to each other. This is illustrated in figure 6.1. As the socioemotional concerns become resolved, the group is able to expend more of its energy on task-related concerns. So, the formation phase gradually gives way to the production phase, although it never completely disappears.

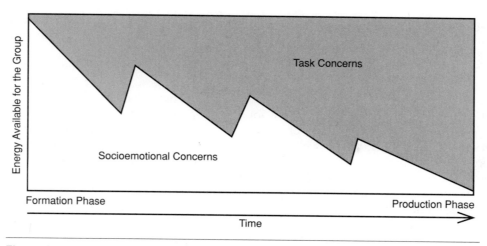

Figure 6.1 Formation and production phases of a group.

The better a group resolves its primary and tertiary tension and develops a stable leadership structure, the more time and energy it has for working on its assignment. The better job the group does on the formation phase, the better job it can do in the production phase.

The example presented earlier involving Mike and Michelle demonstrates how incompletely resolved leadership issues in the formation stage hinder a group's production phase. In the struggle for informal leadership and power, neither student would yield to the other. If Michelle made a suggestion, Mike would counter it and vice versa. The rest of the members couldn't concentrate on creating and implementing the best possible solution in an atmosphere dominated by tertiary tension. Time and energy were wasted in unproductive bickering. Unfortunately, this type of struggle is fairly common.

Rules and Norms

Rules and **norms** are the standards of behavior and procedures by which group members operate. Norms, the informal standards, are not written down. On the other hand, rules are more formal and frequently are written in minutes or by-laws, or explained by group facilitators as steps in special procedures (we discuss such procedures in chapter 11). Norms and rules establish limitations for behavior by indicating what behavior is *not* permitted (e.g., "The seat at the head of the table is reserved for the group's chair and no one else may occupy it"). They also prescribe certain behavior by specifying what *is* supposed to occur (e.g., "Members should call each other by their first names," or "The designated leader is responsible for finding an appropriate meeting place"). Rules and norms are different from each other only in their degree of formality, with rules being more formally stated. Norms are enforced by peer pressures, whereas rules are usually enforced by the designated leader. Rules and norms belong to the group as a system rather than to any individual.

What functions do rules and norms serve for the group? They help group members know what is and is not acceptable behavior as a member, thus reducing the uncertainty members feel about how to act. They establish procedures for working as a coordinated team. In the long run, productive rules and norms help the group achieve a high level of efficiency and quality control so that it can accomplish its assigned task well. Can you imagine how hard it would be if, every time you had a meeting, you had to negotiate the procedures by which the group should operate? You would be wasting all your valuable time deciding *how* you should work instead of getting your job done.

Formal rules are constructed in a couple of ways. First, the parent organization that created the group may give the group rules prescribing its operation. For example, many large organizations use the procedures in *Robert's Rules of Order* to govern meetings. If a committee is created by such an organization, then that committee must operate using *Robert's Rules* for committees. By the way, *Robert's Rules* for committees are *not* the same as parliamentary procedures for large assemblies. Instead, they are geared to the informal discussion and decision by consensus that most small groups use. We mention this here because some individuals mistakenly insist that parliamentary procedures be used in small groups. We believe such insistence may represent an attempt to control the group by intimidating other members.

Sometimes committees and other small groups establish their own formal rules by deciding what they want the group to accomplish and how this can best be done. Frequently, organizations establish by-laws, which include the operating rules for the small groups that operate under their authority.

Norms usually are not discussed openly, but nevertheless they have a strong effect on the behavior of the group members. For example, in *The Breakfast Club,* the students do not talk about establishing a norm whereby they will protect each other against the teacher. However, when the teacher asks the students *who* closed the library door, none of the students tattles on Bender. Even though the rest of the students do not like Bender at that point, they will not rat on him to the "enemy" teacher. This is evidence of a strong norm operating, which might be stated thus: "No matter what our personal feelings are, we must not rat on each other to adult authority figures."

Development of Group Norms

If *The Breakfast Club's* students did not discuss what they considered to be appropriate behavior for their group, how did the members know how to behave? How do norms develop? There are a number of ways norms are established in a small group[3] (see table 6.2).

Table 6.2 How Group Norms Form

Primacy: Behaviors and events occurring early in the group's history
Explicit statements: Statements made by the other members or the group's leader about what is and is not expected behavior
Critical events: Important happenings that indicate what is or is not acceptable behavior
Carry-over behaviors: Expectations about appropriate and inappropriate behavior that is part of the general culture, or environment, of the group

Primacy, behaviors that occur early in the group's history, often set norms for the group. When group members first meet, they feel uncertain and uncomfortable. Anything that reduces the uncertainty is welcomed. Thus, what first occurs in a group can easily become habit because it helps reduce the feeling of uncertainty. For example, imagine you serve on a committee that includes faculty and students. If you aren't sure whether to address the faculty members by their first names, and you hear a fellow student member addressing them by titles, chances are you will follow that lead. A norm is becoming established whereby students call faculty members *Professor* or *Doctor,* but faculty members address students by first names.

However, early group behaviors that become norms can cause problems later on. Recall that when members first meet, they experience primary tension which makes them so polite and stiff that they do not confront or disagree with each other. This can easily develop into a norm of "no conflict," which stops members from expressing disagreements or doubts. As you have seen from the chapter on critical thinking, this "no conflict" norm can be extremely detrimental to the group's later decision-making abilities.

Sometimes norms are established by *explicit statements* that a leader or another member makes. For example, one member might tell a new member, "The chair likes to have proposals in writing. If you want to make a suggestion about work procedures at the staff meeting, you should bring a handout for everyone to use." This statement relays information about the group leader's preferences and also subtly lets the new member know that suggestions are supposed to be well thought out before being presented to the group. Explicit statements like this also help reduce the new member's uncertainty about appropriate behavior.

Some norms are established through *critical events* that occur in a group. For example, one of your authors once taught a graduate seminar of nine people who came to trust each other, often revealing personal information in the class. Two of the students told nonmembers some of what occurred in the class. When the other members discovered this, they felt angry. At the next class meeting, members expressed their feelings of betrayal. Before the critical incident, some members thought it was all right to reveal in-class information to selected outsiders, but after the meeting it was clear to *all* members that such behavior was a serious violation of a group norm requiring confidentiality.

Finally, many norms are taken from the general culture in which the group members live. For example, you know some ways to behave as a student, no matter what the class. True, some professors are more formal than others, but certain standards of behavior (such as raising your hand when you have a question or a comment, not calling the professor or other students by rude names, and so forth) carry over from one class to another. Thus, many *carry-over behaviors* in a group are ones we have learned as members of a particular culture. This source of small group norms becomes especially troublesome when we interact with members from different cultures. For example, we have observed students from Eastern and Oriental cultures behave very meekly in groups with American students. These foreign students are following the norms of their native cultures, just as are the American students. Likewise, African-Americans and Hispanics tend to use the vocal backchannel (saying things like *mmhmm, okay,* and so forth while another is speaking) more frequently than European Americans. Lack of understanding of another's cultural norms can cause problems in a group.

Enforcement of Group Norms

If norms are not written down, how do group members learn them? Observant group members pay attention to how other members act. From this information, norms can be inferred. In particular, you should pay attention to two types of behaviors: those that occur regularly, and those that incur disapproval.

Behaviors that occur consistently from one meeting to the next probably reflect a group norm. For example, if at every meeting each group member sits in the same seat and waits for the leader to start the discussion, you are seeing evidence of two norms.

Behaviors that are punished by peer pressure also indicate norms. The strongest evidence of a group norm is members' negative reaction to a particular behavior. For example, if several members make sarcastic comments or gestures when another member comes late to a meeting, you are right in guessing that the latecomer has violated a group norm. Most peer pressure will come in the form of nonverbal signals, as group members roll their eyes at each other, glare, shake their heads, or turn away from the violator. Sometimes they will pointedly ignore the offending member's contributions. For example, one of your authors attended staff meetings where an important norm was that newcomers should not criticize long-standing procedures until they had "paid their dues" to the group. Unaware of the norm, one new member spoke as freely as if she had belonged to the group for years. The "old-timers" threw sidelong glances at each other whenever she spoke and did not reply to her suggestions. She never realized that she had violated a norm. Instead, she concluded that the rest of the staff members were not interested in creative solutions, so she stopped sharing her ideas, many of which were potentially valuable. All she needed to do was wait until the rest of the members accepted her. Because she didn't wait, and other members did not explain the norm to her, she was never fully accepted.

Not all norms are enforced equally, for some are more important than others. Norms related to the group's survival and those that express values central to the group are likely to be enforced more vigorously than other norms.[4] For example, many organizations have rules requiring attendance—members can be dropped from the organization if they miss too many meetings. Required attendance is frequently a crucial group norm because it is directly related to the group's ability to survive—if members do not attend meetings, the group system will eventually die. For this reason, attendance norms are likely to be strongly enforced.

Norms that help define a group and distinguish it from other groups also are enforced vigorously. For example, a friend of one of the authors had a job interview for a management position with a trend-setting retail store. Like other applicants, she was well qualified. Part of her interview included a group interview with the staff members with whom she would be working. She reasoned that since the company prided itself on being on the cutting edge of the fashion industry, her conservative "power" suit would not do. Instead, she splurged on a trendy outfit. Her strategy worked; the members of the management group who interviewed her also were fashion trendsetters. They felt comfortable with her in part because she seemed to *fit in* with an important, group-defining norm, and they offered her the job.

Dealing with Deviants

Group members are uncomfortable with **deviants,** members who consistently violate important group norms. To group members, deviants seem to thumb their noses at the group by implying that their own needs and wishes are more important than the needs of the group. The other members will try to force the deviants to fall in line by applying increasing pressure to conform (see table 6.3).[5]

First, groups try to reason with the deviant by explaining the necessity for conforming to the norm. They address a large share of the group's remarks to the deviant in an obvious effort to persuade. These remarks gradually increase in emotional intensity. If reasoning fails, members try to tease the deviant into agreeing with them. Gradually this escalates into coercion, as the other members apply increasingly forceful tactics.

While these persuasive efforts are occurring, solidarity increases among the rest of the members in opposition to the deviant. The harder the members try to convince the deviant to see the error of his/her ways, the more they convince themselves they are right. They develop a united front.

Finally, if all efforts to force the deviant to conform fail, the rest of the members ostracize the deviant. In essence, the group kicks the deviant out, figuratively or literally. Since humans are social creatures needing the companionship of their own kind, this is a particularly harsh form of punishment.

Table 6.3   How Groups Deal with Deviant Members

First, members try to persuade the deviant member to conform to the group norms.
    By reasoning with the deviant
    By attempting to persuade the deviant
    By attempting to coerce the deviant
Second, solidarity builds among the other members against the deviant.
Third, members ignore and will eventually isolate the deviant.
    The deviant is treated as if invisible.
    The deviant is given the most undesirable group tasks.
    The deviant may be kicked out.

We have observed this sequence many times. For example, these steps were followed almost exactly by a student group one of us observed while in graduate school. Groups were formed to complete an extensive group project. One group consisted of three female graduate students, all working hard to achieve high grades, and a male undergraduate who was unconcerned about grades. Rob missed several early group meetings. The little work he contributed was sloppy. The three women politely explained to him the importance of being a responsible group member. When that didn't work, the women tried to shame him into working harder with teasing and sarcasm, which eventually escalated into name-calling. They tried to establish firm rules, but Rob consistently violated them. The solidarity among the women increased. While they waited for Rob, they discussed his unacceptable behavior and patted each other on the back for their responsible attitudes and contributions. Toward the end of the quarter, Rob realized that if he wanted to share in the group grade he needed to do some work. By this time, the graduate students were so disgusted with him that is wouldn't have made any difference even if he could have walked on water. They ignored his suggestions and acted as if he were invisible. Finally, they let him redeem himself somewhat by allowing him to compile, type, and make copies of their group paper (all 60 pages). In short, groups deal with deviants in predictable ways that become increasingly intense. The deviant who does not conform will be removed from the group, physically or psychologically.

Just because groups usually pressure a deviant to conform does not mean that the deviant should automatically cave in to such pressure. Sometimes groups consider people deviant if they disagree or won't go along with a group's plans. However, such people can actually be helpful to a group if they cause the other members to examine information and ideas more carefully. Even so, the other members may not recognize that such disagreement, or *idea deviance,* can be helpful, and will try to force agreement. This pressure can be hard to resist, even when the deviant has a good case. We present more information about the effect of idea-deviant disagreement in chapter 10, which describes conflict in small groups.

Table 6.4 Changing a Group Norm

Prepare

1. Make sure you are seen as a responsible, loyal member of the group; others won't appreciate your comments if you have been unreliable, or act "holier than thou."
2. Ask yourself, "What harm is the norm causing?" Observe the *effects* of the group norm on the members and the group as a whole; count the offending behaviors and make notes of your observations.

Confront Constructively

1. Select an appropriate time to share your information with other members.
2. Share your observations about the effects of the unproductive norm on the group; explain what you have observed the norm to be, and the problems it causes.
3. Ask whether others also have observed these effects or share your concerns.
4. Express yourself supportively, not defensively:
   a. *Defensive comment:* "I'm sick and tired of always being on time while the rest of you wander in any time you please!"
   b. *Supportive comment:* "For the past four meetings we have started between 15 and 25 minutes late. We seem to have developed a norm that scheduled starting times do not need to be observed. Two of us have had to leave these meetings before they were finished in order to go to class. As a result we have missed several key decisions, and the rest of you have had to bring us up to date on what happened. Does anyone else see this as a problem?"

Encourage the Group to Eliminate or Modify the Norm

1. Ask *all* group members to share their observations.
2. Ask *all* group members for their suggestions about correcting the unproductive norm.
3. Encourage all members to enforce the new norm by reminding the group as needed.

Changing a Group Norm

What can you do if you believe that a norm your group has developed is harming the group in some way? Although it isn't always easy, there are ways of changing unproductive group norms. An effective approach is to focus the group's attention on the norm and the harm it is creating rather than on the person violating the norm. In addition, do not try to *force* your suggestions for changing the norm down the other members' throats. They are likely to become defensive, refuse to change, and resent your attempt to control them. Instead, you want the *group* to think of ways to change the norm so that all the members participate in establishing a more productive group norm. Only the *group* can make a lasting change in a norm. The guidelines in table 6.4 will help you. Although changing a norm may seem like a hassle, it is worth taking the trouble if it helps the group become more productive.

Group Roles

Your **role** is the part you play in a group. The role you perform in any particular group is a function of your personality, behavior, expectations, the expectations of other members, and any formal titles or instructions you may have been given regarding that group. Just like an actor has a role in a play, so do we all have a part to play in each group we belong to. And just as an actor has different parts in different plays, so do we have a unique position in each group we join. Although we display certain personality traits no matter what the situation, we adapt our behavior to different groups.

Types of Roles

There are two main types of member roles, *formal* and *informal*. *Formal* refers to roles that are assigned on the basis of a member's formal position or title. Formal roles are sometimes called *positional* roles. For example, one member may hold the title of *secretary* for the group. In that case, *secretary* is a formal role that carries with it certain requirements and expectations. The group's rules will state something like this: "The secretary shall write and distribute to all members minutes of all meetings held by the group. At the end of each year the secretary shall provide a written summary of the group's work during that year to the President of the Student Senate." In addition to a position's required duties, many of us have expectations about how the person occupying a particular role should behave. For example, how do you think a group's chair or president should behave? Don't you expect that person to schedule meetings, call the group to order, stop long-winded participants, keep the meeting on track, summarize, and make sure that all members have an equal opportunity to express their views? In the next chapter we will discuss in detail how effective designated group leaders behave.

Informal roles, sometimes called *behavioral roles,* are those parts people play that reflect their personality traits, habits, and behaviors in the group. Even if they hold the same title or position, different people will behave somewhat differently, reflecting their unique personalities. Through trial and error, every member of a group begins to specialize in certain behaviors within the group. For example, one of us belonged to a work group that included an individual who joked, teased, and refused to take anything seriously. It was difficult for the group to accomplish any work when he was there (which fortunately wasn't very often). This person played the role of *playboy* in the group. A member in the same group knew how to use data bases to find pertinent research reports. She became the group's *bibliographer,* as well as its *prodder* by constantly encouraging everyone to finish assignments when promised. Such informal roles emerge as group members interact. A specific role results from an interplay between the individual's characteristics and other members of the group.

Role Functions in a Small Group

Members' roles in small groups are categorized according to what they *do* for the group: "How does this behavior help or hinder the group in achieving its goal?" There are three main categories of behavior into which small group roles are typically classified: *task, maintenance,* and *individual.* The first two are helpful to the group, the third is not.

A task-oriented behavior is one that contributes directly to accomplishment of the group's task. Task behaviors that occur frequently in small group interactions include initiating, coordinating, making suggestions, asking task-related questions, providing answers, elaborating on someone else's idea, taking notes, and so forth. You probably can think of many more task-related behaviors you have seen performed in groups. In *The Breakfast Club,* the obnoxious Bender performed a number of task-related behaviors. For example, he organized the trip through the school's hallways. Without his efforts, that particular collection of students might never have become a group. Recently, one of us served on a church building committee trying to find a new place to meet. One member said, "Let's make a list of all the possibilities in our price range." After the committee completed the list, the member said, "Now, let's split up the list and each visit one or two before our next meeting. Who will volunteer to look at the two buildings on Glenstone Avenue?" These remarks, which suggested procedure and also helped coordinate the work of the group, are examples of task behavior. A partial list of task-related behaviors is contained in table 6.5.

Maintenance behaviors are those that help the group maintain harmonious relationships and a cohesive interpersonal climate. Behaviors like harmonizing, gatekeeping, supporting, agreeing, showing solidarity, and relieving tension help accomplish this. In *The Breakfast Club,* Claire provided several maintenance behaviors. For example, she stuck up for Brain (the nerd) when he admitted he was a virgin, and she transformed Alison's appearance for the better by convincing her to change her heavy makeup to something more subtle. Such behaviors, which say "I value you" to the others, improve relationships among members. A member of the building committee mentioned earlier welcomed one of us back from a three-week trip by saying, "It's great to have you back! Here's a summary of everything we did while you were gone. We held off making a decision until you got back, because we really wanted to know what you thought." These remarks demonstrate a gatekeeping function by allowing the absent member to contribute to the discussion, and they also show solidarity and support. Table 6.6 is a partial list of maintenance behaviors.

Individual roles consist of self-centered behaviors. The self-centered member places his or her needs ahead of the group's. These roles do not help the group in any way; they may be extremely harmful to it. Things like interrupting, blocking progress, attention-seeking by excessive storytelling and kidding, withdrawing, and name-calling hinder a group. The playboy described earlier was enacting an individual role. Table 6.7 contains a partial list of individual behaviors.

Table 6.5 Task-Related Behaviors

Initiating: Proposing goals, activities, or plans of action; prodding the group to greater activity

Orienting: Defining the group's position in relation to other groups or its goal

Information giving: Offering facts, information, evidence, personal experience, and knowledge pertinent to the group task

Information seeking: Asking other members for information, facts, evidence, and personal experience

Opinion giving: Stating beliefs, values, interpretations, judgments; drawing conclusions from evidence

Opinion seeking: Asking other members for their opinions

Clarifying: Explaining vague statements or interpreting issues

Elaborating: Developing ideas by giving examples, illustrations, and explanations

Evaluating: Expressing judgments about the relative worth of ideas or information; proposing or applying criteria

Summarizing: Reviewing what has been said previously; reminding others of items previously mentioned, discussed, or decided

Coordinating: Showing relationships between or among ideas; organizing the work of other members; suggesting how members can work as an efficient team

Consensus testing: Asking whether the group has reached a decision acceptable to all; suggesting that agreement may have been reached

Recording: Keeping records on board or paper, preparing reports and minutes; serving as group secretary

Suggesting procedure: Proposing an agenda of issues, outline, problem-solving procedure, or special technique to follow

---

Table 6.6 Maintenance-Related Behaviors

Establishing norms: Suggesting rules of behavior for members; challenging unproductive ways of behaving as a member; giving negative responses when another violates a rule or norm

Gatekeeping: Helping another member get the floor; suggesting or controlling speaking order; asking if someone has a different opinion

Supporting: Agreeing or otherwise expressing support for another's belief or proposal; following another's lead

Harmonizing: Reducing tension by reconciling a disagreement; suggesting a compromise or new alternative acceptable to all; combining proposals into a compromise alternative; conciliating or calming an angry member

Tension-relieving: Introducing and making strangers feel at ease; reducing external status differences; encouraging informality; joking; stressing common interest and experiences

Dramatizing: Making comments that evoke fantasies about people and places other than the present group and time, including storytelling and fantasizing in a vivid manner; testing a tentative value or norm through a fantasy or story

Showing solidarity: Expressing positive feeling toward other group members, or reinforcing a sense of group unity and cohesiveness

Table 6.7 Individual (Self-Centered) Behaviors

Withdrawing: Not participating; avoiding important differences; refusing to cope with conflicts; refusing to take a stand; covering up feelings; giving no response to the comments of others

Blocking: Preventing progress toward group goals by constantly raising objections, repeatedly bringing up the same topic or issue after the group has considered and rejected it (It's not blocking to keep raising an idea or topic the group has not really listened to or considered.)

Status and recognition seeking: Stage-hogging, boasting, and calling attention to one's expertise or experience when that is not necessary to establish credibility or is not relevant to the group's task; game playing to elicit sympathy; switching the subject to area of own personal expertise

Playing: Refusing to help the group with the task; excessive joking, dramatizing, and horsing around; making fun of members who are serious about the task; interfering with the group's work

Acting helpless: Trying to elicit the sympathy of other members by constantly needing help to complete assigned task; showing inability for independent thought or action; forcing other members to complete, or redo, work turned in

Individual Roles and the Hidden Agenda

We noted earlier that individualistic roles occur when group members consider their own needs to be more important than the needs of the group. Frequently, these harmful self-centered behaviors occur as a result of a **hidden agenda** item—an unstated, often unconscious reason for belonging to a group, or a private goal a member wants to achieve through the group. The public agenda refers to the group's explicit, stated purposes. Members have the opportunity to discuss or modify it. The hidden agenda is not stated to the group. The total hidden agenda combines all the individual hidden agenda items members bring to the group. For example, LaDonna may want to say on a résumé that she chaired a particular committee. If she is determined to be the leader at any cost, she will make strong attempts to control and direct the activities of the group, even if the group does not want those efforts. In such a case, the behavior may lock the group in a power struggle over the position of *chair*.

The individual with a hidden purpose may be motivated by either tangible or psychological self-interest. For example, a manufacturing manager may argue against a change in procedures that determine how bonuses are calculated by saying that new procedures will be too confusing to implement when the *true* reason is that new procedures will decrease the amount of money available to the manager's division (i.e., the hidden agenda item). In that instance, there is specific, tangible reason—money—for the self-interest. On the other hand, the marketing manager whose division will be equally hurt by new procedures may argue in favor of them because of a strong need to perceive herself as fair-minded and reasonable. This person argues from psychological self-interest to the *benefit* rather than the harm of the group. Thus, a hidden agenda item does not automatically create problems for a group. If an individual's hidden purpose happens to mesh with what the group requires, this marriage of individual and group needs can be a happy one. Whether hidden agenda items are harmful or helpful to the group, they do affect individual's behaviors in the group and the roles they perform.

The Emergence of Roles in a Group

Through communication with each other, members gradually develop their unique contributions and roles. Stop and think for a moment about the groups you belong to. Do you act exactly the same way in each one of them? Probably not. There are variations in your behavior because each group brings out different combinations of your skills, abilities, and personality characteristics. Normal people *want* to contribute their unique talents and abilities so they will be valued by the group. When the other group members appreciate and reward those behaviors, they perform them more often. In that way, roles and a division of labor occurs in the group.

Let's look at an example of how this occurs. Jan had a gift for storytelling. Because Jan felt uncomfortable whenever there was a lull in her seminar's discussion, she generally filled the silences with a story. Stories about her extensive travels easily captured the other members' attention and relieved the uneasiness that silence sometimes caused. The rest of the group encouraged her to relate her stories. Because of both Jan's ability to entertain and the other members' desire to listen, she carved out an informal (behavioral) role as the group's *storyteller*.

Note that the other members of the group *must* reinforce a member's behavior if a role is to become stable and strong. If the other members had not been eager to set aside their work momentarily to listen to Jan, they would not have encouraged the development of her storyteller role despite her skills. Instead, they would have discouraged her by paying little attention or reminding her that she was deflecting the group from its task. Then, Jan would have downplayed her storytelling and searched for another way to contribute. For example, she also was an active listener who clarified and summarized what others said. If she had not won such esteem as the group's storyteller, she might have become the group's recorder or *memory*. From this example you can see how a member's role in a group depends on that member's characteristics as well as how the other members respond.

It is possible to construct *role profiles* for members of a group by observing their behaviors, categorizing them, and naming the role patterns that emerge. Look at figure 6.2, which has two hypothetical role profiles. The first is a profile typical of an *information specialist* in the group. Note that more than half of this individual's remarks to the group give information to the other members. The rest of the behaviors consist of giving opinions, clarifying and elaborating ideas, seeking information and supporting. This person freely shares information and ideas in the group. The second profile is for Jan, our storyteller. You can categorize any individual's behaviors to determine the particular role that a person plays in a group.

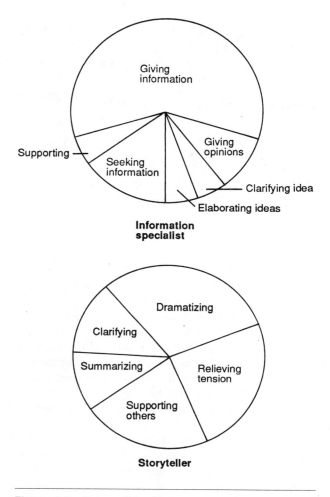

Figure 6.2 Role profiles of two group members.

Development of the Group's Culture

Undoubtedly you have noticed that each group to which you belong has a unique "personality." No two groups will be the same. Each has a different combination of roles, norms, and member personality characteristics that makes it unique. We have already discussed the types of norms and roles that differentiate one group from another, but the group's personality is an intangible pattern of interacting that contributes to the **group's culture.** *Culture,* a term borrowed from sociology and anthropology, is an all-encompassing term that refers to shared behaviors and beliefs of a group. These include the roles, norms status hierarchy, patterns of interacting, deeply held values, and so forth, that characterize a group.

During the development of the group's rules and norms, the members converge on a set of values that guide the group's interactions. Successful groups develop a unity of spirit and a unique identity. They have a clear sense of "who *we* are, what *we* do, and what *we* value." Such values may be inferred by observing how members act with each other. For example, a group that values egalitarianism will insist that members call each other by their first names and will not permit a leader to become too directive or controlling. A group that prides itself on clarity of thinking will likely have discussions characterized by heated intellectual argument.

How does a group define its values and express its unique personality? Although there are many factors that contribute to the development of a group's culture, two are extremely important: fantasy themes and group climate.

Fantasy Themes

You probably have observed that even in the most hardworking task-oriented groups, members do not stick to business all the time. Frequently they will get sidetracked, as if they have made a tacit agreement to "take a work break." Whenever a group is not talking about the here-and-now of the group, it is engaged in **fantasy.** It is important to note that this technical definition of *fantasy* does not mean unreal or untrue. It simply means that the group is not discussing the present work of the group, but is talking about an apparently unrelated topic. For example, at a recent committee meeting where members had been talking about the church budget, Char noticed how healthy all the plants looked in the office. She said, "Wow, look at that spider plant! It looks really happy." This introduced the fantasy to the group.

Sometimes when one member introduces a fantasy, other members will pick it up and add to it. This group storytelling is called a **fantasy chain.** For instance, after Char mentioned the spider plant, other members jumped in and added their comments about how good *all* the plants looked, including the ones in the sanctuary and the lobby. The motif of the discussion, or the **fantasy theme,** was the health of the plants. This discussion of plants continued for two or three minutes before the chair got the group back on track again. The process of creating a fantasy chain is similar to the party game most of us played as children. One person started a story, the person to the left added something, and this continued around the room until eventually each person had contributed to the final story. During a fantasy chain, the tempo of conversation increases and members become more animated and excited than usual. Then, when the fantasy chain has run its course, the group returns to its task and the tempo returns to normal.

While it may appear that during a fantasy chain a group is goofing off, it may, in fact, be accomplishing something quite important. These storytelling sequences help form and convey the group's culture in two ways. First, they help the group define itself by creating symbols that are meaningful and help determine its values.[6] Second, they enable a group to discuss indirectly matters that might be too painful or difficult to bring out into the open.[7]

For example, the church committee that sidetracked into a discussion about healthy plants was defining the environment of the church as one that was good for plants and, by implication, other living things: "We have a nurturing environment here that helps living things, such as plants and people, grow strong and healthy." In another extended example, one self-help group of high school students was disturbed because the two adults serving as coleaders were not providing the students with any direction or guidance on how to proceed.[8] One girl, beginning the fantasy chain, related a recent personal experience. She had been kicked out of her house and forced to scrounge for a place to live for several months. However, she said that even though the painful experience had initially been a "hassle," she was glad it had happened because now she knew that she could take care of herself. The other students began to relate similar experiences. For example, because of the illness or death of their fathers, two different boys had been saddled with adult responsibilities. Although initially they had felt inadequate to handle them, in the end they had risen to the occasion and felt they had attained adulthood. Each of the other students contributed stories with the common theme that "being forced to be an adult is at first frightening, but ends up strengthening the individual." This important fantasy theme served to create this particular group's reality. In effect the students were saying, "We don't like the lack of leadership in this group, but we've been in positions before where adult responsibilities have been thrust upon us and we've come through better in the end. Thus, we can learn to take over the leadership of this group ourselves, and we'll probably learn more than we would have if the facilitators had done it for us." The students did not state this *directly,* but came to that understanding *indirectly* via the fantasy. This fantasy theme was about *competence.* Even though the students initially resented the responsibilities forced on them, they knew from the past experiences they had just shared that they were capable of handling them and learning from the task.

Fantasy chains also help the group deal with emotionally "heavy" information. One of us observed a group of students at the end of a semester-long, intensive group discussion class with a much-revered professor. At one session the students spent a lot of time discussing their parents' divorces, deaths of people close to them, and endings of relationships. Finally, one of the students noticed that they had been contributing to a fantasy chain with *separation* as its theme. What they *really* had been discussing, at the psychological level, was their sadness to see the semester end with the subsequent "abandonment" by their professor. This topic, initially too emotional to discuss directly, was dealt with in the fantasy theme.

Fantasy chains and themes are effective ways in which groups create their shared images of the world, each other, and what they are about as a group. They are difficult to detect when you are participating in them. However, if you listen to a tape recording of your group's interaction, you can hear the increased pace and excitement level that often indicates that a fantasy theme is being discussed. Frequently, you will develop a sudden insight into what the psychological content of the fantasy theme has been, what the fantasy theme is saying about the group, and how the chain represents the group's own reality and, hence, contributes to its culture.

Group Climate

Group climate refers to the psychological atmosphere or environment within the group. You probably have attended group meetings where you felt the warmth and affection of the members for each other. Conversely, you probably also have observed meetings where you felt tension and distrust. These are but two examples of different types of group climates. There are many dimensions of a group's climate. We have chosen to explain three we consider most important—trust, cohesiveness, and supportiveness.

Trust

Trust refers to the general belief that members can rely on each other. When group members trust each other, they do not have to worry that others might be lying to them or may have secret reasons for their behavior. Instead of being suspicious and secretive, members who trust one another are more likely to create an open climate where people can share freely in a group. There are two kinds of trust that are particularly important to groups: task related and interpersonal. Both forms of trust affect the ultimate output of the group.

A member who is trustworthy regarding the task can be counted on to complete assignments and produce excellent work for the group. The higher the quality of the individual work that members do for the group, the higher will be the quality of the group's outputs. One behavior that can destroy trust quickly is failure to complete assignments for the group. A member who does not come through for the group forces the other members to pick up the slack. This is one of the most common sources of conflict and can poison a group's climate.

Interpersonal trust refers to the belief that the members of the group are operating in the group's best interests, and that they value their fellow members. Assume that a member you trust says to you, "I think there are lots of problems with your idea." You are likely to ask that member for reasons and to pay careful attention to the reasons given. On the other hand, if the same statement comes from someone you *don't* trust, you may wonder what's behind the statement, ignore it, get into a shouting match, or try to find subtle ways of sabotaging that member's suggestions. Members who appear to operate from hidden agenda motives are seen as untrustworthy by others. So are "politicians," who always seem to have some personal angle for their behavior that has nothing to do with the group. In fact, politicians can be so destructive to a group that Larson and

LaFasto, who studied excellent groups, recommended that the group leader get rid of them as soon as possible.[9] Lack of interpersonal trust can lead to unrestrained competition, which can tear a group apart. In contrast, groups with a high degree of trust are free to disagree and work cooperatively at the same time. This is the ideal situation for creating a top-notch group product.

Trust is something that a group needs to develop. It is easier at first to trust people who seem to be similar to you. For example, Claire and Andy develop trust quickly because they recognize each other as belonging to the "cool" crowd. However, the entire group, even Bender, eventually develops trust. First the members had to get to know each other. Then they began to perceive each other as unique individuals who had things in common, including their shared dislike of the teacher. As they began to let down their guard with each other, trust started to develop. They continued to learn about each other and to come through for each other. Therefore, when the rest of the group did not rat on Bender for closing the door, trust was established. Cohesiveness is easily developed among members who trust each other.

Cohesiveness

Cohesiveness refers to the attachment members feel toward each other and the group, and the bonds that hold the group together. In a highly cohesive group members feel a strong sense of belonging, speak favorably about the group and the other members, and conform to the norms of the group. In a group that is not cohesive, members do not attend faithfully or feel much sense of belonging. Many members may leave the group if they find other groups more rewarding.

The climates of high- and low-cohesive groups are noticeably different. Members of cohesive groups respond more directly to each other and express more positive feelings for each other and the group. Usually, highly cohesive groups are productive, although some cohesive groups have work norms that keep rates of production low.

You probably have observed the meetings of cohesive groups and felt the warmth and closeness between the members. Terry, elected to office in a campus organization, was excited because she envied the obvious cohesiveness expressed by the previous year's officers. She said she wanted to be part of a group like that. Similarly, at the end of *The Breakfast Club,* the students have come to appreciate each other. They have discovered a number of feelings and experiences they share and, finally, have been able to express their positive feelings. Two events demonstrate their newly-found affection. Claire gives her earring to her former tormentor, Bender, and Brian writes the essay which represents the group's discovery that each of them is an athlete, a brain, or a princess. This group has become a cohesive unit. Table 6.8 provides suggestions you can use to increase the cohesiveness of a group.

Table 6.8 Increasing Cohesiveness in a Group

Develop a strong group identity.
1. Encourage group traditions, such as annual parties, special greetings and handshakes, and rituals.
2. Develop in-group insignia like tee shirts and sweatshirts, pins, or hats.
3. Refer to the group members as "we" and "us."

Give credit to the group as a whole when representing the group to outsiders or other groups.

Give credit to individuals within the group itself for contributions they make toward the group's goal achievement.

Support both disagreement and agreement by encouraging openness and freedom of expression.

Create a climate of supportiveness where every individual feels appreciated and believes his or her ideas are valued.

Set clear and attainable goals for the group.
1. Goals should be difficult enough to provide a challenge and produce group pride when they are met.
2. Goals should not be so hard that they are nearly impossible to attain because failure will lower cohesiveness.

In general, cohesive groups are more effective as well as more satisfying for their members than noncohesive groups, but sometimes highly cohesive groups develop norms that harm the group and its decisions. *Groupthink,* which we discuss in detail in chapter 10, refers to the tendency of a highly cohesive group to accept information and ideas without subjecting them to critical examination.

Supportiveness

In a *supportive* climate, members encourage each other, care about each other, and treat each other with respect. On the other hand, in a *defensive* climate, members try to control, manipulate, and criticize each other.[10] In a supportive climate members feel safe to express themselves. They believe their opinions are valued by the group, even when other members disagree. They feel appreciated. Because members feel safe from psychological assault, they are free to direct most of their energy toward helping the group accomplish its task. On the other hand, if members are afraid that they will be attacked by another member, they will hesitate to offer their opinions. They will spend so much time defending themselves or being on the alert for psychological assault that they cannot pay much attention to the task of the group. A list of supportive behaviors with their contrasting defensive behaviors may be found in table 6.9.

Notice that there is an element of negative evaluation in all the defensive behaviors. These are *judgmental* behaviors of a type that do not belong in a group. Instead of critically evaluating ideas, members are *critical of each other* as persons. Notice, also, the relationship between cohesiveness and supportiveness. It is hard to feel strongly attached to a group if you don't know from one moment to the next when *you* are going to be attacked. Perhaps you also can see the

Table 6.9   Defensive and Supportive Communication Behaviors

Defensive Behaviors	Supportive Behaviors
Evaluation: Judging the other person; indicating by words or tone of voice that you disapprove	**Description:** Desiring to understand the other's point of view; describing *your own* feelings and beliefs without making the other person wrong
Control: Trying to dominate or change the other person; insisting on having things your way	**Problem orientation:** Trying to search honestly for the best solution without having a predetermined idea of what the solution *should* be
Strategy: Trying to manipulate the other person; using deceit to achieve your own goals	**Spontaneity:** Reacting honestly, openly, and freely
Neutrality: Not caring about how the other group members feel	**Empathy:** Showing by your words and actions that you care about the other group members
Superiority: Maximizing status differences that exist; "pulling rank" on other members with title, wealth, expertise, status, etc.	**Equality:** Minimizing status differences; treating every member of the group as an equally valued contributor
Certainty: Being a "know-it-all;" acting *positive* that your way or belief is the only correct one	**Provisionalism:** Being tentative in expressing your opinions; being open to considering others' suggestions fairly

relationship to open-mindedness—a supportive group consists of members who are willing to listen actively to each other and who are egalitarian in their approach to others. Open-minded members will probably not demand that the group perform in a particular way, the one and only *right* way. Can you begin to see how each element of the group system is related to all the other elements?

It is especially important that each member feels appreciated by the other members. Most members do not need to feel they have high status or power so long as they know that their contributions make a difference. The ideal culture reinforces the value of each individual; it is *supportive*. A group will "work" if each person knows he or she has an esteemed place in the group.

Summary

This chapter dealt with how a group develops from an initial collection of individuals to an entity we call a *group,* with its own distinct personality. Even though each group is unique, all groups develop norms, rules, roles, and a group culture. Groups normally experience two major phases in their development. During the formation phase they find ways of managing primary tension and the interpersonal relationships among members. In the production phase, they cope with secondary tension by directing most of their attention toward the accomplishment of their goals.

Rules and norms, the standards of behavior for members of the group, differ only in their degree of formality. They help members know what is and is not acceptable behavior. Group norms, or informal rules, are established through primacy, explicit statements members make, critical events in the group's history, and carry-over behaviors from the culture at large. Norms that directly affect the group's survival and those that express "who we are" are more likely to be strictly enforced. Groups try to control members who deviate from norms by making increasingly intense attempts to persuade them to change. The deviant who does not conform risks ostracism. Unproductive norms can be changed if their harmful effects are pointed out, then all members together discuss and agree on an acceptable norm.

Roles are functions members perform in the group. Formal roles, like *chair* or *secretary,* carry with them certain requirements as well as expectations of behaviors. Informal roles develop from the personal characteristics of the members and through interaction. Roles are classified into task, maintenance, and individualistic categories. The first two types are necessary to the effective operation of the small group. The third, which may stem from a member's hidden agenda or unconscious motive, can harm the group.

The group's culture reflects the deeply held values and beliefs of the group. Two factors which contribute to the development of a group's culture are fantasy themes and group climate. Fantasy themes help the group create a shared sense of reality and allow members to discuss painful or difficult matters indirectly. Two important aspects of a group's climate include cohesiveness, the degree to which members feel attracted to each other, and supportiveness, the extent to which members express feelings of appreciation and liking to each other. In time each group develops a unique organization of rules, roles, and culture through interaction among members.

Review Questions

1. Give an example of primary, secondary, and tertiary tensions. How do they differ from each other? What might you do to help a group manage each type?
2. What kinds of activities would members perform in each of the two main phases of group development? What kinds of statements would you expect to hear in each phase? What is likely to happen to a group that is unsuccessful in the first phase?
3. Give three examples each of group rules and group norms. What are the four common ways norms develop? Give an example of each.

4. Assume that members of a group you have joined have a habit (norm) of interrupting one another before the speaker has had a chance to express his or her ideas completely. What are the steps you could take to change this counterproductive norm? What would you say to the other members?
5. How does a group treat an individual who fails to conform to group norms? If you have experienced deviant behavior in a group, how did your group handle it? Would you do anything differently today?
6. From your own experience, give two examples of formal roles. What were the requirements of each? What expectations, beyond the minimum requirements, did you have of the individuals who occupied the roles?
7. From your own personal experience, give two examples of informal roles. How did these roles develop in the group? What behaviors did the individuals perform? What personality characteristics may have contributed to each person's performing each particular role?
8. Give three examples of hidden agenda items that could interfere with a group's performance.
9. Explain the characteristics of a fantasy theme and the functions it performs for a group. If you can recall a fantasy theme from your own experience, what function did it perform for your group? What was the topic of the fantasy theme?
10. Describe the differences between defensive and supportive group climates. List three specific behaviors that contribute to each climate. How is a defensive climate harmful to the group?

Bibliography

Bormann, Ernest G. *Discussion and Group Methods: Theory and Practice*. 2d ed. New York: Harper & Row, 1975, chapters 8, 9.

Brilhart, John K., and Galanes, Gloria J. *Effective Group Discussion*. 7th ed. Dubuque, IA: Wm. C. Brown, 1992, chapter 8.

Fisher, B. Aubrey and Ellis, Donald G. *Small Group Decision Making*. 3d ed. New York: McGraw-Hill, 1980, chapter 6.

References

1. The terms *primary* and *secondary* tension were first used by Ernest G. Bormann; elaboration of the concepts may be found in Bormann, *Discussion and Group Methods: Theory and Practice,* 2d ed. (New York: Harper & Row, 1975): 181–190.
2. Robert F. Bales, "The Equilibrium Problem in Small Groups," in *Working Papers in the Theory of Action,* eds. Talcott Parsons, Robert F. Bales, and Edward A. Shils (New York: Free Press, 1953): 111–161.
3. Daniel Feldman, "Development and Enforcement of Group Norms," *Academy of Management Review* 9 (1984): 47–53.
4. Feldman, "Development and Enforcement of Group Norms."

5. Stanley Schacter, "Deviation, Rejection, and Communication," *Journal of Abnormal and Social Psychology,* 46 (1951): 190–207; and Harold Leavitt, *Managerial Psychology,* 2d ed. (Chicago: University of Chicago Press, 1964): 270–274.

6. Catherine Cobb Morocco, "Development and Function of Group Metaphor," *Journal for the Theory of Social Behavior* 9 (1979): 15–27.

7. Ernest C. Bormann, Jeri M. Pratt, and Linda L. Putnam, "Power, Authority, and Male Responses to Female Dominance," *Communication Monographs* 45 (1978): 119–155.

8. Morocco, "Development and Function of Group Metaphor."

9. Carl E. Larson and Frank M. J. La Fasto, *Teamwork: What Must Go Right, What Can Go Wrong* (Newbury Park, CA: Sage Publications, 1989).

10. Jack R. Gibb, "Defensive Communication," *Journal of Communication* 11 (1961): 141–148.

CHAPTER SEVEN

Perspectives on Leading Small Groups

CHAPTER OUTLINE

Leadership and Leaders

Leadership

Sources of Power in the Small Group

Leaders

Designated Leader

Supervisory Leader

Peer Leader

Emergent Leader

Myths about Leadership

Current Ideas about Leadership

The Functional Concept of Group
Leadership

Leader as Completer

The Contingency Concept of Group
Leadership

*Leadership Adaptability as the Key to
Effectiveness*

STUDY QUESTIONS

1. What is the distinction between *leaders* and *leadership?*
2. What are the sources of interpersonal influence?
3. What are the differences among the three types of designated leader?
4. What is the distinction between a designated and an emergent leader?
5. What are three pervasive myths regarding leadership?
6. What is the functional approach to leadership and what is the leader's primary function in this approach?
7. What is the contingency approach to leadership and what are some common contingencies to which a leader should adjust?

KEY TERMS AND CONCEPTS

Contingency Concept

Coordinator

Designated Leader

Emergent Leader

Expert Power

Functional Concept

Influence

Interpersonal Power

Leader

Leadership

Legitimate Power

Peer Leader

Punishment Power

Referent Power

Reward Power

Supervisory Leader

When Marcos was appointed chair of the membership committee of his service club, he and Luis were the only experienced members on the committee; the other three members were new to the club. The membership committee was responsible for recruiting new club members and helping them become integrated into the club. The inexperienced members were excited about working on the committee, but they were not aware of all the club's activities, procedures, and past efforts. Marcos faced a challenge. He did not want to stifle the enthusiasm, dominate the group, or do most of the work for the group. On the other hand, he did not want to lose valuable time while the new members felt their way along. While he preferred to chair a committee where all members could contribute equally to the decisions and the work, he believed that initially this group needed strong direction from Luis and himself.

Marcos and Luis worked together between the committee meetings to establish an agenda and select some of the early goals and activities of the committee. During meetings, Marcos kept fairly close control over the agenda and the discussion of each topic. He assigned the members specific tasks, but he always made sure the assignments were acceptable to each member. He and Luis worked closely with each member between committee meetings. This saved the new members time and frustration as they learned about their responsibilities. While the group was developing, Marcos encouraged the newer members to contribute suggestions and ideas until they were able to speak up frequently on their own. When he felt that the group members were becoming capable of acting without his direction, Marcos began gradually to encourage the members to take on more decision-making responsibility, and he turned over more of the decision making to the committee as a whole. As the members accepted more responsibility, Marcos became less involved in individual details of the committee's work. Instead, he focused his attention on the process of discussion and decision making during the committee meetings. By the end of his year as chair, Marcos was functioning as the committee's coordinator rather than its director.

This true story, related by a student, illustrates an important aspect of small group leadership. To be effective, the leader of a small group must be able to *adapt* his or her behavior to fit the circumstances of the group. There is no ideal leadership style that will fit a group's needs perfectly at all times. Our story highlights two important concepts. First, Marcos had to be *flexible* if he wanted to be a successful leader. Leaders need to adapt their behavior, not just from one group to another, but sometimes at different stages during the life of the same group. Marcos used his knowledge of the club's activities and procedures to help the group members avoid mistakes when learning new tasks. He did this initially by tightly controlling the activities of the members. Later, as the members became more knowledgeable, Marcos stopped controlling details and began to be a more democratic leader. As you can see, adaptability requires the leader to analyze member and group needs and modify his or her actions to fit the circumstances.

Second, *flexible leadership makes substantial demands of the group's leader.* When Marcos chose to meet with the new members between committee meetings to help them become proficient in their new duties, he was spending much more time on committee-related business than were the rest of the members. He was functioning like a teacher or a coach, guiding the rest of the members and working with them until they could work on their own. Becoming a leader of a group does not mean that you can sit back and order other people around; frequently it will require much more of your time than it does of the other members. In addition, this type of leadership will require you to pay attention at all times to group needs and help members achieve the personal satisfaction that comes with performing well. Marcos' goal, a worthy one for all group leaders, was to develop the individual group members so that the group as a whole could function effectively without his being present. As good parents help their children grow up so they can live independently, good group leaders help their groups grow so that they, too, can operate effectively without needing the direction of a strong leader. Good leaders develop leaders. Thus, to be effective, groups need leaders who are perceptive, flexible, and energetic.

In this chapter we examine some important concepts and theories about leaders and leadership in the small group. We look at how the concept of *influence* is related to leadership as well as at several of the myths many people hold regarding leadership. We conclude with a discussion of current approaches to leadership.

Leadership and Leaders

There is a difference between a group's *leader* and its *leadership*. *Leader* refers to a person in the group, most often one who holds a title that carries both special responsibilities and authority. *Leadership* refers to behaviors or functions performed by *any* individual in a group (including but not limited to a person appointed or selected as leader) which help the group achieve its goals. We begin our consideration of these two concepts with the more general one, *leadership*.

Leadership

Leadership is typically defined as "interpersonal influence, exercised in a situation and directed, through the communication process, toward the attainment of a specified goal or goals."[1] Several things are implied by this definition. First, *group* leadership consists of behaviors that are directed toward helping the group attain *its* goals. Thus, when we examine leadership within the group, we concern ourselves only with *behaviors that are helpful to the group as a group.* A group rebel, even one whom others admire and follow, would not be considered a leader *of the group* if the rebellious actions prevent the group in any way from accomplishing its goal. Second, leadership is accomplished through communication. Leadership does not involve physical force or coercion of any sort to compel a group. Instead, the group's leadership is enacted through discussion with the leader influencing the group through the give-and-take of person-to-person communication. Third, to be most useful, the leader must adapt to the situation of the group. Leadership is a dynamic process of exchange, not a fixed quality or set of behaviors. Finally, this definition promotes the idea of **influence** as the heart of group leadership: the exercise of interpersonal power to bring about actions of other members that help the group achieve its goals. For example, notice that Marcos did not manipulate, bully, or coerce his fellow group members into performing the work of the group. Nor did he *use* the group to serve his strictly personal goals. Rather, he used his interpersonal skills to guide, teach, and help the other members perform for the benefit of the group. His power came from the willing support others gave his efforts to lead.

Sources of Power in the Small Group

Interpersonal power is another term for "influence" in a small group. As Hackman and Johnson say in their book about leadership, "Leadership is impossible without power since a leader must modify attitudes and behaviors."[2] Raven and French have identified five sources of interpersonal power.[3] We believe that four of these sources—*legitimate, reward, expert,* and *referent*—provide the power that true leaders use in a group. The fifth, the power to punish, also serves as a source of influence in a group, but we do not think it is the most appropriate source for the leaders we discuss in this book. Coercion breeds resentment, making group members less productive than they could be. Understanding these sources of influence can help you establish and use power appropriately for the good of the group (see table 7.1).

Legitimate power refers to the influence that exists when someone has a position or title that others believe gives that person the right to exercise influence. The leader may have been elected by the members themselves, appointed by someone from the group's parent organization, or have a title (such as "Dr." or "President") that confers power. For example, Marcos was elected vice-president of his service club, which automatically made him the chair of the membership committee. As an elected "official," Marcos was perceived by the membership to have the right to control or direct some of the activities of the members.

The types of rewards and punishments a leader can give depend on the type of group, the parent organization, and the leader's position with respect to the other members. For example, if you are the elected leader of a group of your peers you will probably have to rely mostly on positive, intangible methods for rewarding members—praise, attention, smiles, and so forth. However, if you are the office manager controlling a group that consists of staff members who report to you, you have more ways of rewarding or punishing the members. You can still reward with praise, but now you also may control what your staff members' salaries are, whether they will be promoted, selected for special training, or

Table 7.1   Sources of Power and Influence

Legitimate Power	Leader is elected or appointed; has a title (chair, coordinator, etc.)
Reward or Punishment	Leader can give or take away items of value; may be tangible (money, promotion, titles) or intangible (praise, acceptance)
Expert Power	Leader has information, knowledge, or skills needed and valued by the group
Referent Power	Leader is admired and respected; other group members try to copy his/her behavior

receive year-end bonuses. The additional legitimate power provided by the organization gives you a greater variety of rewards and punishments at your disposal. However, even if you can exercise **punishment power,** genuine leadership relies more on influencing members through **reward power** than pressuring them with explicit or implied threats. We suggest that you motivate members with encouragement and support. Use the threat of punishment only as a last resort. You want to be the kind of leader others *choose* to follow.

Another source of power is expertise. An individual with **expert power** is perceived by the other members to have knowledge or skill valuable to the group. Marcos possessed expert power as a long-standing, active member of his club because he knew how things worked, whom to see for specific information or help, and what had been tried in the past. His expertise was valued by the other members. Instead of resenting him for initially taking charge, the new members appreciated his willingness to share his expertise to get the group off to a good start. Both of us assign group tasks in our classes. Frequently the student identified by the rest of the members of the group as being the leader is a person with specialized knowledge that the group needs. For example, a good writer is valued for the ability to serve as overall editor for a group-written paper, and a senior becomes influential in a group of freshmen because he or she is familiar with the campus.

Finally, a person whom others admire and want to be like has *identification* or **referent power.** Most of us want the people we like and admire to like us, too. That desire provides a great source of power for leaders. Because their good opinions of us matter, we have a tendency to act like the people we admire. In high school, one of us belonged to a social group that had an informal leader with considerable referent power. The rest of the group accepted this person's opinions on a variety of issues such as how to dress, whom to date, and what school activities to join. In another example, many people who knew John F. Kennedy say he had *charisma,* a type of referent power. He was so admired that many were eager to support his suggestions.

A group leader's influence usually stems from more than one of these power sources. Marcos, for example, was the legitimate leader of the group, but he also had expert power. In addition to referent power, President Kennedy possessed legitimate power and the power to reward and punish. As you can guess, the more sources of power an individual has, the greater that person's influence in the group.

Notice, also, that it is the *perceptions of the members* that determine an individual's influence within the group. A group leader may not *really* have the power to promote someone to a new position, but if the other members *believe* the leader holds that kind of power, they will grant that person more influence in the group. For example, one of our classroom groups had a member who convinced the other people in her group that she was proficient in using the school's computer to analyze data. The other members believed Sandra and deferred to her judgment on this and a variety of other matters. Unfortunately, Sandra was *not* proficient at using the computer. By the time the group realized this, it was too late to turn in a good project report. Nevertheless, for a long time Sandra was quite influential in her group because other members *perceived* her to be expert. Influence comes from the amount of power other members attribute to you, not just from your actual skills and legitimate authority. You can *lead* only if other members are *willing* to be influenced by you.

Leaders

Any person who exercises interpersonal influence *to help the group attain its goals* can properly be termed a **leader;** she or he is certainly *leading* the other members. There are several important implications to this statement. First, this definition of leader implies that *all* individuals in a group can supply some of the needed leadership services. Second, it does not require that a leader hold a particular title or office. The group's leader *may* possess a title such as *chair* or *president,* but as we saw earlier, such a formal role is only one source of leadership power (legitimate power). Any member of the group, with or without a title, can at times function as the group's leader. Third, this definition indicates that communication is the process through which a person leads others. Rather than assuming that leaders are born or must have particular titles, the definition suggests that leaders *perform behaviors* that help the group achieve its goals. Leaders lead by what they say and do. They make choices about their communication behavior that are crucial to our understanding of leadership.[4] It is possible for an individual to be called the "leader," yet fail to lead the group. We will now examine several types of leaders frequently found in small groups, and define terms frequently found in writings about small group leaders (see table 7.2).

Designated Leader

The **designated leader** is the group's legitimate leader, an individual who holds a title, such as *chair, coordinator, moderator, facilitator,* or *president,* that identifies him or her as having a specific leadership role to play within the group. Usually

Table 7.2 Types of Leaders in the Small Group

Designated Leader:	Legitimate leader: elected or appointed to the position
Supervisory Leader:	Has supervisory responsibility for the members of the group: has power to reward and punish; may be able to "hire and fire" group members
Peer Leader:	Holds title but has same status as other members of group; relies on legitimate, expert, and referent power to influence; principal duties involve coordination
Coordinator:	Has same status as other members but may not have a title; relies on expert, referent, and some legitimate power, coordinates other members
Emergent Leader:	Starts out with equal status in a group of peers but emerges as leader in a natural process; combines blend of task- and people-related behaviors preferred by the particular group

group members expect the designated leader to perform a variety of coordination functions for the group, which we will describe in detail in the next chapter. The designated leader may be elected to the position by the other members of the group or may be appointed by the parent organization that established the group. Designation as group leader invariably confers some legitimate power to the role. Considerably different limitations are placed on two major subtypes of the designated leader: *supervisory* and *peer*.

Supervisory Leader A **supervisory leader** has considerable legitimate power to reward and punish the members of the group. An individual who functions as a supervisor may be called *department head, manager, supervisor, foreperson, coach* or similar title. Frequently, supervisors are the bosses of the individuals in the groups they lead; they often have direct power to determine such things as salary, promotion, and working conditions. For example, one of our students is a member of a creative group in an advertising agency that is led by her boss. Her supervisor, and other leaders like him, can legitimately exert a great deal of power in the group, even to the point of hiring and firing group members. But not even a supervisor can force *willing* support, where members choose freely to give their very best efforts. Hackman and Johnson distinguish between "managing" and "leading." They point out that supervisors can lead, whereas subordinate employees may lead but cannot legitimately supervise each other. As managers, supervisors are concerned with such things as maintaining productivity and solving everyday work problems. Leaders *find* problems others have not recognized. They move the group toward change and innovation.[5]

Peer Leader The **peer leader** has the same status as other individuals in the group, but has been selected by the group members themselves or appointed by an outside authority to coordinate the work of the group. Such leaders are often called *coordinators* or *chairs* (e.g., the chair of a governmental task force created

"I was just going to say 'Well, I don't make the rules.' But, of course, I do make the rules."

The supervisory leader *does* have the power to make the rules. (Drawing by Leo Cullum; © 1986 The New Yorker Magazine, Inc.)

by the mayor, the coordinator of the high school prom committee, the fraternity president). In our initial example, Marcos was this type of leader. As you can imagine, successful peer leaders function in different ways from supervisors. Because they have less power to reward and punish members, peer leaders must rely heavily on expertise and referent power, with only those legitimate powers granted specifically to the role of "leader" by the group and/or parent organization.

Coordinators are types of peer leaders found frequently in business, industry, and governmental organizations. They help organize the work of the group but do not make the group's important decisions. A coordinator is usually elected or officially appointed. Occasionally the person is given coordination responsibilities in an informal way. For example, a boy who gathers his friends together to play soccer or a woman who takes it upon herself to organize a neighborhood watch committee are functioning as coordinators of autonomous groups. These individuals usually rely especially heavily on expertise and referent power to exercise influence within the group. Usually coordinators have little power to punish. A supervisor who depends on expertise instead of the power to reward and punish functions more as a coordinator than as a traditional "boss."

Emergent Leader

An **emergent leader** is a person who starts out as any other member in a group of peers, but who gradually emerges as leader in the perceptions of the other members by providing leadership services they value. Although most of the groups to which you belong have a designated leader, understanding the typical process of leadership emergence will give you insight into what constitutes effective group leadership. Even appointed or elected leaders must win the willing support of the other members. Much of what we know about the emergence of a leader in an initially leaderless peer group comes from a series of studies conducted by associates of Ernest Bormann at the University of Minnesota.[6] These researchers observed groups of college students placed in leaderless task groups. Their findings show that at first all members of an initially leaderless group have the potential to be recognized by others as the leader of the group. However, members who don't speak up or are uninformed are quickly eliminated as possible leader. Next to be eliminated are members who, compared to the rest of the group, are overly bossy or dogmatic. Remaining in consideration are frequent speakers who are well informed on the issues facing the group, open-minded, democratic, sensitive, and skilled in expressing ideas for the group. The individual who ultimately emerges as the group's leader is the member who seems able to provide the best balance of task and people skills for that particular group. Especially important is the ability to coordinate the work of other members by communicating effectively with them.

Even though you may rarely encounter a leaderless group outside the classroom setting, two important points learned from studies of emergent leaders have a direct bearing on groups that *do* have designated leaders. First, a person who emerges as a leader in one group will not necessarily emerge as a leader in another. Because each group's situation is different, each group requires a unique blend of leader skills. The type of task the group has to complete and the personalities and preferences of the members help determine what is appropriate leadership for the group. For example, members who are highly task-oriented tend to be uncomfortable with relationship-oriented leaders. One group might select a task leader who is all business and helps the members complete their tasks without wasting any time on chit chat. Another group composed of extremely sociable members may perceive a highly task-centered coordinator as hostile and uncaring. The particular individual who emerges does so because of the way the individual components of that particular group mesh as a system.

Second, emergent leaders influence people with primarily referent, expert, and reward power. They do not have a title with a job description or set of duties to fall back on, and so must rely mostly on their communication skills to lead the group. Emergent leaders, by definition, have the support of the other members of the group. This is something to which designated leaders should pay attention. Even though you may hold a title in your group (chair, coordinator, president, and so forth), you should strive to be the person who would also emerge as the acknowledged leader. A designated leader without the support of the other members of the group will probably fail. Therefore, even when you are the official leader of the group, you should tune in to the needs and expectations of both the other members and the group as a whole. If you do this, the others will *choose* you to lead, and you will be a more influential leader as a result. The guidelines for performing as a *group-centered democratic leader,* presented in chapter 8, will help you emerge as the leader in groups of peers.

Myths about Leadership

When we have asked our students what they think group leaders should do, usually they say that leaders "control the actions of the other members," "give orders," and generally "tell people what to do." While that style of leadership may be effective for some groups, "acting bossy" in a group of peers will get you and the group into trouble! In this section we examine several other pervasive myths about leadership (see table 7.3). We also present historical information about the study of group leadership.

1. **Leadership is a personality trait that individuals possess in varying degrees.** From Plato to the 1950s, the study of leadership consisted of a search for the traits that made people leaders. Traits thought to be related to leadership included intelligence, attractiveness, psychological dominance, and size. Although some researchers still continue to examine the relationship between certain traits and leadership, most people agree that there is no difference between group leaders and the other members. Strict trait approaches to studying leadership are flawed in several ways. First, there is no trait or set of traits that leaders in general have but followers do not. For example, although some studies found that recognized leaders are more intelligent than the average of the members, the leader is not necessarily the most intelligent individual in the group or even particularly intelligent.

   A second flaw in the trait approach to leadership is the underlying assumption that all leadership situations call for the same trait or set of traits. Think about this for a moment. Are you a leader in every group to which you belong? Are you always a follower? Do you think, for example, that the leader of a classroom discussion group must possess the same traits as the leader of a military platoon? You can begin to appreciate the fact that there is no one set of traits that will identify the best leader for any given group or situation.

   A third flaw in the trait approach relates directly to the concept of *trait* as something innate. Another way of saying this is "Leaders are born, not made," which assumes that if you are not born with the characteristics of a leader (whatever those may be) you will not become a leader. Instead, leadership consists of *behaving in ways that can be learned* (at least up to a

Table 7.3 Myths of Leadership

Leadership is a Trait That Individuals Possess in Varying Degrees

1. Prevalent theory from Plato to 1950s.
2. Involved searching for the trait or traits that distinguished leaders from others.
3. Problems:
   a. There is no trait that leaders have that others do not.
   b. Assumes that all leadership situations demand the same trait or traits.
   c. Implies that leaders are born and that leadership behavior cannot be learned.

There is an Ideal Leadership Style That All Leaders Should Use

1. Prevalent from late 1940s to late 1960s.
2. Involved searching for the ideal leadership style suitable for all situations.
3. Improvement over trait approach; leadership consists of behaviors that are learned.
4. Problems:
   a. Assumes that all leadership situations demand a single leadership style.
   b. Assumes that a single group's needs do not change over time.
   c. Cannot reconcile inconsistent research findings about what the best style is.

Leaders Get Other People to Do Their Work for Them

1. Prevalent up to present time.
2. Involves trying to coerce, manipulate, or persuade other group members to submit to the leader's will.
3. Problems:
   a. Ignores the chief value of having a group solve a problem.
   b. Ignores the importance of the leader's service to the group.

---

point). Consider, for a moment, Candy Lightner, the woman who developed MADD, **M**others **A**gainst **D**runk **D**rivers. Ms. Lightner was an ordinary single parent, not a recognized leader, before her daughter was killed by a drunk driver. Nothing in her previous background or experience could have predicted that she would become the leader of a national organization like MADD. But she cared enough to do the hard work of learning to lead. So can you.

2. **There is an ideal leadership style no matter what the situation.** Since the 1950s, a number of researchers have examined the behaviors associated with leadership, including the styles displayed by various leaders. Several studies indicated that leaders performed two different types of behaviors, *task-oriented* and *relationship-oriented*.[7] Leaders performed behaviors high on either one, neither, or both of the dimensions. Many people believed that the ideal style of leadership was one which was high on both dimensions, so many organizations instituted training programs to teach their employees how to be simultaneously task- *and* relationship-oriented.

Other researchers have examined three general styles of people in leadership positions: autocratic (authoritarian), democratic (participatory), and laissez-faire (noninvolved). *Autocratic* leaders are primarily task-oriented people who personally make the decisions for the group and control the group's process. They alone decide the group's agenda, select procedures the group will follow, and decide who will speak when. In one such group observed by one of us, the group's leader was also the supervisor for the rest of the members of the group. Instead of asking for input in developing the group's agenda, the leader prepared it and presented it to the group. The leader called upon the other members to speak, one by one. He made comments on each person's report. If he decided that a subject had been discussed enough, he arbitrarily moved the group to the next agenda item. The members were bored and frustrated. Although as individuals they had some good ideas they wanted to present, they believed it was futile to bring them up in discussion. As one member said, "What difference would it make? If it isn't Bob's idea, he won't support it and it won't get done." These group members, who were expert, creative, and potentially enthusiastic, were being stifled by the style of the designated leader.

Democratic leaders want all the group members to participate in decision making, and so are more relationship-oriented than autocratic leaders. Democratic leaders try to discover the wishes of the group members and help them achieve their common goals. They encourage members to develop the group's agenda as well as to determine what procedures the group will use. Discussants can speak freely within the group. When members propose ideas, they are considered to be the property of the group as a whole. Democratic leaders suggest but do not compel or coerce. They try to help the group achieve consensus in solving problems. Democratic leaders see their function as helping the group accomplish what the members want, as long as it is part of the group's purpose or the charge given to the group by the parent organization. They do not manipulate the group into doing only what the *leaders* want. Members of groups with leaders who function democratically tend to be more satisfied, participate more actively in meetings, demonstrate more commitment to group decisions, and are more innovative than members of groups with either autocratic or laissez-faire leaders.[8]

Laissez-faire "leaders," who consider themselves to be no different from the other members, display a hands-off style which really does not provide much leadership. They create a void that forces the other members to step in or flounder without coordination. Occasionally the other members blend their efforts to lead the group successfully, but more often such groups end up wasting a lot of time or following the structure provided by an autocratic leader who emerges and takes charge. Only groups of highly motivated experts tend to be more productive and satisfied with laissez-faire leaders than democratic structuring leaders.[9]

Research that attempted to describe an ideal leadership style came up with inconsistent findings. While most group members preferred the democratic rather than the autocratic style, some groups composed of authoritarian members preferred the more authoritarian style. Moreover, autocratic groups sometimes completed more work than democratic groups. About the only consistent finding was that groups preferred either the democratic or the autocratic style to the laissez-faire style.

The styles approach assumes that there is a best style of leadership for all occasions. Research was aimed at discovering what that best style was, and training programs were established to teach workers the ideal style. However, this assumption oversimplifies the complexities of groups as open systems. For example, consider the following two groups: (1) an advertising agency's creative group, where the members have worked together successfully for two years, and (2) an outdoor survival group of young adolescent boys, strangers to each other, none of whom has ever been camping. Would you recommend the same style of leadership to the coordinator of the creative group and to the adult advisor of the survival group? Everything suggests a democratic approach with the creative group and a more controlling approach with the young boys. Most of us would agree that no one style is right for all situations.

Another assumption underlying the search for the ideal leadership style is the notion that a particular group will have the same needs over its lifetime. However, not only do different groups vary in their needs for different leadership services, but over time a single group's needs will change greatly as well. Recall Marcos, the chair of his club's membership committee. His group's initial needs were different from its later needs. The inexperienced members appreciated how Marcos structured their work and took charge of the early decisions. As they became more experienced, they needed less control from Marcos and more freedom to work in their own ways.

Most people today discredit the idea that there is an ideal leadership style no matter what the occasion. Rather, a number of factors such as the experience of the members, how long they have been together, how successful they have been in the past, how interesting the job is, and whether or not there is an impending deadline all contribute to determining the most appropriate style.

3. **Leaders get other people to do the work for them.** When some of our students are elected or appointed to leadership positions, they assume that their job is to tell other people what to do. They often seem surprised that the other students resent their attempts to control and that merely ordering someone to do something is no guarantee that it will get done. Recently, the president of a campus organization was disgusted that a colleague of hers failed to complete an assignment for the organization. "I told her what to do, and I told her we needed the information for today's meeting," she said. Little did she realize that her own attitude, which assumed that the

other student was obligated to carry out her orders, was part of the problem. If you think your position as leader makes your job easier, think again! As we saw with Marcos, early in a group's life the leader can expect to put in more work and time than the other members of the group. Effective leaders expect to provide *service* to the group. The leader should either provide or arrange for someone else to provide whatever the group needs to accomplish its goals. Leaders are responsible for seeing that the job gets done, not necessarily to do it themselves.

Current Ideas about Leadership

Now that you know that small group leadership isn't a trait, a style, or bossing people around, let's discuss what it *does* involve. There are several contemporary ideas about leadership that will help you to be more effective as a group leader. The ideas we discuss next complement each other. We hope that you will think about group leadership in a new way as you understand how different aspects of the group as a system should influence a leader's behavior and appreciate the special work that effective leaders contribute to a group's progress.

The Functional Concept of Group Leadership

The **functional concept** of leadership contains two premises. First, this concept assumes that certain important functions (jobs) must be performed if the group is to be successful in reaching its goals. These functions are usually classified as task-related or people-related functions. Several of these functions were described in chapter 6. Task-related functions, such as *initiating* discussion or action, *offering opinions, making suggestions, elaborating* on other members' ideas, and so forth, are behaviors that are directly related to getting the group's job done. People-related functions, such as *harmonizing, gatekeeping,* and *relieving tension,* are behaviors that help members work as a team.

Another important premise of function theory is that performing the needed functions is the responsibility of *all* the group members, not just the individual who is designated as the group's leader. The functional concept of group leadership recognizes that, in addition to the group's leader, other members of a group can and must provide leadership services needed by the group. It is impossible and unfair for one individual to perform all the services a group needs. That would require a perfect person and we haven't seen anyone with *all* needed knowledge and skills. Remember, people *want* to contribute and to be appreciated for their participation. *Every* member of a group needs to know that he or she is considered a valued member of the group. When that occurs, members tend to be committed and loyal, and group cohesiveness is high.

The abilities of all members are needed in a group. For example, in a committee one of us observed, the chair summarized discussion and kept the group's work organized. Another member was particularly good at devising compromises that all members could support. Yet another member's irreverent sense of humor helped the committee relieve tension when conflicts threatened to get personal or out of hand. The functions approach to group leadership encourages members to use their special strengths in supplying needed leadership for the group, yet it puts a special responsibility on designated leaders to provide essential functions that aren't being provided by some other member.

Leader as Completer

"Okay," you say, "I accept the principle that leadership should be functional, but just what is *my* job if I'm appointed or elected leader of some group such as a class project group or committee in student government? If *all* members are responsible for providing needed leadership functions, what is expected from the leader?" One answer is that the leader's job is to supply any needed functions (services) that other members are *not* providing or at least to see that someone does supply these services.[10] This gives the designated leader a lot to do. The leader is responsible for constantly monitoring the group's progresss to identify what the group needs at any point in time, deciding whether those functions are currently being performed adequately by other members, and if not, providing needed services or encouraging someone else to provide them. For example, if the leader sees that one member has not offered an opinion about an important issue considered by the group, the leader could *gatekeep* by asking that member's opinion. If the group seems confused, the leader should summarize, clarify and reorient the group or ask that someone else do so. If secondary tensions are mounting, the leader should try to relieve them before they cause harm, perhaps by cracking a joke or suggesting a ten-minute break.

Far from downgrading the position of leader, the functional approach to leadership is demanding of designated leaders. This approach requires that the leader be able to determine what functions are needed as well as to supply them. The leader must constantly be aware of what is happening in the group. The functions concept assumes that people can learn a variety of leader behaviors and that all of us should learn to function as leaders in certain circumstances.

"*Just a few more pages, Hansen, and we'll take a short break.*"

Relieving tension by suggesting a short break can help keep the group working effectively. (Drawing by C. Barsotti; © 1989 The New Yorker Magazine, Inc.)

The Contingency Concept of Group Leadership

A related contemporary concept about leadership is the **contingency concept,** which holds that appropriate leadership behavior depends upon the situation. As we noted earlier, it doesn't seem reasonable that the same leadership style should be used for a classroom discussion group as for a platoon during a fire fight. Marcos' actions, in our introductory example, illustrate a practical application of the contingency approach. At first, Marcos' fellow members were unused to the procedures and workings of the service club, and therefore benefited from a directive style of leadership. Later, as they became more knowledgeable, a highly directive style would have limited their contributions, squashed their enthusiasm and devalued their expertise. So Marcos switched to a more appropriate democratic style. There are several contingency approaches; we will focus on those developed by Hersey and Blanchard, and Chemers.

Contingency approaches suggest that leaders should consider several factors before deciding the specific leadership services appropriate for the group. Among these factors are the type of task, how well the members work together, how well members work with the leader, and so forth.[11] A major factor that affects the way a leader should act is the maturity level of the followers.[12] Hersey and Blanchard have provided a model, shown in figure 7.1, to help you assess appropriate leadership behaviors after you have taken into account the maturity level of the followers. In general, the more experienced, interested, and motivated the members are, the less direction is needed from the leader.

We believe it is important for you to be able to *adapt* your behavior in a way that is appropriate for your group. Hersey and Blanchard's model, tempered with your common sense and knowledge of group leadership, should help you determine how best to lead your group in different times and circumstances.

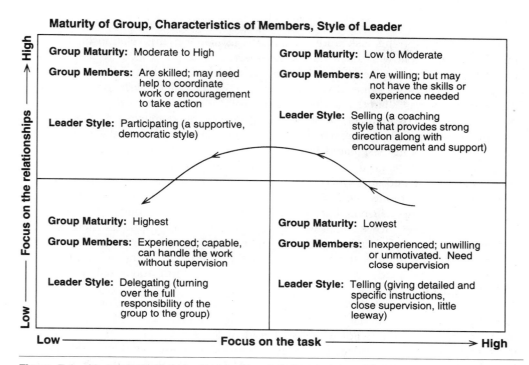

Maturity of Group, Characteristics of Members, Style of Leader

Group Maturity: Moderate to High **Group Members:** Are skilled; may need help to coordinate work or encouragement to take action **Leader Style:** Participating (a supportive, democratic style)	**Group Maturity:** Low to Moderate **Group Members:** Are willing; but may not have the skills or experience needed **Leader Style:** Selling (a coaching style that provides strong direction along with encouragement and support)
Group Maturity: Highest **Group Members:** Experienced; capable, can handle the work without supervision **Leader Style:** Delegating (turning over the full responsibility of the group to the group)	**Group Maturity:** Lowest **Group Members:** Inexperienced; unwilling or unmotivated. Need close supervision **Leader Style:** Telling (giving detailed and specific instructions, close supervision, little leeway)

Focus on the relationships — High / Low (vertical axis)

Low ⸻ **Focus on the task** ⸻⟶ High

Figure 7.1   Model of situational leadership. (Based on Paul Hersey/ Kenneth Blanchard, *Management of Organizational Behavior: Utilizing Human Resources,* 4th ed., © 1982, p. 152. Reprinted by permission of Prentice-Hall, Englewood Cliffs, New Jersey.)

If group members are unable, unwilling, or don't have enough information to complete the task on their own, *telling* can be an effective leadership style. Such members are said to be low in maturity. The leader will need to give them specific instructions and provide close supervision of their work. The leader tells the members what, how, and when to do something, and the members have little say in the matter. *Telling* demonstrates high-task and low-relationship behavior.

If group members have low to moderate maturity, they are usually willing but do not have the skills or experience necessary to perform well. In this case, the leader takes a *selling* approach, where much of the direction is provided by the leader, but members' enthusiastic support for this direction is sought. Two-way communication occurs as the leader encourages members to ask for explanations and additional information. The leader's goal here is to promote the enthusiasm of the members while providing guidance needed to complete the task well. This *selling* style is *both* high-task and high-relationship oriented. You may recognize this as the style Marcos initially used with his membership committee. In that case the members were willing to work and enthusiastic about the club, but did not have the necessary information or confidence to perform their jobs well at first.

With members of moderate to high maturity the leader can pay less attention to the demands of the task and concentrate instead on the relationships among members. Here, followers have the skills to perform the job, but may feel insecure about taking action or need coordination to work out a set of roles and division of labor. The leader's supportive, democratic style is called *participating* because decision making is shared and the leader's role is mostly one of facilitation and coordination. Marcos gradually adopted this style with his committee as they became true peers. When members reach this level of maturity, *anyone* in the group could probably serve as its designated leader. All members share in leading the group.

In a fully mature group, members are both able and willing to perform. They need little task-related supervision or encouragement. In this situation, the *delegating* style is appropriate, where the leader turns over the responsibility for the group to the group. *All* members (including the leader) are coequals in responsibility. This relatively low-task, low-relationship style is appropriate where a more active leadership style might be perceived as interference. However, even when the group is fully mature, the leader must still monitor the changing conditions of the group and be ready at any time to step in to perform additional services the group may need.

Most of us have styles of leading and small group services we prefer to perform. Moreover, we are not infinitely capable of altering our behavior, and some of us are more flexible than others. For example, President Reagan was noted for his delegating managerial style. This seemed so much a part of his personality that some believe it is doubtful he could have taken charge had a crisis threatened the nation. Some leadership experts advise us to look for situations that need our preferred styles or to encourage supportive and capable members of the group to assist the leaders.

Leadership Adaptability as the Key to Effectiveness

The theme uniting the contingency and functions approaches to leadership is the concept of *adaptability*. The search for *the* best leadership style or the perfect set of leader traits is fruitless. Currently, group theorists accept the ideas that different groups require different leader behaviors, and the same group will require different behaviors at different stages of its development. By now you may feel overwhelmed with all the information a "mere human" has to process to be an effective group leader. Being an effective group leader in varied situations demands your ability to perceive what is happening with the individual members and the group as a whole, and to adapt your behavior accordingly. Being perceptive requires listening well, knowledge of group processes and procedures, and analytical ability. Adapting your behavior requires mastering a variety of leader skills.

Before you throw your hands up in despair at the complexity of being an effective small group leader, we present one final contingency concept we think will help you organize your thoughts about how to lead. That concept is Chemers' *Integrative Systems/Process Model* of small group leadership (see table 7.4).

Table 7.4   Using Chemers' Approach to Help You Analyze Your Group Situation

---

Input Factors

Task

Is the task clearly structured or vague? How much freedom does the group have?
Is there a *best* solution, or could any one of several solutions work equally well?
How much time do you have to complete the task?
Is it important that all members are satisfied with the final product, or is it more important that the
 task be completed?

Members

How much do the members know about how to perform the work?
Are the members enthusiastic about the task?
Have the members been together for a long time and are they used to working together as a team?
What do the members expect from the leader? What do the members prefer?
Do the members, collectively, have the informational and other resources to complete the task
 successfully?

Yourself as Leader

Do you understand the task?
How well do you know the members, their abilities, and preferences?
What is your preferred behavior as a leader? Is it compatible with this situation? If not, can you
 encourage one or more of the members to supply what you lack?
What are your sources of power? Do you have the authority you need to complete the task?

Process Factors

Task-Oriented Behaviors

What task-oriented functions are currently being performed?
Are there any gaps, or group needs that are going unmet?
Can you as leader provide these, or will you enlist the help of group members?
How adequate is the problem-solving procedure being followed by the group?
How well are critical-thinking processes and standards being applied to major decisions made by the
 group?

Relationship-Oriented Behaviors

What relationship-oriented functions are currently being performed?
Are there any gaps, or group needs that are going unmet?
Can you as leader provide these or will you enlist the help of one of the group members?

General Behaviors

Is there an appropriate balance between the task-oriented and relationship-oriented behaviors *for this
 particular group at this time?*
How are the members behaving toward each other? Is their behavior helping the group achieve its
 goals?
How are you as leader behaving toward the members? Is your behavior helping the group achieve its
 goals?

Table 7.4   Using Chemers' Approach to Help You Analyze Your Group Situation (continued)

Outcome Variables

Group Performance

Are members completing their assignments on time, with appropriate quality? If not, what is the reason—lack of motivation, lack of information, or something else?
How adequate are group decisions? How well have possible solutions been evaluated for effectiveness and possible negative outcomes?

Satisfaction

Are members satisfied with their performance?
Are you as leader satisfied with the group's performance?
Will the parent organization be satisfied with the group's work?

Cohesiveness

Are members working smoothly with each other?
Do they seem to want to work together?
Are there any deviants or scapegoats who need to be managed?
Is the level of cohesiveness affecting the group in a positive or a negative way?

Chemers' approach encourages you, as a group leader, to conduct a continuous and systematic analysis of your group as a changing system to determine what an effective leadership approach might be. Chemers' model is consistent with the systems view of small group communication that we presented in chapter 2. Input variables to consider include both the leader's and the members' personal characteristics, the task, cultural and situational factors, and expectations. Process variables include leader and member skills, group history, and culture. Output variables include the group's current performance, satisfaction, and feedback. Using this as a basic framework can help you select the most helpful leadership behaviors for your group. That's why we stressed the models of open systems theory and group development. The better you understand how a group is "running," the better you can adapt your behaviors to the needs of the moment as the group continuously changes. With practice you can learn to do this increasingly well.

Summary

In chapter 7 we have explained and supported the proposition that leaders must be adaptable to other group members, the group as a whole, and the group's situation at each point in time. We made a distinction between *leadership* and *leaders. Leadership* refers to goal-directed interpersonal influence within a group, which may be exerted by any member of the group. It is different from supervising or managing. A *leader* is a specific individual, often with an official leadership position or title, who behaves in ways that help the group achieve its goals, and who is perceived by the other members as the leader. Five common sources of a leader's power are legitimate authority, the ability to reward and to punish, expertise, and referent power. A designated leader is a person who, by appointment or election, holds an official leadership title. This individual may coordinate group efforts as a supervisor or peer. An emergent leader is a person who becomes the group's leader through a process of elimination and selection. The emergent leader is usually the individual who is perceived by members to have the best blend of behaviors for the particular group.

We have found three myths about leadership especially prevalent: that leadership consists of certain traits leaders possess in varying degrees; that there is a best style of leadership appropriate for all situations; and that leaders get other people to do all the work for them. Some researchers believe that the democratic leadership style is more productive than the autocratic, but research findings have been inconsistent. Rather than getting other people to do things for them, leaders perform services for group members to facilitate accomplishment of the group's task. They certainly do not sit back and "just let it happen." One currently-accepted idea about group leadership is the functional approach, where each member of the group is encouraged to perform whatever functions the group needs. The leader serves as a completer, supplying whatever necessary functions the other members are not providing. The most effective type of leadership for any particular group depends on the contingencies facing the group. With the functions and contingency approaches, the burden is placed on the leader to analyze the group, its members, and its needs, and act accordingly. We strongly urge you to be sensitive and flexible. Provide whatever functions are needed at any point in time—a *completer* of the group as a total system.

Review Questions

1. Describe the five sources of leader power and give an example of each one.
2. What are the differences between supervisory leaders and peer leaders? What sources of power are associated with each type of designated leader?
3. Describe the process of elimination by which a leader can emerge from an initially leaderless group. What can a *designated* leader do to be perceived as the group's emergent leader?
4. What is the trait approach to leadership? What are the underlying assumptions and flaws in this approach?
5. Describe the three major styles of leadership. Why is there no *best* style of leadership for all situations?
6. Describe the functions and contingency ideas about leading. What does this imply for a designated leader?
7. Explain the idea that an ideal small-group leader is an "integrative *completer* of a system in process."

Bibliography

Cathcart, Robert S., and Samovar, Larry A. (eds.). *Small Group Communication: A Reader.* 5th ed. Dubuque, IA: Wm. C. Brown, 1988, section 7.

Hackman, Michael Z. and Johnson, Craig E. *Leadership: A Communication Perspective.* Prospect Heights, IL: Waveland Press, 1991.

Larson, Carl E., and LaFasto, Frank M. J. *Teamwork: What Must Go Right, What Can Go Wrong.* Newbury Park, CA: Sage Publications, 1989.

Stogdill, Ralph M. *Handbook of Leadership.* New York: The Free Press, 1974.

References

1. Robert Tannenbaum, Irving R. Wechsler, and Fred Massarik, *Leadership and Organizations: A Behavioral Science Approach* (New York: McGraw-Hill, 1961): 24.

2. Michael Z. Hackman and Craig E. Johnson, *Leadership: A Communication Perspective* (Prospect Heights, IL: Waveland Press, 1991): 76.

3. John R. P. French and Bertram Raven, "The Bases of Social Power," in *Group Dynamics: Research and Theory,* 3rd ed., eds. Dorwin Cartwright and Alvin Zander (New York: Harper & Row, 1968): 259–269.

4. H. Lloyd Goodall, Jr., "The Skills of Leading Small Groups in American Business and Industry," in *Small Group Communication: A Reader,* 5th ed., eds. Robert S. Cathcart and Larry A. Samovar, (Dubuque, IA: Wm. C. Brown, 1988): 532–545.

5. Hackman and Johnson: 11–12, summarizing the writing and thinking of numerous leadership theorists.

6. Ernest G. Bormann, *Discussion and Group Methods: Theory and Practice,* 2d ed. (New York: Harper & Row, 1975): 253–269; John C. Geier, "A Trait Approach to the Study of Leadership in Small Groups," *Journal of Communication* 17 (1967): 316–323.

7. Ralph M. Stogdill, Carroll L. Shartle, Willis L. Scott, Alvin E. Coons, and William E. Jaynes, *A Predictive Study of Administrative Work Patterns* (Columbus: The Ohio State University, Bureau of Business Research, 1956); Ralph M. Stogdill and Alvin E. Coons, eds., *Leader Behavior: Its Description and Measurement* (Columbus: The Ohio State University, Bureau of Business Research, 1957); Robert Blake and Jane Mouton, *The Managerial Grid* (Houston: Gulf Publishing Co., 1964).

8. Hackman and Johnson: 26–27.

9. Hackman and Johnson: 27.

10. William C. Schutz, "Leader as Completer," in *Small Group Communication: A Reader,* 3d ed., eds. Robert S. Cathcart and Larry A. Samovar (Dubuque, IA: Wm. C. Brown, 1979): 454–460.

11. Fred Fiedler, *A Theory of Leadership Effectiveness* (New York: McGraw-Hill, 1967).

12. Paul Hersey and Kenneth H. Blanchard, *Management of Organizational Behavior,* 4th ed. (Englewood Cliffs, NJ: Prentice-Hall, 1982).

CHAPTER EIGHT

Applying Leadership Principles

CHAPTER OUTLINE

What Groups Expect Leaders to Do

Administrative Duties
> *Planning for Meetings*
> *Following Up on Meetings*

Leading Group Discussions
> *Initiating Discussions*
> *Structuring Discussions*
> *Equalizing Opportunity to Participate*
> *Stimulating Creative Thinking*
> *Stimulating Critical Thinking*
> *Fostering Meeting-to-Meeting*
>   *Improvement*

Developing the Group
> *Establishing a Climate of Trust*
> *Developing Teamwork and Promoting*
>   *Cooperation*

Managing the Group's Written
Communication
> *Personal Notes*
> *Group Records*
> *Written Notices and Visuals*
> *Reports and Resolutions*

**Group-Centered Democratic
Leadership: A Special Case**

KEY TERMS AND CONCEPTS

Group-centered democratic leadership

STUDY QUESTIONS

1. What do most people expect a small group leader to do?
2. What are the characteristics of group-centered democratic leadership and why are they important to understand?

When TerryAnn was elected president of her college service club as a junior, she was thrilled. She wanted the club to continue experiencing the same success she witnessed when she was a member. Unfortunately, such was not to be the case. TerryAnn and the rest of the executive committee met soon after their spring election to make plans for the upcoming fall. Although many good ideas surfaced at this meeting, no one wrote them down. TerryAnn was somewhat intimidated by all the seniors on the executive committee, and she was reluctant to ask the other members to do things or to assign tasks. Consequently, no one knew who was supposed to do what, so committee members lost summer planning time. When fall came, they had to scramble to catch up.

TerryAnn's reluctance to take charge affected both the executive committee and the regular organizational meetings. She made no effort to start the meetings on time, so members got into the habit of coming late. Because there was no agenda, members did not know what they would be discussing or what materials they should bring to the meetings. Discussion was haphazard, jumping from one topic to the next without ever finishing a single subject. No minutes of meetings were ever compiled or distributed, so members weren't sure what actions had been decided or who was assigned to what tasks. As a result of the disorganization in the executive committee, service club members became disenchanted with the organization. Membership decreased. As the frustrating year drew to a close, TerryAnn was increasingly depressed because her high hopes for the club had not come close to being realized.

This true story could have had a different ending if TerryAnn had known what the other members expected of her. Because she was reluctant to act like a dictator, she did the opposite. But the group members would have welcomed some direction from TerryAnn. They were practically crying for her to provide them with structure and organization and to see to it that certain group tasks were completed. In this chapter we will explain what the typical duties of designated small group leaders are and what most group members expect from their designated leaders.

What Groups Expect Leaders to Do

We emphasized repeatedly in the last chapter that the leader has a lot of work to do, sometimes more than any other member of the group. There are specific services most groups in the U.S. expect their designated leaders to provide. Four major categories into which these services fall are: administrative duties, leading group discussions, developing the group, and managing the group's written communication.[1] The following information can serve as a kind of leader's manual for you whenever you find yourself elected or appointed to a leadership position in a group.

Table 8.1   Administrative Duties of the Group Leader

Planning for Meetings

Define the purpose of the meeting.
List exactly what you want to accomplish at the meeting.
Establish the starting and stopping times.
Make sure members know the purpose, what is to be accomplished, starting and stopping times,
    location, and necessary preparation.
Advise and prepare resource people in advance.
Make all necessary physical arrangements.

Following Up on Meetings

Keep track of member assignments.
Serve as liaison with other groups.

Administrative Duties

Certain administrative duties must be performed for the group to run efficiently. These include planning for meetings, following up on members' assignments, and serving as liaison with other groups, including the parent organization (see table 8.1). Terry Ann's performance was particularly weak in these areas.

Planning for Meetings

Leaders must plan meetings in advance so they don't waste other members' time. Here is a set of guidelines you can follow:

1. **Define the purpose of the meeting and communicate it clearly to the members.** Don't have a meeting if there is no reason for it. If a meeting is needed, make sure you state the purpose clearly. For example, "To talk about what we're going to do this year" is too vague; "To establish a list of priorities we want to accomplish within the next six months" is clear and specific. Moreover, tell the members exactly what outcomes should be produced at the meeting, such as a written report, an oral recommendation, plans for a party, a decision made, and so forth. Highly successful groups have clear goals that are understood and supported by every member.[2] You may need to notify some members of where and how they can locate information needed for the meeting or of other steps they can take to prepare.
2. **Make sure members know the place, starting time, and closing time for the meeting.** Tell members in advance when the meeting will begin and end so they can arrange their other activities as needed. Then, *make sure you stick to those starting and ending times!* Consistently starting meetings late or running overtime kills enthusiasm and lowers attendance, as TerryAnn discovered.

"How about some little pads and pencils?"

It's the leader's responsibility to make sure members have all the supplies they need. (Drawing by Levin; © 1985 The New Yorker Magazine, Inc.)

State exactly where the group will meet. A vague place such as at "the library" may cause confusion, as it did in one of our classroom project groups. Some of the members found each other in the lobby, while others assembled in the student lounge area. Each subgroup blamed the others for not attending!

The leader is responsible for communicating this information to members, though it can be delegated to someone else (i.e., a secretary). Still, it is the leader's responsibility to be sure everyone knows when and where to meet.

3. **If special resource people are needed at the meeting, advise and prepare them.** Groups often need information and advice from specialists. A personnel committee may need the advice of an affirmative action specialist; a student group may need to consult with the parking services manager before recommending changes in parking policies; a collective bargaining committee may want to talk with an insurance expert before presenting its demands. Make sure invited guests know what to expect at the meeting and what information they will be called upon to provide.

4. **Make all necessary physical arrangements.** You should make sure the room is reserved, the seats are arranged properly, and needed materials (i.e., notepads, pencils, microphones, tape recorders, etc.) are on hand.

Following Up on Meetings

Generally two kinds of follow-up are needed: reminding group members of assignments and preparing necessary reports.

1. **Keep track of member assignments.** The leader needs to make sure that members know what their assignments are and by what date they are to be completed. The group should keep written records of assignments, perhaps as part of the regular written records (minutes). (Keeping written records is such an important responsibility that it is dealt with separately in a later section of this chapter.) In addition, the leader may need to keep in touch with members by telephone to keep track of each member's progress and to remind them of upcoming meetings. Recent studies of successful teams have found that group members' most common and serious complaint was that the designated leader failed to confront and correct group members who were not performing adequately.[3] Had TerryAnn done these things at the initial planning meeting following her election, her term might have been memorable for positive rather than negative reasons.

2. **Serve as liaison with other groups.** The leader is the group's spokesperson. Usually this means the leader will represent the group to other groups, answer questions about the group and its work, and keep the parent organization informed. For example, the chair of an organization's membership committee may want to explain recruitment plans to the promotion committee so publicity efforts can be coordinated. The chair makes all reports and motions for a committee at meetings of its parent organization. Sometimes the leader will be interviewed by public media.

Leading Group Discussions

One of the most important duties of a designated leader is to coordinate discussions so that they are productive. Leaders should plan how they will initiate the meetings, keep the discussion organized, encourage all members to participate, and stimulate both creative and critical thinking in the group. They also should monitor the group so that what is not accomplished at one meeting can be addressed at the next. This was TerryAnn's most crucial failing during her term as president. These suggestions are summarized in table 8.2.

Table 8.2   Tips for Leading Group Discussions

Initiating Discussions

Help reduce primary tensions.
Briefly review the purpose of the meeting, outcomes to be achieved, limitations to be observed.
Give members informational handouts as needed.
Make sure special roles (such as *recorder)* are established.
Suggest procedures to follow.
Ask a clear question to help members focus on the discussion issue.

Structuring Discussions

Keep the group goal-oriented; watch for digressions and topic changes.
Put the discussion or problem-solving procedure on the board or in a handout.
Summarize each major step or decision.
Structure the group's time.
Bring the discussion to a definite close.

Equalizing Opportunity to Participate

Address comments to the group as a whole.
Control compulsive, dominating, or long-winded speakers.
Encourage less-talkative members to participate and listen with interest.
Do not comment after each member's remarks.
Bounce questions of interpretation back to the group before you offer an opinion.
Remain neutral during arguments.

Stimulating Creative Thinking

Suggest techniques (such as brainstorming) designed to tap a group's creativity.
Encourage members to search for other alternatives.
Discuss components of a problem one at a time.
Be alert to suggestions that open up a whole new line of thinking.

Stimulating Critical Thinking

Encourage members to evaluate information and reasoning.
Make sure all members accept the standards, criteria, or assumptions used in making judgments.
Evaluate all solutions thoroughly before making them final.

Fostering Meeting-to-Meeting Improvement

Review personal notes of the meeting.
Decide how the meeting could have been improved.
Establish specific improvements as goals for the next meeting.
Adjust behavior to help meet these new goals.

Initiating Discussions

Opening remarks set the stage for the meeting and help members begin to focus on the group's task. Here are guidelines for you to follow.

1. **Help reduce primary tensions, especially with new groups.** Members may need to be introduced to each other. Nametags or tents may be needed. An icebreaker or other social activity may be used to help members get to know one another.

2. **Briefly review the purpose of the meeting, the specific outcomes desired, and the area of freedom of the group.** Although members should have been informed of these prior to the meeting, some members may want clarification. Discussing them early helps prevent misunderstandings later.

3. **Give members informational and organizational handouts.** These may include informational sheets, an agenda, outlines to guide the discussion, copies of things to be discussed, etc.

4. **See that special roles are established as needed.** Most groups keep written records of meetings and establish a recorder role for this purpose. Decide what roles are needed and how they will be handled. For example, will the position of *recorder* be rotated or handled only by one individual?

5. **Suggest procedures to follow.** Members should know whether decisions will be by consensus or majority vote, and whether the group will follow the small group procedures recommended by *Robert's Rules* or any other group technique. We recommend that you suggest procedures to the group, then ask the members to accept, modify, or suggest alternative procedures. (If bylaws or other laws impose specific procedures on the group, such as on a jury, you won't have this flexibility.)

6. **Ask a clear question to help members focus on the first substantive issue on the agenda.** This helps launch the group into the substantive portion of the meeting. You may want to refer to the examples of discussion questions in chapter 4 (see table 4.2).

Structuring Discussions

Once the group members are familiar with each other and oriented to the task, the leader can help them function efficiently by organizing the discussion. While effective leaders help maintain productive relationships among the members, their primary focus should be on the group's task. That includes constantly monitoring the group's *process* and making needed adjustments. The following are some suggestions for you:

1. **Keep the group goal-oriented; watch for digressions and topic changes.** Be sure the members understand and accept the goal. If a digression occurs, you can help bring it back on track with statements like

THE FAR SIDE By GARY LARSON

"And so you just threw everything together? ...
Mathews, a posse is something
you have to *organize*."

The main thing a leader does is help the group get organized. (THE FAR SIDE. Copyright 1987 FAR
WORKS, INC. Reprinted with permission of Universal Press Syndicate. All rights reserved.)

these: "We seem to be losing sight of our objective," or "What does that
have to do with what we were discussing?" Topic switches are common, so
you'll need to be on constant watch for them. When you notice one, point
it out and suggest that the group finish one topic before going on to
another: "We're jumping ahead. Let's finish our parking recommendation
before we start talking about scholarships." When a change of issue or
irrelevant topic crops up, or when a member suggests a solution
prematurely, ask if that person would mind waiting until the group has
finished its analysis of the current issue.

2. **Put the discussion or problem-solving procedure on the board or in a handout.** If the group is using a procedure such as the nominal group technique or brainstorming, you'll help the group remember the steps by summarizing them briefly in writing. This helps keep comments to the point.

3. **Summarize each major step or decision.** It is easy for members to lose track of what the group is doing. Before the group proceeds to the next issue or agenda item, ensure that all members understand what the group just decided or concluded by summarizing and asking members whether they accept the summary as accurate and complete. In many cases, a secretary can help summarize. This also helps make a clear transition to the next step in the discussion.

4. **Structure the group's time.** Nothing is more frustrating than running out of time before you have a chance to discuss an issue important to you! Since members often get caught up in a discussion, it is up to the leader to keep track of time to remind the group of what still needs to be done and how much time is available.

5. **Bring the discussion to a definite close.** Do this no later than the scheduled ending time for the meeting, unless *all* members agree to extending the time. In your conclusion include a brief summary of all progress the group has made, a review of assignments given, a statement of how reports of the meeting will be distributed to members and others, comments about preparation for the next meeting, commendations for a job well done, and your evaluation of the meeting to improve the group's future interactions.

Equalizing Opportunity to Participate

Along with keeping the group's discussion organized, the leader is responsible for seeing to it that everyone has an equal opportunity to speak. There are several things you can do to produce such equality:

1. **Address your comments to the group rather than to individuals.** Unless you are asking someone for specific information or responding directly to what a member has said, speak to the group as a whole. Make eye contact with everyone, especially the less-talkative members. Such eye contact shows that you *expect* them to speak. It is natural to pay the most attention to those who talk a lot, but this may further discourage quiet members.

2. **Control compulsive, dominating, or long-winded speakers.** Occasionally a member monopolizes the discussion so much that others give up. This imbalance can destroy a group. The other members expect the leader to control domineering members and will thank you for it. You may try several techniques to control such members. First, avoid direct eye contact. Second, sit where you can overlook them naturally when you ask questions of the group. Third, cut in tactfully and say something like: "How do the *rest* of

you feel about that point?" Fourth, help the group establish rules about how long someone may speak, then establish a timekeeper to keep track of members' remarks. Fifth, you can describe the problem openly to the group and ask the members to deal with it as a group. Sometimes, even more drastic measures may be needed, such as talking with the offending individual privately or even asking the person to leave the group. This is a last resort; use it only when other measures have failed.

3. **Encourage less talkative members to participate.** Quiet members may feel overwhelmed by talkative ones. Encourage less-talkative members: "Roger, finances are your area of expertise. Where do you think the budget could be cut?" or "Maria, you haven't said anything about the proposal. Would you like to share your opinion?" As leader, you should make a visual survey of members every minute or two to look for nonverbal signs that a member wants to speak, that someone seems upset, or that a member disagrees with what someone else is saying. Give such members a chance to speak by asking a direct question such as, "Did you want to comment on Navida's suggestion?"

   Other techniques for increasing the participation of quiet members include assigning them to investigate needed information and reporting back to the group, or inviting them to contribute with their special areas of knowledge or skill. You might say, "Kim, you're a statistical whiz. Will you take charge of the data analysis for the project?" Listen with real interest to what an infrequent participant says and encourage others to do so as well. Nothing kills participation faster than perceived lack of interest.

4. **Avoid commenting after each member's remark.** Some discussion leaders comment after each person has spoken. This produces a *wheel* network of verbal interaction. Eventually members start waiting for the leader to comment, and this inhibits the free flow of conversation. Listen, speak when you are really needed, but as a rule don't repeat or interpret what others say.

5. **Bounce questions of interpretation back to the group.** Some groups follow the designated leader's opinions. Especially in a new group, you should hold back until others have had a chance to express their views. Then, offer yours only as another point of view to be considered before the group makes a decision. If a member asks, "What do you think we should do?" you can reply, "Let's see what everyone else thinks first. What do the rest of you . . . ?"

6. **Remain neutral during arguments.** If you are heavily involved in an argument, you will have a harder time being objective, seeing that each person has a chance to participate, and that each point of view is represented. If evaluation is needed, try to get the other members to provide it. If you stay neutral, you can legitimately serve as a mediator for resolving disputes. Of course, feel free to support decisions as they emerge and encourage critical thinking by all members.

Stimulating Creative Thinking

Many problem-solving groups create mediocre solutions. Sometimes inventive solutions are needed. A few special techniques may help:

1. **Suggest discussion techniques that are designed to tap a group's creativity.** Several techniques, such as *brainstorming,* are designed especially to help a group create inventive solutions. (Brainstorming is described in chapter 11.) These techniques employ the *principle of deferred judgment*—the group is encouraged to postpone evaluation until all possible solutions are presented. When people know that their ideas will not be judged, they feel freer to suggest "wild" and "crazy" ideas, many of which may turn out to be useful.

2. **When the flow of ideas has dried up, encourage the group to search for a few more alternatives.** You might use these idea-spurring questions: "What *else* can we think of to . . . ?" or "I wonder if we can think of any more possible ways to . . . ?" Often the best ideas are suggested late in a period of creative brainstorming.

3. **Discuss the components of a problem one at a time.** For instance, ask "Is there any way to improve the appearance of . . . ?" or "the durability of . . . ?"

4. **Watch for suggestions that open up new areas of thinking, then pose a general question about them.** For example, if someone suggests putting up signs in the library that show the cost of losses to the users, you might capitalize on that idea by asking, "How *else* could we publicize the cost of losses to the library?"

Stimulating Critical Thinking

The importance of critical thinking was covered in detail in chapter 5. We want to remind you here of the designated leader's responsibility for ensuring that group members carefully evaluate the decisions they make. Here are specific suggestions:

1. **Encourage group members to evaluate information and reasoning.** You can ask questions to make sure that the group evaluates the source of evidence ("Where did that information come from?" "How well respected is _____ in the field?"); the relevance of the evidence ("How does that apply to our problem?"); the accuracy of the information ("Is that information consistent with other information about the issue?" "Why does this information contradict what others have said?"); and the reasoning ("Are the conclusions logical and based on the information presented?"). You may be able to bring in outside experts to challenge the views of the group or help evaluate information.

2. **See that all group members understand and accept the standards, criteria, or assumptions used in making judgments.** Fair, unbiased judgments are based on criteria that are clear to all members. You might ask, "Is that criterion clear to us all?" "Is this something we want to insist on?" or "Do we all accept this as an assumption?"

3. **See that all proposed solutions are tested thoroughly before they are accepted as final group decisions.** Make sure that group members discuss tentative solutions with relevant outsiders, that pros and cons of each solution have been evaluated, and that members have had a chance to play *devil's advocate* in challenging proposals. For a major problem, you might propose holding a *second chance meeting,* where all doubts, concerns, or untested assumptions, can be explored.

Fostering Meeting-to-Meeting Improvement

Effective group leaders spend time evaluating each meeting to discover how it could have been improved. Sometimes, they may ask the group itself to participate in evaluating the meetings. More often, leaders will privately review their meeting notes to determine whether the major meeting goals were met and how smoothly the meeting went. Then, good leaders establish their goals for improving future meetings and adjust their behaviors accordingly.

1. **Review personal notes of the meeting.** A leader should keep personal notes (discussed later) of important happenings during the meeting. After the meeting, the leader should ask him- or herself: "Did we accomplish our purpose?" "Did everyone have a chance to participate?" "Did anyone hog the floor?" "Was the group both creative and critical in its thinking?" and, most important of all, "What could I personally have done to ensure a better meeting?"

2. **Decide how the meeting could have been improved.** The answers to the previous questions will guide the leader here. For example, if Sonya believes that the group jumped on an early solution just to end the meeting without carefully assessing the problem just to get the meeting over with, then she might decide that the group needs to look at the problem again. If TerryAnn had evaluated her meetings, she would have discovered that the group needed more direction and guidance than she was providing.

3. **Establish specific improvements as goals for the next meeting.** After determining where the meeting could have been improved, the leader should then incorporate this information into planning for the next meeting. Sonya, for example, could place the problem back on the agenda, explain to the group that she perceived a lack of critical thinking, and invite the group to assess the problem again.

4. **Adjust behavior accordingly.** Once leaders have diagnosed areas of group communication where improvement could occur and decided what needs to be done, they should then adjust their behavior to help ensure improvement. For example, TerryAnn needed to be more clear, direct, and concise in her communication. She also needed to keep the group on track instead of letting them digress. Notice that these are *communication* behaviors (*not* personality characteristics) that TerryAnn should change. Several studies of effective leaders have shown that good leaders do adjust their behavior from one meeting to the next, depending on what the specific goals of the meeting are. Good leaders monitor their own and the other members' behaviors so they can modify their own behaviors to help the group.

We now consider some specific areas in which the designated small group leader can foster improvement by helping the group develop.

Developing the Group

One of the most important functions of the leader is to assist in the development of the group from a collection of individuals to a productive unit. This involves such things as establishing a climate of trust, promoting teamwork and cooperation, and evaluating the group's process. These are summarized in table 8.3.

Establishing a Climate of Trust

Groups perform more effectively when members trust one another. The following suggestions can help you establish a climate of trust:

1. **Establish norms that build trust.** Norms that build trust encourage respectful active listening, cooperation, confidentiality, getting assignments done on time, and the freedom to disagree without being considered deviant. Many leaders are far too slow to speak to members who are manipulative, do poor work, or act out of self-interest harmful to the group.[4]
2. **Function as a coordinator rather than a dictator.** You can foster a climate of trust if you act as though your job is to serve the needs of the group, not to order people around or serve your personal interests. That way, members will feel free to express themselves and to develop skills needed by the group. Ask for volunteers to do jobs for the group rather than ordering: "Cal, get the . . ."
3. **Encourage members to get to know each other.** Usually, members will trust each other and feel safe in the group if they get to know one another as individuals. Sometimes an unstructured period where members get

Table 8.3 Tips for Developing the Group

Establishing a Climate of Trust

Establish norms that encourage trust.
Function as a coordinator, not a dictator.
Encourage members to get to know one another.
Confront members who violate other members' trust, including goof-offs.

Developing Teamwork and Promoting Cooperation

Use "us" and "we," not "I" and "you."
Develop symbols of group identification.
Watch for hidden agendas that conflict with group goals.
Use appropriate conflict management approaches and procedures.
Share rewards with the group.
Lighten up; share a laugh with the group.

acquainted with each other's beliefs, values, backgrounds, and attitudes helps create a sense of teamwork. You may want to schedule social gatherings and outings that provide the opportunity for this to occur.

Developing Teamwork and Promoting Cooperation

Although the leader's principal responsibility is to see that the group accomplishes its task, the development of teamwork can help group members work productively. Here are suggestions you may use:

1. **Speak of "us" and "we," rather than of "I" and "you."** Calling the group members "we" implies commitment to the group and its values. Ask what it means if another member speaks of the group as "you."

2. **Develop a name or other symbol of group identification.** Shared identification can be displayed by such items as T-shirts, logos, "inside" jokes, slogans, and so forth. For example, one advertising agency's creative group that had a long string of successful ad campaigns called itself the "Can Do" group.

3. **Watch for evidence of hidden agenda items that conflict with group goals.** If you suspect a hidden agenda item is interfering with the group's agenda, promptly bring it to the attention of the group. Avoiding such problems makes them worse, not better.

4. **Use appropriate conflict management approaches and procedures.** Conflict does not have to hurt a group, but if it is allowed to proceed too long or to become personal, it can cause lasting damage. Help prevent this by keeping arguments focused on facts and issues, and by *immediately* stopping members who attack another's personality or character. When there

are two or more competing subgroups, look for a larger issue that can bring them together. Find a *superordinate* goal—more important to the members than their individual subgroup goals—behind which the subgroups can rally.

Sometimes, despite the best intentions of the leader, a group may become deadlocked. If this happens, look for a basis on which to compromise. Maybe you can synthesize parts of one person's ideas with parts of another's to create a compromise or consensus solution. Perhaps you can serve as mediator. At any rate, if you have been performing your job well as the group's leader, you have remained detached from the fray. You should therefore have a broader perspective from which to create a solution that all parties can accept. We present specific conflict management procedures in chapter 10.

5. **Share rewards with the group.** Leaders often receive praise from authority figures or the group's parent organization. Wise leaders give credit to the group. Your comments about what *the group* has done, your pride in membership, and your acknowledgement of the service provided by members fosters cohesiveness and team spirit.

6. **Lighten up; share a laugh or joke with the group.** Don't let the discussion get so serious that people can't enjoy themselves. Humor helps reduce tensions and makes people feel good about each other. Most groups take mental "work breaks" where they digress from the task. Wise leaders let the group develop fantasy chains that enrich the group's life and help establish shared beliefs and values. The result of such tension-relieving activity is more concerted work effort in the long run. Bring the group back to the task once the joke is over or the fantasy has chained out.

Managing the Group's Written Communication

Although the majority of communication among members of a small group is oral, the group needs written messages to provide continuity from meeting to meeting, to keep the parent organization informed about its activities, and to coordinate activities with other groups. Leaders may not be the ones who actually carry out these activities, but it *is* their responsibility to see that they are performed by someone. Once again, if TerryAnn had asked someone (either the club's secretary or a volunteer) to keep minutes of their first planning meeting, the executive committee might not have floundered in confusion and wasted the summer planning months. The four basic categories of a group's written messages are personal notes, group records, written notices and visuals, and group reports and resolutions. These are summarized in table 8.4.

Table 8.4   Managing the Group's Written Communication

Personal Notes

1. Should be kept by leader and each individual member as well
2. Should include facts, proposals, interpretations agreed to by the group
   a. decisions made by the group
   b. assignments and responsibilities given

Group Records

1. Must be kept for continuing groups; should be kept by one-meeting groups
2. May be prepared by the designated leader, secretary, or a member who volunteers or is appointed
3. Begin with a heading that recaps the attendance, time, and date of meeting
4. Minutes should include:
   a. a summary of all relevant information and criteria agreed to
   b. assignments given
   c. decisions made
   d. plans for future action
5. Minutes should *not* include:
   a. sensitive information
   b. who proposed each course of action
   c. how anyone voted
6. Summary reports of one-meeting groups include same basic information as minutes, but may be less formal.

Written Notices and Visuals

1. Meeting notices include:
   a. name of group
   b. date, time, and place of meeting
   c. purpose of meeting and specific outcomes to be achieved
   d. agenda
   e. specific facts, procedures, or other preparation needed
2. Subcommittees or individuals submitting reports to the group should distribute copies of charts, graphs, tables, printed materials, lists, drawings, and so forth to members (in advance if possible).

Reports and Resolutions

1. Committees and task forces often submit written reports of their findings or recommendations to other groups, such as the parent organization.
2. Oral report is usually given to CEO and executive committee along with written report.
3. If report is submitted as a resolution or motion, group's leader presents the resolution or motion; group members should attend to answer questions, counter objections.

Personal Notes

During meetings, taking notes helps the leader (and other members) keep track of what is going on. Making brief notes helps you focus your listening so you won't forget what the group is discussing. Your notes may include important facts about a problem, proposed ideas, major interpretations that the group has decided upon, assignments you and others have accepted, and anything else that may be important to the discussion. Figure 8.1 is an example of personal notes made during such a problem-solving discussion.

April 8, 1992 --- Everyone present

<u>Discussion topic</u>: what topics should we include in our class
presentation on group polarization?

<u>Main criteria</u>:

Judy & Bill --- to get an "A" info must be accurate
Bart --- has to have practical application
Bev --- Dr. Brilhart wants innovative presentation
Everybody should have a part in presenting the topic to the class.

<u>Topics</u>

* Definition of group polarization (all agreed)
 Risky shift (Hal says can become a cautious shift w/ cautious
   members --- this term is outdated)
* Exercises to demonstrate when group takes risks + when it becomes
   cautious --- Judy says there's a bunch of these in a book she has
* Need to show how this applies in real life.

* Decisions Made
Assignments: Me (application); Judy & Bill (library research);
Hal & Bev (exercises -- w/ Judy's book)

Next meeting --- Wed., April 15.

Figure 8.1 An example of personal notes.

Group Records

The chair of any committee should keep careful notes of what occurs during each meeting so that accurate and clear minutes can be written and distributed to members. Although minutes are the responsibility of the group's leader, someone else (a secretary or a volunteer) may be designated to perform this duty. In some organizations, a professional secretary may attend the group's meetings specifically to take notes and prepare minutes.

Written records of each meeting are essential for all continuing groups. Otherwise, members will find they are redoing work, forgetting important information, failing to consider some proposals, and not completing assigned work. Disagreements over what was reported or decided will be common. Wasted time and effort, and needless tensions, will result.

Minutes of April 10, 1992 Meeting of Committee A

Committee A held a special meeting at 1:30 P.M. on Friday, April 10, 1992 in room 14 of the Jones Library.
Attendance: Walter Bradley, Marlynn Jones, George Smith, Barbara Trekheld, Michael Williams.
Absent: Jantha Calamus, Peter Shiuoka

1. The minutes of the April 4 meeting were approved as distributed.
2. Two nominations for membership in the graduate faculty were considered. A subcommittee of Bradley and Trekheld reported that their investigation indicated that Dr. Robert Jordon met all criteria for membership. It was moved that Professor Jordon be recommended to Dean Bryant for membership in the graduate faculty. The vote was unanimously in favor.

   The nomination of Professor Andrea Long was discussed; it was concluded that she met all criteria, and that the nomination had been processed properly. It was moved that Professor Long be recommended for appointment to the graduate faculty. The motion passed unanimously.
3. Encouragement of grant activity. Discussion next centered on the question of how to encourage more faculty members to submit proposals for funding grants. Several ideas were discussed. It was moved that we recommend to President Yardley that
   a. A policy be established to grant reduced teaching loads to all professorial faculty who submit two or more grant proposals in a semester.
   b. Ten percent of all grant overhead be returned to the department that obtained the grant for use in any appropriate way.

   This motion was approved unanimously.

Report of Second Meeting of Polarization Instructional Group

Date of Meeting: October 22, 1992
Time and Place: 3:35 P.M. in our regular classroom, CBA 202
Attendance: Beverly Halliday, Bart Bonn, Hal Darling, Judy Hartlieb; Bill Miklas, absent.

Report of Previous Meeting

Judy distributed copies of the last meeting's record to the group members; it was approved.

Phone Numbers

Phone numbers of all members were exchanged.

Test Ideas

Hal read some ideas for test questions from a book he had borrowed from Professor Brilhart. The group discussed criteria for a test question and determined that a question that was "close to home" and applicable to the class members should be sought. The issue was to be considered further when the group next met.
The meeting was adjourned at 3:45 P.M. with plans to meet again on Thursday, October 29, during class.

Figure 8.2 Two Examples of Group Minutes

Minutes of small group meetings should contain a summary of information shared during the meeting and pertinent to the problem that was discussed, all ideas considered by the group, any criteria agreed upon, all decisions, all assignments, and any plans or procedures for future action. Special summaries or attached copies of procedures for future action should also be included. Minutes begin with a heading in memo form, the time and place of the meeting, and a report of attendance. They should be signed by the writer and a copy sent to each member as soon as possible after the meeting. Two examples of minutes are shown in figure 8.2.

A report of one-meeting groups is usually needed, but not necessarily in the same form as minutes. The designated leader usually prepares a summary report of the meeting that includes the same basic information as minutes. A copy goes to each member with additional copies to other concerned people.

Because members of committees and task forces need to express themselves freely, there are some things that should *not* be reported in minutes or reports. Confidentiality should be protected. You should not report who proposed or moved some course of action, how anyone voted, or who provided what information. Some sensitive information would not even be recorded. You *should* include all conclusions, decisions, and assignments.

Written Notices and Visuals

Notices of meetings that have been called should go to each member in plenty of time for each to prepare. Usually a meeting notice should include the following information:

1. Name of group and of person to whom the notice is being sent.
2. Name of the person sending the notice or calling the meeting.
3. Place of meeting.
4. Time the meeting will begin and end.
5. Purpose of the meeting and specific outcomes that must be achieved.
6. Agenda, if more than one item will be discussed, and a statement about whether the agenda is open for additional topics or problems.
7. Any specific facts, reading sources, or other preparation members may need, and special techniques or procedures to be followed.
8. In the event this is a one-meeting conference, a list of all who will attend (if that is available).

An example of a meeting notice is shown in figure 8.3.

When subcommittees or individual members have conducted special research for a group they should usually give a copy of their major findings (including a list of all sources) to all members. These may include such information as tables of statistics, graphs, duplicated copies of print material, lists, and drawings. All of these are easy to produce in this age of computers and fax machines. Such visual aids are best distributed in advance of a meeting but can be handed out during an oral summary given at the meeting. Likewise, visual aids such as display charts, diagrams, graphs, and so forth enhance any oral report. Many of these investigative reports can be incorporated into the minutes.

Reports and Resolutions

Frequently groups must prepare written reports of their work, including findings or recommendations. For example, a President's task force may investigate and make recommendations about national problems such as pornography, ocean

Date: March 30, 1990
To: Curriculum Committee (Drs. Berquist, Bourhis, Drale, Jackson, Persky, Shankar, Stovall, Spicer)
From: Dr. Galanes, Chair
Re: Curriculum Committee meeting

The next meeting of the Curriculum Committee will be on Friday, April 20, at 11:00 A.M. in Craig 320.

Purpose of meeting: We need to: (1) decide what our departmental assessment's focus will be (student outcomes, student perceptions, alumni perceptions, or something else); (2) decide what areas of the department will be assessed; and (3) establish subcommittees for each area.

Bring: The assessment guidelines provided by the Center for Instructional Assessment and any other material you think is relevant.

Figure 8.3   An Example of a Meeting Notice

pollution, and the quality of public schooling. Corporations have teams of researchers and designers developing new products. The end product is usually a major written report accompanied by a brief oral report, often given to the CEO and a group of executives.

Although the designated leader is responsible for submitting the group's report by a certain deadline, normally one or two members of the group do the actual writing of the report. A first draft is given to all members for suggestions and revisions, followed by discussion and agreement on the final version. Each member of the committee signs the final report. You may have to complete something like this as a requirement for your small group communication course.

Sometimes the final written product is a resolution or motion the committee's chair makes during a meeting of the parent organization. For example, a committee to study faculty morale develops recommendations; the committee's chair moves that the recommendations be accepted by the faculty senate. Often, members of the committee accompany the chair to the meeting of the parent organization to answer questions, make supporting speeches, and counter objections. A common format for motions and resolutions may be found in any comprehensive parliamentary manual, such as *Robert's Rules of Order, Newly Revised,* or the organization may have its own manual for such reports.

As you can see, any group's designated leader will be expected to perform a variety of duties that are associated with the title *leader.* Far from being the person who orders others around, the leader instead becomes a servant to the group by making sure that the group has what it needs.

Group-Centered Democratic Leadership: A Special Case

We believe that effective leaders adapt their leadership styles to suit the particular conditions of their groups. Sometimes a controlling form of leadership is appropriate, but often (especially for discussion and problem-solving groups) a participatory, or democratic, style will work best. Now that we have said that, we would like to stress another bias we share. We believe that many effective group leaders are like teachers or coaches, gradually guiding the group to a point of maturity where it can function independently of the leader. In other words "good leaders develop leaders." Effective leaders are like ideal parents who help their children learn to make decisions on their own and take care of themselves without the parents' help. We think this is a worthy goal for leaders to adopt. Even if it is unrealistic to think that certain groups will ever be able to run without coordination by a leader, we are in favor of leaders exercising the *minimum* amount of control necessary to get the particular job done. We support the idea of the leader gradually teaching the other members how to help the group function smoothly and effectively. TerryAnn wanted to function as a democratic leader; she got into trouble because she expected group members to coordinate themselves *before* they had clear notions of what their duties were. She did not realize that group members needed coaching and direction from her in order to become a functioning group system.

In addition, it is likely that many of the groups to which you belong will be composed of peers—coworkers, colleagues, fellow students, neighbors, and so forth. In such groups, it is inappropriate to behave like a dictator or a domineering parent. The other members will probably resent it and the potential benefits of group discussion will be lost if only one person's opinion—the leader's—counts.

For these reasons, we advocate the use of group-centered democratic leadership as most appropriate *for the kinds of groups that depend upon discussion among relative equals*. This includes most problem-solving, discussion, learning, and decision-making groups. A **group-centered democratic leader** concentrates primarily on the group's task, secondarily on the group's interpersonal relationships, shares leadership functions wherever possible, encourages full participation of the members, and sees his or her major function as providing whatever services the group needs. In other words, instead of assuming that the group exists to help the leader achieve personal goals, the group-centered democratic leader is the servant of the group. Even if the group you are leading is not fully mature with members who can function on their own, group-centered democratic leadership is a worthwhile goal toward which to strive. Like the ideal parent, you'll be helping the group grow from infancy to mature adulthood. Leaders who operate this way reflect a basic ideal of a democratic society such as ours: that all people are created with equal rights as persons.

Table 8.5   Guidelines for the Group-Centered Democratic Leader

Be an active participant in the group.
Focus primarily on the task, not the social relationships.
Be perceptive and analyze the needs of the group.
Be adaptable in your behavior.
Be knowledgeable about group processes and group techniques.
Be respectful of and sensitive to others.
Follow the group rules.
Be an effective communicator.

Some important guidelines for serving as a group-centered democratic leader follow. These characteristics are not inborn traits that you either do or do not have; rather, they are patterns of behavior that can be acquired with desire and effort. We think these guidelines will be helpful to you (see table 8.5). Use your common sense in applying them in your group, and modify them to fit the specific needs of specific groups.

1. **Be an active participator in the group.** Effective discussion leaders participate but they are not incessant talkers. You cannot influence a group if you do not participate. Recall that the first criterion for eliminating someone as emergent leader is lack of participation. If you want to sustain your influence in the group and be considered a valuable member, you must contribute. However, you should balance your talking with active listening so you won't be dominating the group. Don't fall into the trap we see with many of our students who think that the leader is supposed to comment on everything. This "I-gotta-say-something-after-each-member-speaks" syndrome can make group sessions deadly.

2. **Focus primarily on the task, not the social relationships.** The person most likely to be identified as the leader in a leaderless group is the individual who is task-oriented and clearly helps the group achieve its goals. This should be the focus for a designated leader, too. Effective leaders have a good grasp of the problem facing the group, help members concentrate on achieving the task, and don't permit time to be wasted with lengthy digressions.

3. **Be perceptive: analyze the needs of the group.** Effective leaders understand people. They know how to help others motivate themselves to contribute their best to the group. They can sense what members need. They are exceptionally active, focused listeners who pay attention to what's going on in the group. For example, if group members appear confused, you know that the group should spend some time clarifying the discussion.

If the members keep saying the same things and reaching no conclusions, you might conclude that the members need a suggestion that will provide direction for the group. Consider the following dialogue:

Jerry: Yeah, we've got to finish everything Monday night, the charts and all, with the easel, and get the stuff to Maryann. Our presentation on Tuesday should be pretty good.

Maryann: (Becoming agitated and visibly upset) That's not going to give me nearly enough time to type them! I have to have them by Friday at the latest! How can you expect me to type the charts, fix the table of contents, copy the paper, and have it ready to turn it on Tuesday if I don't get the stuff until Monday?

Sheri: (Trying to calm Maryann, while also somewhat annoyed at her tone of voice) Lighten up, Maryann. It won't take that long—we've only got two charts to do, and I can help you.

Darryl: (The group's coordinator, sensing that this argument stems from a misunderstanding, clarifies) Hold on, guys. I think we're talking about two different sets of charts. If I remember right, we promised we'd get the data tables that are supposed to go into our written report to Maryann by Friday so she can type them over the weekend. But I thought Sheri and I were supposed to make the two chart posters for our class presentation on Monday night. Isn't that what we decided?

In the preceding example, Darryl senses that the argument is over a misunderstanding and attempts to clarify it for the group. Notice that he states his clarification ("If I remember right" and "Isn't that what we decided?") in such a way that other members can disagree or improve on his understanding if he has been mistaken. Darryl could perform this function for the group only because he had been paying attention and focusing his listening.

4. **Adapt your behavior to fit the needs of the group.** As we have noted previously, groups need different things at different times. In addition to being able to analyze what the group needs at any given time, the effective leader has enough behavioral flexibility to be able to provide a variety of functions. If one approach seems unsuccessful with a particular group, the leader tries a different approach. For example, Terrell tries to stifle Cissy, an incessant talker, by not making direct eye contact with her, but that doesn't work. Terrell later cuts off Cissy after she has made *one* point when he says, "What do the rest of you think of that proposal?" That helps, but Cissy still interrupts and tries to dominate. Terrell then talks to Cissy privately, explaining what effect her chatter is having on the other members. Terrell has been willing to adapt his behavior for the good of the group, and (we hope) can convince Cissy to do the same!

5. **Be knowledgeable about group processes and group techniques.** This may seem obvious, but it has been our experience that many designated group leaders have no idea how to lead a group, what is reasonable to expect from group members, or what are useful group techniques for solving specific problems, such as brainstorming or the problem census. All too often, a manager may appoint a subordinate to head a committee without ensuring that the subordinate has adequate training to perform well. You may be willing to do the job, but if you don't know what you are doing you can make a shambles of what could have been a productive group. Effective group leaders know in general what to expect, such as the overall phases a group experiences. They also are familiar with a variety of group techniques designed for specific purposes, and suggest these techniques when they would be useful. They never quit trying to develop new skills and techniques. (We present a number of these techniques in chapter 11.)

6. **Be respectful of and sensitive to others.** Groups are effective problem solvers because several heads are usually better than one at solving complex problems. However, this works only if all members contribute. Members will be reluctant to speak up if they believe they will be ridiculed or ignored. We have observed numerous groups that contained such a member. One person was so used to having his suggestions "shot down" by the leader that he ceased to participate. In another group, one extremely critical member had silenced almost all the other members. As a result, these groups lost a lot of potentially valuable information and insights, all because one member was disrespectful of the others. In contrast, effective leaders tune in to the verbal and nonverbal cues given by the members and adjust their own behavior accordingly. They are sensitive and attentive to others, patient, and are critical thinkers at appropriate times.

7. **Follow the group rules, just as you expect other members to do.** While group members often give the leader some leeway in following rules that other members are expected to observe, effective leaders do not abuse this privilege. If others are expected to arrive on time, so should the leader. If the leader chastises other members for not finishing assignments, then the leader *must* make sure his or hers are completed on time. Effective leaders are model members.

8. **Express your ideas clearly and concisely.** Good group leaders think and speak clearly and concisely. They are able to get to the heart of the matter being discussed, to clarify, and to summarize what is being said. They do not ramble but are well organized, coherent, and pertinent. The ability to verbalize the goals, procedures, ideas, values, and ideals of the group is an important leadership skill.

We conclude this section on group leadership by relating a story one of us heard several years ago. A crowd of people rushed down the street. At the tail end of the crowd was a man hurrying to catch up with the group. A bystander asked him why he was following the crowd, to which he replied, "I am their leader, therefore I must hurry to follow them." This story sums up what we believe effective group leadership is—not coercion or manipulation of the group in the leader's preferred direction, but a willingness to serve the *genuine* needs of the group for the benefit of all.

Summary

We introduced this chapter by relating the experience of TerryAnn, who wanted to be a respected group leader, but failed to perform the tasks the group needed from her. Group members expect acknowledged leaders to perform a variety of services on behalf of the group, and if TerryAnn had done these, her term might have ended differently. These tasks include providing administrative duties for the group, such as planning for meetings and following up on assignments, structuring the group's discussions, helping the group develop as a team, and managing the group's written messages. This last function includes seeing to it that records are kept for the group and distributed to appropriate individuals, and making sure that group reports and resolutions are completed on time and presented to other groups or the parent organization. We advocate group-centered democratic leadership, especially for most groups of peers.

Review Questions

1. What are the major responsibilities of the leader in most groups?
2. For what kinds of situations is group-centered democratic leadership appropriate? What are the characteristics of such a leader? From your own experience, give examples of leaders who have or have not behaved as group-centered leaders.

Bibliography

Brilhart, John K., and Galanes, Gloria J. *Effective Group Discussion.* 7th ed. Dubuque, IA: Wm. C. Brown, 1992, chapter 10.

Cathcart, Robert S. and Samovar, Larry A. *Small Group Communication: A Reader.* 6th ed. Dubuque, IA: Wm. C. Brown, 1992, section 8.

Larson, Carl E., and LaFasto, Frank M. J. *TeamWork: What Must Go Right, What Can Go Wrong.* Newbury Park, CA: Sage Publications, 1989.

Robert, Henry M. *Robert's Rules of Order, Newly Revised.* Glenview, IL: Scott, Foresman, 1981.

Tropman, John E. *Effective Meetings.* Beverly Hills: Sage Publications, 1980.

References

1. Much of the following information is discussed in detail in John K. Brilhart and Gloria J. Galanes, *Effective Group Discussion*. 7th ed. (Dubuque, IA: Wm. C. Brown, 1992): 206–227.
2. Carl E. Larson and Frank M. J. LaFasto, *TeamWork* (Newbury Park, CA: Sage Publications, 1989): 27–33.
3. Larson and LaFasto: 136.
4. Larson and LaFasto, especially chapters 6, 9, and 10.

CHAPTER NINE

Procedures for a
Problem-Solving Group

CHAPTER OUTLINE

Scientific Method as the Basis for Problem Solving

Characteristics of Problems

Definition of *Problem*

Problem Solving versus Decision Making

Problem Characteristics

Task Difficulty
Solution Multiplicity
Intrinsic Interest
Member Familiarity
Acceptance Level
Area of Freedom

The General Procedural Model for Problem Solving

1. Describing and Analyzing the Problem
2. Generating and Explaining Possible Solutions
3. Evaluating Possible Solutions
   Criteria for Evaluating Solutions
   Narrowing a Long List of Proposed Solutions
   Charting the Pros and Cons
4. Deciding on a Solution
   Different Ways to Make Decisions in Groups
5. Planning How to Implement the Solution

Applications of the General Procedural Model for Problem Solving

KEY TERMS AND CONCEPTS

Consensus

Criterion (Criteria)

General Procedural Model for Problem Solving

Problem

Problem Solving

Scientific Method

STUDY QUESTIONS

1. What are four reasons for having a group rather than an individual solve a problem?
2. What is a *decision by consensus?* How does it differ from a *decision by majority vote?*
3. What are three important reasons why a group should follow a clear-cut procedural outline when engaging in problem-solving discussion?
4. What are the three major parts of every problem?
5. What are six problem characteristics to consider when you determine what type of problem-solving procedure to use?
6. What are the five major stages in the General Procedural Model for Problem Solving? What goes on during each of these stages?

Humans are natural problem solvers. Nog and his associates could chip a stone axe head in an hour, cut and shape a handle in another hour, cut sinews from a large animal, and then fasten the axe head to the handle with the sinews. Not counting the time spent gathering the materials, it took over three hours to produce one stone axe. This tool could then be used to cut small trees and shape rough wooden objects, split animal skulls to get brains for tanning, chop vines for weaving baskets, kill an enemy, or solve other problems. But such stone axes were heavy, could cut only small trees, crushed a lot of fibers, and sometimes broke into pieces. Descendents of Nog developed bronze to replace the stone heads, which made a better cutting edge that wasted less meat or wood and was far easier to attach to a handle. Still later problem solvers figured out how to make iron, and then how to refine it into steel that could hold a fine cutting edge. Think of other improvements in tools and life-styles made possible by new inventions.

Inventing, as you've probably noticed, is another name for problem solving. Solving woodcutters' and butchers' problems resulted in the invention of crosscut saws, power saws, and other tools to increase the efficiency and quality of their work.

However, solutions to problems may have both predictable and unexpected impacts on human and earth systems. Many of these changes prove to be more harmful than the problem they were supposed to solve. What solves one person's, group's, or nation's problem often creates problems for others. For instance, consider how we generate electrical power—primarily by burning coal. Because coal smoke deposited soot on the countryside near the plants, tall chimneys were built to send the soot high into the atmosphere. But hundreds of miles downwind, lakes began to die, crop yields decreased, and older trees turned brown from acid rain. The tall stacks that "solved" air quality problems in Chicago, Omaha, and St. Louis were creating horrific problems in New England, Canada, and other points northeast.

The moral of this brief history of problem solving is that every change in any system affects the rest of the system, whether that system is a stone-age group of hunters and gatherers, a continent, or the entire living earth. As Shakespeare put it, "Pluck a rose and you affect a star." Our story of problem solving has several implications for small task groups:

1. Problems need to be solved and re-solved continually as changes in systems occur. There are no permanent, everlasting solutions. In one sense, a solution is just an adjustment, which will have to be redone as conditions change—the same way a steering correction solves a momentary directional problem when you drive.
2. Feeling that some condition could be improved is a situation that precedes human problem solving. For a long time no one felt unhappy with stone axes. Asking "What is unsatisfactory?" is basic to inventing new ways, new solutions.

3. Every invention/solution will have effects in addition to the desired ones. Problem solvers should try to understand all potential outcomes before they act in order to avoid making a situation worse than it was before the "solution" was implemented. We call this step *applying criteria, evaluating possible solutions,* or *testing solutions.* For many complicated problems, testing requires more knowledge and skills than any one person can apply.
4. In any problem-solving procedure, definite steps should be taken to improve the immediate and long-range benefits of proposed solutions. To avoid physical conflicts ranging from fistfights to wars, problem solvers should take into account the needs and interests of *all* people affected by proposed changes. For instance, a company contemplating a major change in its benefits program should consult with employees at all levels before making final decisions regarding the change. In a crowded world with overloaded life systems we have little room for serious errors.

To illustrate the previous ideas about problem solving, think about the impact of dumping trash into the oceans, fluorocarbons into the stratosphere, and carbon dioxide into the air. Harmful side effects of such practices include skin cancers, dead fish, disease-causing oysters, and a warming of the entire earth. In a more ordinary example, the person who planned the evening classes where one of us worked scheduled the classes thirty minutes earlier, which was more convenient for the students. However, this earlier time overlapped with the late daytime classes, thus creating a space problem—not enough classrooms to accommodate all the scheduled classes. Sometimes solutions, no matter how well intended, have negative side effects.

As we said in chapter 1, groups usually produce superior solutions to complex problems than individuals do; they also produce greater member understanding and more satisfaction.[1] Groups frequently achieve what is called the *assembly effect,* in which the group solution is superior both to the choice of the group's most expert member and to an averaging of opinions of all members. Verbal interaction among the members is the essential ingredient for this superior output.[2] However, group problem solving is not always better. The relative advantages and disadvantages are listed in table 9.1. Groups can do a lot to improve the quality of both problem-solving procedures and outputs. High cohesiveness and high performance norms ("We'll do nothing but the best!") both help.[3] So do orderly, systematic problem-solving procedures, which produce better solutions and decisions than less organized procedures.[4] Chaotic conversation interferes with critical thinking. Chapter 9 identifies the nature of problems, and describes procedures for improving group discussion aimed at solving those problems.

Table 9.1   Advantages and Disadvantages of Solving Problems in Groups

Advantages	Disadvantages
Solutions for complex problems are usually superior; groups have more resources, including information and methods.	Groups take more time.
Members accept the solution more readily; satisfaction is higher.	Participation may be uneven: some members may dominate, others withdraw.
Members understand the solution more completely.	Primary tension and conformity pressures may interfere with critical thinking.

Scientific Method as the Basis for Problem Solving

Since the earliest prehistoric times people have invented gods as the causes of their blessings and calamities. Once a cause has been identified, someone can think of a solution. So with "god" as the cause, people invented worship rituals to solve problems involving weather, food, and other people.

Later in the development of human problem solving, people began to take a different approach. They started to observe what natural events occurred close together. For example, certain types of dark clouds often preceded a thunder shower. Such observations as the basis of knowledge was called *science* (from Latin *scire,* "to know"). The **scientific method** uses this discipline of observation in a systematic procedure designed to gain knowledge about the physical world as a basis for solving problems. Today more and more people are learning to apply the generalized procedure of science as a way of solving problems, from the most personal to those of worldwide scope such as AIDS and the greenhouse effect.

Many times humans are quite unsystematic in how they attempt to solve problems. As a result they often overlook key elements of a problem or possible outcomes of various solutions. For example, you would question a physician who gave a shot of penicillin for chest pain without first listening to the patient's chest, taking CAT scans or X rays, performing blood tests, and asking whether the patient was allergic to penicillin. This unsystematic approach would not be based on real science.

Much personal problem solving is done at an unconscious or preconscious level that we sometimes call *intuition.* For example, you may be wondering what to do about an assignment, then suddenly the answer will occur to you while you're taking a shower. Such intuitive problem solving can be valuable and lead to creative breakthroughs for solving problems. However, intuition used alone has serious limitations for problem solving. Ideas derived through intuition must be examined critically before they are implemented. Critical thinking can reveal flaws in solutions that may not be apparent at first.

No matter *how* a group discovers the possible solutions to a problem—through intuition, logic, or some other avenue—it is essential that the group use the scientific method (of which critical thinking is a specialized application) to check out how well the solutions will work. We believe the time-tested method of science should be used by any group with a major problem to solve.

Characteristics of Problems

To help you plan problem-solving procedures, we next explain the nature of problems. Some components are common to all problems; other elements vary. You should consider both types of characteristics when devising a problem-solving procedure.

Definition of *Problem*

"Problem" refers to the difference between what exists and what is expected or desired. For instance, if your room door is open when you expect it to be locked, you have a problem. Every problem situation has the three major components shown in figure 9.1. A group needs to understand these components completely in order to develop an appropriate solution for a particular problem.

1. **An undesirable existing situation.** If people feel that something is perfectly satisfactory as it is, there is no problem. For example, you may be frightened of crossing the street in front of your campus, but another student who has dodged worse city traffic for many years may perceive no problem. To understand a problem you must first be able to describe exactly what is unacceptable to you in the existing situation.

2. **Goal or desired situation.** At the start, a goal may vary from a vague image of some better condition to a very precise, detailed objective. Part of the problem-solving effort should be directed at specifying the precise goal in a way that is both acceptable to all members and achievable. Outstanding groups have clear goals that all members support.[5] For example, your goal might be to achieve some way to cross the street in which no pedestrian could be injured by a passing vehicle.

3. **Obstacles to change.** These are conditions and forces that must be overcome in order to achieve the goal. Typical obstacles include the competing interests of other people, lack of tools or skills, insufficient funds, or anything you must overcome in order to reach the goal. For example, your goal of achieving a safe crossing for your campus may be blocked by lack of interest on the part of the city council, lack of city or college funds, lack of knowledge and skill in pedestrian safety, and other projects that have higher priority with traffic department officials.

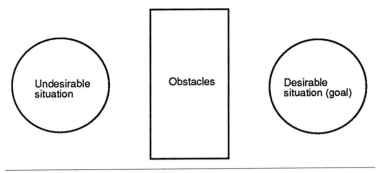

Figure 9.1 Components common to all problems.

Problem Solving versus Decision Making

Before proceeding further with our study of problems and problem solving, we need to distinguish between the concepts *problem solving* and *decision making*. **Problem solving** is what you do to move from the existing situation to the goal. Hence a *problem-solving procedure* is a sequence of steps or actions taken to solve a problem, including: defining the problem, identifying or creating possible solutions, and choosing among the solutions. *Decision making* refers to the act of selecting one or more options from those available; it does *not* involve sizing up the problem or creating possible options. Problem solving is a more comprehensive procedure that includes decision making (choosing). Indeed, the entire process of problem solving often involves making many decisions, such as how to define the problem, what solutions to consider, which to suggest or act upon, how to carry out the solution, and so on. As in most situations, the steps you take and the order in which you do them influence the quality of the product. Can you imagine cutting out material for a coat without first having some pattern to guide your scissors? Next, turn your attention to the nature of problems as a further basis for explaining problem solving procedures.

Problem Characteristics

There are several characteristics of problems you should consider when deciding on a procedure for problem solving. A great deal of research has gone into determining characteristics crucial to the exact problem-solving procedure. We have summarized the findings of this research.

Task Difficulty

A problem can vary from complicated (e.g., how to get astronauts and their cargo to and from Mars) to simple (which color of pencils to buy). The procedural outline of steps in problem solving should reflect the complexity of the problem. The more complex a problem is, the more information the group will need in order to understand the existing situation adequately.

Solution Multiplicity

The number of possible options may vary from one or two to infinity. The procedures you choose in problem solving should reflect this characteristic of a problem. For example, brainstorming, a technique for creating large numbers of novel solutions, is beneficial when there are many possible options (i.e., high-solution multiplicity) but is too time-consuming when there are only a few possibilities. (The guidelines for brainstorming are presented in chapter 11.)

Intrinsic Interest

This term refers to the level of interest group members have in the problem assigned to them. Berkowitz found that the more fascinated and involved members were with a problem, the less strict procedural control they wanted from a designated discussion leader.[6] When members are first interested in the problem, they want to express their feelings and opinions about it with little regard for procedure. After they have ventilated these strong feelings they will more willingly accept procedural guidance through the steps necessary to achieve quality outcomes.

Member Familiarity

Not surprisingly, groups with knowledgeable, experienced members tend to perform better than groups with less-experienced members. The less members know about the problem the more time they will first need to spend in becoming familiar with its details. The early part of any problem-solving discussion should be spent in sharing knowledge until everyone has the same understanding of the problem. This *mapping* procedure is illustrated in figure 9.2.

Acceptance Level

This term refers to the degree to which a solution chosen must be acceptable to the people it will affect. For instance, it may seem logical to reduce tobacco-caused illness and death by simply making it a crime to sell or use tobacco in any form. But past experience indicates that people using tobacco would not likely accept this solution. Instead, prohibiting the sale and use of tobacco would add another illegal drug to the market, leading to more crime, exorbitant prices,

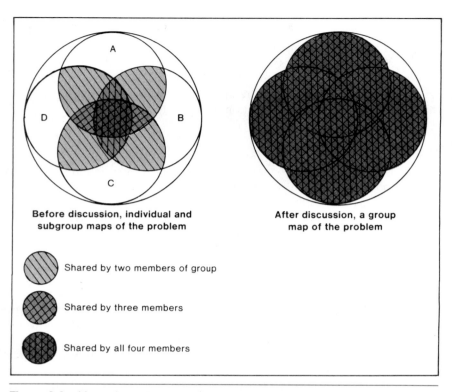

Before discussion, individual and subgroup maps of the problem

After discussion, a group map of the problem

Shared by two members of group

Shared by three members

Shared by all four members

Figure 9.2 Maps of a problem before and after members discuss it.

need for prison space, and less control on the quality of tobacco products. Therefore, outlawing tobacco would not likely be accepted any better than was the prohibition of alcohol in the early 1900s. In contrast, most drivers don't care how a bridge is built so long as it is functional, safe, and cost effective. Thus, if acceptance of a proposed solution is essential to its success, then the problem-solving procedures should include some way of testing how people will react. This can be done by including key representatives in the group or pretesting potential solutions before they are implemented.

Area of Freedom

As defined earlier, the area of freedom is the amount of authority given to a group by its parent organization. The procedure followed by a group will depend on how much of the total problem-solving procedure it has the authority to undertake. A fact-finding group may be asked only to investigate a problem, not solve it. Another small group may have authority only to interpret information, as in the case of a jury which can decide guilt or innocence but not the penalty for guilt. Many advisory committees and conferences can recommend a solution but not make it binding, or a group may be commissioned to select among solutions generated by another group.

It is vital that members understand the exact charge to the group before they proceed to work on any problem. Otherwise, members may become frustrated or angry. A committee one of us observed was charged with making recommendations about the types of student activities on campus. Instead, this committee created a sweeping proposal to fire certain individuals and restructure the student activities department. Even though committee members worked long and conscientiously to develop the plan, it was not accepted because the committee went far beyond what it was supposed to do. You can see that it is critical for group members to understand what they are supposed to do, and what they are *not* supposed to do.

The General Procedural Model for Problem Solving

We have noted that acting as a scientist means beginning with careful observations of what exists, what is happening, what events are related to other events, and so forth. Observation, not wishful thinking, is the key to acquiring and evaluating information using the scientific method. This is the method used by individuals and groups who are effective problem solvers.

Many people have studied how good problem solvers work. One of the more famous of these people was the American philosopher John Dewey, who asked students to think about a problem they had faced and solved, then to try recalling the sequence they used to solve the problem. From their reports he created a general sequence of mental steps he called *reflective thinking,* which implied that this was systematic rather than intuitive or haphazard behavior. According to Dewey, the sequence of individual problem solving usually goes like this: first we become aware of some difficulty, then we define and describe it, think of some possible solutions, evaluate these potential solutions, and make a decision about what to do. If possible, we evaluate the action taken to see whether it is effective, then continue or replace it after further testing.[7] Various versions of this set of steps have been recommended in books about small group communication. Procedures such as *Reflective Thinking, Ideal Solution,* and *Standard Agenda* are examples designed to foster methodical, orderly problem solving.

Researchers investigating problem solving by small groups have demonstrated the advantages of using a planned organization for problem-solving discussions in such small groups as task forces, committees, and quality circles. In an early line of research involving one of us, the general conclusion was reached that using *any* systematic procedure or outline produces better decisions than using no procedure.[8]

Why do step-by-step procedures improve the quality of solutions? Poole concluded that these sequences often remind group members of something they would otherwise forget to do; the sequence specifies logical priorities and steps that must be taken.[9] Recent evidence indicates that much of the increase in the quality of solutions results from thorough analysis of the problem, generation of a variety of solutions, and detailed assessment of both positive and negative aspects of the alternative solutions being considered by the group.[10] In other words, the group benefits from using an outlined procedure for problem solving because the procedural steps remind the members to: (1) do a thorough job of investigating, describing, and diagnosing the problem; (2) generate a variety of alternatives from which to choose; and (3) predict as completely as they can all the positive and negative outcomes likely to occur with each option. Without a procedure to follow, a group is likely to overlook important questions or facts, or forget to evaluate each option critically and completely.

The **General Procedural Model for Problem Solving** applies all the principles we have learned about effective problem solving by individuals and groups. The model provides a framework to guide each phase of the problem-solving process and is flexible enough for you to adjust it to suit the special needs of your group. Also, it reminds the group to investigate and analyze the problem thoroughly before trying to solve it, and to think critically about the positive and negative outcomes likely to occur with each alternative solution. The five steps in this general problem-solving procedure are summarized in table 9.2 and are presented in detail below.

1. Describing and Analyzing the Problem

During the first stage of problem solving the group concentrates on thoroughly understanding the problem. Members should consider all three major elements of the problem: what is unsatisfactory, what is desired, and what obstacles exist. This phase of problem solving may require nothing more than sharing the knowledge members now have (such as the *mapping* procedure illustrated earlier) or may require extensive research. The description and analysis of a problem should never be rushed; however, many of us have a tendency to begin thinking about a solution as soon as someone names a problem. We sometimes propose solutions without adequate knowledge of the facts, limiting factors, and possible negative consequences of the solutions we proposed so quickly. Often we resist listening to objections others have to our initial ideas. Here are several principles to guide your thinking and discussion in step 1 of problem solving.

a. If you are a committee created to work for some organization or administrator, be sure you understand the *charge* precisely. The charge is your assignment of both responsibility and limitations, given by the organization or person who created the group. Getting the charge straight is what you do when you make sure you understand an assignment exactly as

Table 9.2 Steps in the General Procedural Model for Problem Solving

1. Describe and analyze the problem.
2. Generate and explain possible solutions.
3. Evaluate all solutions, emphasizing probable positive and negative effects.
4. Decide on a solution.
5. Plan how to implement the solution.

intended. It's a good idea to get the charge in writing. A committee should ask for clarification of any unclear terms from the person(s) making the charge. For instance, you need to know what form your final product is to take: a recommendation, a motion at a general membership meeting, a research report, a blueprint with perspective drawings, or some other tangible object. You will certainly need to know what limitations are placed on your freedom, such as what information you can obtain from company records, legal restraints, spending limits, etc. You will want to know when your work must be done; deadlines are part of most charges to groups. So be sure the charge is clear to all members, and it is understood alike by the small group and the parent organization.

b. Work out a statement of the problem as a single, clear *problem* question. We discussed this in detail in chapter 5, but we again remind you of it here. A question that suggests the solution biases the group and limits its effectiveness. "How can we convince the administration to put in a new parking lot?" is a *solution question* that assumes the solution to the parking problem is to create a new parking lot. This *problem question* is better: "How can we improve the parking situation on campus?"

c. Focus on the problem before discussing how to solve it. One of the most common sources of poor solutions is getting solution-centered before the problem has been thoroughly investigated, described, and analyzed. In most groups chances are good that some impatient members will suggest a solution early in step 1. The discussion leader or another member should then suggest that the group refrain from any talk about *what* to do until after the group has completed its analysis of the problem.

d. Describe the problem thoroughly. Be sure to answer all questions about what is going on, what you hope to accomplish, and possible obstacles to that goal—the way a successful investigative reporter or detective does. A good way to describe the problem is to think of it as an uncharted map with only vague boundaries. Your first job as a group is to make a complete, detailed map of the problem. Questions you will need to answer are outlined in table 9.3.

Table 9.3   Questions You May Want to Ask As You Analyze the Problem

What are all the relevant facts?

1. Who is involved? When? Where? How?
2. What complaints have been made?
3. What is the difference between what is expected and what is actually happening?
4. What harm has occurred?
5. What exceptions have there been?
6. What changes have occurred?
7. What other information do we need?

What may have produced or caused the unsatisfactory condition?

1. What events precipitated the problem?

What do we hope to achieve?

1. What form will our solution take?
2. What would be a minimum acceptable solution for each person concerned?

---

e. If this is a major problem likely to require extended work over several meetings, the group should make an outline and a schedule based on the General Procedural Model for Problem Solving. This outline and schedule can be modified later, if needed, but at least now the group will reap the benefits of a plan before getting too deeply into the problem analysis.

f. Summarize the problem as a group to be sure everyone now understands it in the same way. In the case of a large problem this summary may be done in writing by one member and edited by the entire group until all members are satisfied with it.

2. Generating and Explaining Possible Solutions

The quality of the solution to a problem will not be better than the quality of the pool of ideas the group considers. Studies of problem solving have shown that the ideas discovered later are more likely to be innovative and of high quality than the ideas first mentioned.[11] So the major issue of step 2 is not "What *should* be done to solve the problem?" but "What *might* be done to solve the problem?"

During step 2 the focus of the group should be on finding and listing possible solutions, not on determining their relative merits or on trying to decide what to do. Now is the time to defer judgment of ideas. The leader may need to remind the group not to argue (yet) the relative merits of proposed solutions. The group engages in *creative* rather than *critical* thinking during this step of the procedure. The technique of brainstorming, discussed in chapter 11, is designed especially to help groups create a large quantity of solutions while deferring judgment on their merits.

During the first major stage of problem solving some possible solutions may have been suggested. Those should have been written down at the time by the group's recorder (often the designated discussion leader). Now they are added to the list.

Although no criticism should be conducted during step 2, ideas may be explained and clarified. Someone may ask "What do you mean?" or "Could you please explain how that would work?" Descriptive explanations help everyone understand the idea and may even stimulate further ideas.

Sometimes while generating ideas a member will recognize details of the problem that ought to be explored more fully. The group may then cycle back for further exploration about that issue. As soon as it is finished, the group should return to the job of generating ideas. You can see how ideas will be forgotten and lost if they are not *all* written down when first mentioned, preferably where everyone can see them.

Even if a problem is low in solution multiplicity (e.g., it has only two possible solutions), it still pays to list the solutions *before* criticizing or evaluating them. As soon as the group has completed the list of alternatives, it is ready to proceed with evaluating them.

3. Evaluating Possible Solutions

During the third stage of problem solving *all* proposed solutions should be evaluated so that the one(s) finally selected are the best ones. Critical thinking by the group is especially crucial during this stage. Test the solution by comparing it to facts brought out during the discussion of the problem, and test for a match with probable causes of the problem, goals of the group, restrictions required by the group's area of freedom, and all other criteria the group has established for a solution. It is especially important to consider all possible *negative* consequences of each solution, such as new problems it might create for the group or other people.

Criteria for Evaluating Solutions

Serious secondary tension may arise as people argue and disagree while they discuss the pros and cons of proposed solutions. To make arguments as constructive as possible and keep personal defensiveness to a minimum, the group should discuss, agree upon, and possibly rank (from most to least important) the criteria for judging the idea. **Criteria** are statements that set standards and limits for comparing and evaluating ideas. For example, our department's redesign of the public relations major was based upon an important criterion: it had to meet the guidelines established for public relations majors by the Public Relations Society of America and the International Association of Business Communicators.

Some criteria are *absolute,* which means they *must* be met (e.g., "The band for our annual banquet must not cost more than $500" is an absolute criterion—the group has no leeway). Other criteria are *important,* but give the group some flexibility (e.g., "The band for our annual banquet should be able to play a variety of music that would appeal to people ranging from 18 to 75 years old.").

There are criteria that are virtually universal in judging among solutions, such as "Will the proposed solution solve the problem?" "Can the proposed solution be done?" "Will the benefits outweigh the costs?" "Is this solution within our area of freedom?" and "How acceptable is this idea to the people most likely to be affected by it?" Such criteria encourage the group to consider whether or not the ideas proposed are legal, moral, workable, within the competence of the group or organization, within the control of the parent organization, and so on.

You have probably noticed that these are general, abstract criteria. You will need to express criteria as specifically and clearly as possible. Here are examples of criteria that are precise so there is likely to be no misunderstanding about their meaning:

The building must be ready to use by July 1, 1996.

Costs must not exceed a total of $50,000.

All employees must have equal opportunity to use the suggestion system.

Narrowing a Long List of Proposed Solutions

When a list of ten or more ideas has been generated by brainstorming or some other technique, the group will need to reduce this list to a manageable size before it discusses the merits of the ideas. This can be done in a number of ways after the group has established its criteria. Here are three useful techniques:

1. Combine any ideas that are similar or overlapping. For example, "Hold a goodwill party" and "Have a get-acquainted cocktail party" could be combined into "Plan a tension-reducing social event."
2. Allow each member (including the leader) to vote for his or her top three choices. Tally the votes. Any proposed solutions that do not have at least two votes may be removed from the list.
3. Give each member five small cards on which to write the number or name of his or her five preferred solutions, one on each card. The cards are arranged from most to least preferred. A *5* is written on the top card, a *4* on the second, and so on down to the last card, which receives a *1.* The cards are collected by the leader or recorder and the ratings tallied for each idea. The ratings are summed and divided by the number of members in the group to give an average rating to each idea. Any idea with no rating is crossed off the list. The group then discusses the pros and cons of only the proposed solutions with the highest ratings.

Table 9.4 Charting the Pros and Cons of Two Proposed Solutions

---

How to Reduce Passenger Injuries in Automobile Accidents

Pass Federal Law to Require the Use of Seat Belts

1. Pros
   a. Would reduce or eliminate many injuries
   b. Would be inexpensive
   c. Precedent exists in many states
2. Cons
   a. Infringes on individual rights; expect a heated legal fight
   b. Difficult to enforce
   c. Some injuries could be worse with seatbelts

Require New Cars to Be Equipped with Airbags

1. Pros
   a. Would be extremely effective
   b. Technology currently exists
2. Cons
   a. Would increase the cost of cars
   b. Infringes on individual rights; expect a heated legal battle
   c. Airbags might inflate incorrectly and cause an accident

---

Charting the Pros and Cons

During the evaluation discussion, a recorder (often the discussion leader) can help greatly by creating a chart of the ideas being discussed, with the pros and cons mentioned for each idea, as shown in table 9.4. Instead of *Pros* and *Cons* the chart headings might be *Advantages* and *Disadvantages, For* and *Against*, or even + and −. Without such a chart it is often impossible to remember the major arguments and evidence for and against each proposed solution. Using such a chart helps the group think critically about the proposals under consideration.

Once the remaining proposals have all been thoroughly evaluated, the group has set the stage for the emergence of a final decision on a solution or policy.

4. Deciding on a Solution

Just as groups experience predictable phases in their overall development, they also go through identifiable phases during decision making. Several well-respected researchers have contributed to our understanding of group decision-making phases.[12] For example, Fisher found that groups first enter an *orientation* phase, proceed to a *conflict* phase when they argue about their various options, and finally enter the phases of *decision emergence* and *reinforcement*.[13] Decision emergence may begin during step 3, as members gradually move toward a consensus and coalesce around one proposal. The members will usually know when this has happened. Often a discussion leader can hasten this by asking something like "I think we may have decided on a solution. Is that right?" If members agree aloud or nod their heads, a straw vote by show of hands or simply asking "Does everyone agree?" or "Does anyone disagree?" can confirm this consensus.

Reinforcement refers to the complimenting and backpatting that members give each other after a job well done. They will say things like "That took a long time, but we really came up with a workable solution," "I really think we did a fine job with that," or "We done good, folks!" Such backpatting expresses and reinforces the positive feelings members have toward each other. Cohesiveness is increased and will carry over to benefit the group in subsequent work.

We don't want to leave you with the impression that all groups experience exactly the same phases during decision making. That would be too simplistic. Poole, for example, found that many factors influence the types of phases groups experience and the order in which they occur.[14] We present the idea of group phases to help you analyze what may be occurring in groups you belong to, but we ask you to remember that the subject is more complex than we have described here.

Sometimes a consensus is hard or even impossible to achieve. We will next consider some ways in which groups make decisions, and what they can do to increase the likelihood of arriving at consensus.

Different Ways to Make Decisions in Groups

A group can make decisions in many different ways, but some methods are likely to produce poorer results than others. In some groups the leader has authority to make decisions and may do so frequently for the group. This sort of leader is called a *boss* or *head*. One person may be perceived as the most expert member on the problem the group is discussing; that person may be asked to make the decision for the group. As a way of avoiding conflict, the group can use some method of chance, such as flipping a coin, drawing straws, or rolling dice. Sometimes numbers can be averaged to produce a decision, such as averaging individual cost estimates to decide how much money to budget for a particular item. Often, groups decide by voting, which is mandatory in committees governed by Robert's "Rules for Committees" (included as a special section of *Robert's Rules of Order*). So what should you do when a decision is needed?

Three common ways of making group decisions are to let the leader or some other designated member decide without consulting the group, for the group leader to consult with other members but then make the final decision, and for the group to make the decision by consensus. **Consensus** refers to decisions where all members agree the choice they have made is the best one they can make that is acceptable to all; it doesn't necessarily mean the final choice is each member's number one pick. The first method is appropriate for minor decisions, such as where to meet, what refreshments to serve, what color of notepads to put in the conference room, or even whom to ask to type the report. It is also appropriate for those decisions where the leader (or designated decision maker) has all the information needed to make the decision, and support from the group members is guaranteed in advance. The consultative method is appropriate when the leader does not have all the needed information, when group members are likely to accept the decision, or when time is short. The consensus method is appropriate for major decisions, such as what policy to recommend or how to solve a complex problem, where acceptance is important and the group has the time to deliberate.

Voting, in which a majority decides for the group, merely weighs the power of numbers, not the relative merits of ideas. A majority is often wrong, and a minority of one member may have the best idea. Further, voting may leave a group split, with some losers who may resent the decision and try to sabotage it. A vote may be required to confirm that a decision has been reached, but whenever possible all members should agree that they have reached the best decision they all can support—a true consensus decision. Even with a large majority, such as 5 to 2, a split vote does not establish such agreement. Scientific research and our experience both confirm that you should make a major decision with a majority vote *only* when the group must make a decision without enough time to reach consensus, or the group has exhausted every possible way of achieving consensus. The next chapter on conflict provides suggestions for achieving consensus.

5. Planning How to Implement the Solution

Sometimes groups break off their discussion as soon as they have decided on a solution without working out a plan to put their decision into effect. They may *feel* finished, but they truly are not. Good leaders see that the group has worked out the details of implementation. During this stage of problem solving, the group answers questions such as the following:

Who will do what, when, and how so our decision is enacted?

How will we write and present our report?

How will we word our motion to the membership meeting, and who will speak in support of it?

What follow-up should we make to monitor how well this solution is working?

Some implementation plans are simple, but others are complicated and detailed. Chapter 11 provides information about a special procedure called PERT that will help you implement the solutions your group has chosen.

Although groups rarely stick exactly to the General Procedural Model for Problem Solving (or to any problem-solving guidelines), if you attempt to follow this sequence in the form of an outline of questions written about the specific problem, you will help guarantee that no important question, issue, or step is overlooked, thereby creating a poor solution. The flexibility of the procedure allows you to tailor it to the characteristics of any particular problem, just as

"You mean no one remembered to bring a rock?"

Implementation requires careful planning to succeed. (Drawing by Chas. Addams; © 1985 The New Yorker Magazine, Inc.)

Chapter 9

scientists adapt the scientific method to the specific problems they face when doing research. So you can understand better how such adaptations are made, we next present examples of actual outlines written, adapted, and followed by problem-solving groups we have observed.

Applications of the General Procedural Model for Problem Solving

The first example of a procedural outline, shown in table 9.5, was created by a self-appointed advisory committee of students concerned about pedestrian safety on a street just east of the campus where we both teach. The group of students first decided on the general problem they wanted to tackle, then created an outline to guide their investigation over an eight-week span. They devised possible solutions, decided on what to recommend, and finally presented their report to both the city council and the president of the university. You will notice that it closely follows the General Procedural Model of Problem Solving. The students' work was tragically timely—shortly after their presentation, a student was killed crossing that very street.

The outline in table 9.6 is much shorter and simpler; it is designed to be used for a brief discussion in class.

Summary

Problem solving is how we invent ways to improve situations we think are less than satisfactory. All human inventions and progress are the results of problem-solving behaviors. However, solutions often create new and different problems, sometimes worse than the ones they fix. So all proposed solutions need to be evaluated critically before they are put into effect. Beginning with superstitions and religious sacrifices to gods, human problem solving has evolved to what we call the *scientific method*. Using the scientific method means using systematic procedures rather than only hunches, intuitions, or chance.

Groups outperform individuals in solving complex problems. This is due to the verbal interaction during which information, interpretations, and critical thinking are exchanged. Furthermore, commitment to making solutions work is greatly increased when people affected by the solutions participate in the problem solving.

A problem consists of a situation perceived to be unsatisfactory, a desired situation or goal, and obstacles to reaching that goal. A problem-solving procedure should be adapted to the characteristics of a specific problem. Groups need to consider such variables as solution multiplicity, complexity, member familiarity, intrinsic interest, acceptance level, and the area of freedom.

Table 9.5   Sample Outline Using the General Procedural Model for a Complicated Problem

Problem Question: What Shall We Recommend That City Council and University Administration Do to Reduce Pedestrian Injuries on National Avenue East of Campus?

I. What is the nature of our problem involving vehicle-pedestrian accidents on National Avenue east of campus?
   A. How do we understand our charge?
      1. What freedom do we have in this matter?
      2. What limits has our instructor placed on us?
      3. To what does the general problem question refer?
   B. How do we feel about this problem?
   C. What do we find unsatisfactory about the way traffic and pedestrians currently affect each other on National Avenue?
      1. Diagram of present street, buildings, crossing, medians, lights, etc.
      2. How serious is the problem of injuries to pedestrians?
         a. What kinds of accidents and injuries have occurred?
         b. When do these accidents happen?
         c. Do they tend to occur at any specific times?
         d. What kinds of persons are involved?
         e. How does this compare to accidents and injuries elsewhere?
         f. Are there any other facts we need to learn?
   D. What seems to be causing these accidents?
      1. Characteristics of the location?
      2. Human behavior?
      3. Other factors?
   E. What do we hope to see accomplished?
      1. In reducing the number of accidents and injuries?
      2. In practices of City Council and Administration?
      3. Any other features of our goal?
   F. What obstacles exist to prevent achieving our goal?
      1. Financial?
      2. Priorities of Council or Administration?
      3. Vested interests, such as businesses?
      4. Other?
II. What might be done to improve the safety of pedestrians crossing National Avenue east of campus?
   A. Brainstorm for ideas
   B. Do we need explanations or descriptions of any of these proposed solutions?
III. What are the relative merits of our possible solutions to accidents and injuries on National Avenue?
   A. What criteria shall we use to evaluate our list of possible solutions?
      1. Costs?
      2. Acceptability to involved persons?
      3. Probable effectiveness in solving the problem?
      4. Appearance?
      5. Other?
   B. Shall we eliminate or combine any ideas?
   C. How well does each remaining potential solution measure up to our criteria and the facts of the problem?
IV. What recommendation can we all support?
   A. Has a decision emerged?
   B. What can we all support?

Table 9.5 Sample Outline Using the General Procedural Model for a Complicated Problem

V. How shall we prepare and submit our proposal?
   A. In what form shall we communicate with Council and Administration?
   B. How will we prepare the recommendation?
      1. Who will prepare the recommendation?
      2. How will we edit and approve this report?
   C. How will we make the actual presentation?
   D. Do we want to arrange for any follow-up on responses to our recommended solution?

Table 9.6 Sample Outline Using the General Procedural Model for Problem Solving for a Simple Classroom Discussion

I. What sort of final exam would we like for Communication 315?
   A. What is our area of freedom concerning the exam?
   B. What facts and feelings should we consider as we discuss what sort of exam to request?
II. What are our criteria in deciding upon the type of exam to recommend?
   A. Learning objectives?
   B. Grades?
   C. Preparation and study required?
   D. Fairness?
   E. Other?
III. What types of exams are possible?
IV. What are the advantages and disadvantages of each type?
V. What will we recommend as the type of final exam?

The General Procedural Model for Problem Solving provides a sequence of major steps and substeps for problem solving based both on the scientific method and extensive research into how groups make high-quality decisions. Procedural outlines based on this model can be tailored to the characteristics of any problem. The model provides for thorough description and analysis of the problem before discussion of possible solutions, listing a variety of proposed solutions before evaluating them, thorough and critical thinking about the possible positive and negative outcomes of every proposed solution before a selection is made, and the plan of action needed to implement the decision is decided. Group decisions can be made by the leader, by the leader consulting with the group, or by the group. Consensus decisions are often superior because groups achieve an assembly effect during discussions. An outline based on the General Procedural Model for Problem Solving can guide discussion of a brief, simple problem, or guide months of research and meetings required for a problem as complex as the failure of space shuttle engines. Groups create an outline of questions and techniques to follow. Examples of such outlines are provided in the chapter.

Review Questions

1. What is the basis for the General Procedural Model for Problem Solving? Why was this basis selected over others?
2. How do groups compare with individuals as solvers of problems for which there is no known best answer?
3. Why is it important to investigate thoroughly and describe a problem before talking about how to solve it?
4. What are the reasons for listing criteria as specifically as possible before evaluating a list of proposed solutions to a complex problem?
5. Describe three ways to reduce a large number of proposed solutions to a few for the group to discuss in detail.
6. How does it help a group to write on a chart arguments for and against each solution?
7. What goes on during each of the five steps of the General Procedural Model for Problem Solving? How can this procedure be adapted and modified into outlines suited to any sort of problem?

Bibliography

Dewey, John. *How We Think*. Boston: D. C. Heath, 1910.

Hall, Jay. "Decisions, Decisions, Decisions." *Psychology Today* (November 1971): 51–54, 86–87.

Hirokawa, Randy Y. "Discussion Procedures and Decision-Making Performance: A Test of the Functional Perspective." *Human Communication Research* 12 (1985): 203–224.

Larson, Carl E., and LaFasto, Frank M. J. *Team Work: What Must Go Right, What Can Go Wrong*. Newbury Park, CA: Sage Publications, 1989.

Maier, Norman R. F. *Problem Solving and Creativity in Individuals and Groups*. Belmont, CA: Brooks/Cole, 1970.

References

1. Jay Hall, "Decisions, Decisions, Decisions," *Psychology Today* (November, 1971): 51–54, 86–87; Jay Hall and W. H. Watson, "The Effects of a Normative Intervention on Decision-Making Performance," *Human Relations* 23 (1970): 299–317; Irving L. Janis, *Groupthink: Psychological Studies of Policy Decisions and Fiascoes*, 2d ed. (Boston, MA: Houghton-Mifflin, 1982); Randy Y. Hirokawa, "Consensus Group Decision-Making, Quality of Decision and Group Satisfaction: An Attempt to Sort Fact from Fiction," *Central States Speech Journal* 33 (1982): 407–415; Lester Coch and J. R. P. French, Jr. "Overcoming Resistance to Change," *Human Relations* 1 (1948): 512–532; and Myron W. Block and L. R. Hoffman, "The Effects of Valence of Solutions and Group Cohesiveness on Members' Commitment to Group Decisions," in *The Group Problem-Solving Process*, ed. L. Richard Hoffman (New York, NY: Prager, 1979): 121.

2. Brant R. Burleson, Barbara J. Levine, and Wendy Samter, "Decision-Making Procedure and Decision Quality," *Human Communication Research* 10 (1984): 557–574.

3. Paul Miesing and John F. Preble, "Group Processes and Performance in Complex Business Simulation." *Small Group Behavior* 16 (1985): 325–338.

4. Hirokawa, "Consensus Group Decision-Making," 407–415; Hirokawa, "Why Informed Groups Make Faulty Decisions: An Investigation of Possible Interaction-Based Explanations," *Small Group Behavior* 18 (1987): 3–29; "Discussion Procedures and Decision-Making Performance: A Test of the Functional Perspective," *Human Communication Research* 12 (1985): 203–224.

5. Carl E. Larson and Frank M. J. LaFasto, *TeamWork* (Newbury Park, CA: Sage Publications, 1989): 27–38.

6. Leonard Berkowitz, "Sharing Leadership in Small Decision-Making Groups," *Journal of Abnormal and Social Psychology* 48 (1953): 231–38.

7. John E. Dewey, *How We Think* (Boston: D. C. Heath, 1910).

8. Among these studies were: John K. Brilhart and Lurene M. Jochem, "Effects of Different Patterns on Outcomes of Problem-Solving Discussion," *Journal of Applied Psychology* 48 (1964): 175–79; Ovid L. Bayless, "An Alternative Model for Problem Solving Discussion," *Journal of Communication* 17 (1967): 188–197; Carl E. Larson, "Forms of Analysis and Small Group Problem Solving," *Speech Monographs* 36 (1969): 452–55; Randy Y. Hirokawa, "Discussion Procedures and Decision-Making Performance," *Human Communication Research* 12 (1985): 203–224.

9. Marshall S. Poole, "Decision Development in Small Groups II: A Study of Multiple Sequences in Decision Making," *Communication Monographs* 50 (1983): 224–225; and "Decision Development in Small Groups III: A Multiple Sequence Model of Group Decision Development," *Communication Monographs* 50 (1983): 321–341.

10. Randy Y. Hirokawa, "Group Communication and Decision-Making Performance: A Continued Test of the Functional Perspective," paper presented at the annual convention of the Speech Communication Association, Boston, 1987; Randy Y. Hirokawa and Kathryn M. Rost, "Effective Group Decision Making in Organizations: Field Test of the Vigilant Interaction Theory," paper presented at the annual convention of the Speech Communication Association, Atlanta, 1991.

11. For example, see Sidney J. Parnes, "Effects of Extended Effort in Creative Problem Solving," *Journal of Educational Psychology* 52 (1961): 117–122.

12. Robert F. Bales, *Interaction Process Analysis* (Reading, Mass: Addison-Wesley, 1950); B. Aubrey Fisher, *Small Group Decisions Making: Communication and the Group Process,* 2d ed. (New York: Harper & Row, 1975); Poole, "Decision Development in Small Groups II."

13. Fisher: 144–157.

14. Poole, "Decision Development in Small Groups II."

CHAPTER TEN

Managing Conflicts Productively

CHAPTER OUTLINE

What Is Conflict?
Myths about Conflict

Groupthink
Symptoms of Groupthink
Preventing Groupthink

Managing Conflict in the Group
Conflict Management Styles
  Avoidance
  Accommodation
  Competition
  Collaboration
  Compromise
Expressing Disagreement
Steps in Principled Negotiation
Breaking a Deadlock
  Mediation by the Leader
  Third Party Arbitration

STUDY QUESTIONS

1. What are three prevailing myths about conflict in small groups?
2. What is groupthink? How does groupthink appear in a small group? How can groupthink be prevented?
3. What are five commonly used conflict management styles and when is it appropriate to use each one?
4. What are the four steps to negotiating principled agreement?
5. What steps can a leader take to help break a deadlock? What can a group do if those steps fail to produce an agreement?

KEY TERMS AND CONCEPTS

Accommodation	Conflict
Avoidance	Devil's Advocate
Collaboration	Groupthink
Competition	Principled Negotiation
Compromise	Third Party Arbitration

In April 1961, a group of Cuban exiles, supported by the United States Navy, Air Force, and CIA, invaded Cuba at the Bay of Pigs.[1] The invasion was a disaster for the Cuban exiles and the United States. Two of the four invading ships were sunk by Cuban Premier Fidel Castro's air force; the other two retreated. Twenty-thousand well-equipped Cuban troops surrounded the invaders. Twelve hundred of the original fourteen hundred exiles were captured and imprisoned. Most of the rest were killed. The decision to invade Cuba is widely regarded as the worst of President John F. Kennedy's administration. The main problem was not just that the invasion failed. After all, any decision, no matter how well conceived, can turn out to be a mistake because of information not known to the decision makers. The problem with the Bay of Pigs decision was that President Kennedy and his advisors should have predicted, *from information available at the time the decision was being made,* that the invasion would fail.

The Bay of Pigs decision was made by a group of intelligent, well-informed policy experts who should have seen the warning signs. Irving Janis' exhaustive study of the decision-making process concluded that these policy experts made several major miscalculations. For example, the American Joint Chiefs of Staff believed that once the invasion was launched Cuban citizens would rise up against Castro in support of the invasion. This support was considered essential to the invasion's success. However, Castro was popular among the Cuban people, who supported *him,* not the invading troops. The few dissidents who *did* support the invasion were quickly jailed. This miscalculation did not represent a failure of American intelligence gathering—Allen Dulles, head of the CIA, revealed after the invasion that he had not expected much support from the Cuban population.

Unfortunately, the intelligence branch of the CIA had not been asked to supply evidence about the *amount of support* the invaders could expect. This important information went unreported. Janis concluded that if Kennedy's policy advisors had shown *any* skepticism about the success of the invasion, the intelligence experts and others would have been happy to share their expertise

Similar to the decision to launch the *Challenger* described in chapter 5, the decision to invade Cuba represents a failure by a decision-making group to think critically. As with the *Challenger* launch, the policy advisors were generally in favor of the invasion. They failed to look for information that might contradict their original biases. Some of the advisors had personal reservations which they did not express during the advisory group meetings. For example, historian Arthur Schlesinger, one of Kennedy's advisors, has said that although he had doubts about whether the invasion could succeed, he did not want to be thought of as a nuisance in committee meetings, so he chose to remain silent. So did others. In other words, the disastrous Bay of Pigs decision represents failure of a group's throughput processes—failure of the advisory group to encourage disagreement and manage conflict effectively during the decision-making process.

In order to make the best decision among possible solutions to a problem, a group must take advantage of the collective thinking skills of the members. When group members think critically, disagreement almost always occurs. Conflict that is expressed and managed appropriately in a group can help members sharpen their thinking and decide wisely. In contrast, unexpressed disagreement contributes to *groupthink,* the term Janis coined to describe the faulty decision-making process employed by Kennedy's advisors. We will discuss the specific elements of groupthink later in this chapter. In addition, we will describe what causes conflict in the small group, how it affects the group, and how it can be managed so that it helps, rather than hurts, a group.

What Is Conflict?

Conflict can range from a simple disagreement to a war. You can observe conflict in a small group when two or more people express incompatible ideas. For example, Marsha suggests that her group present a skit for its presentation, but Silvio feels skits are childish. That conflict must be resolved somehow in order for the group to complete its task of making a class presentation. Most of the conflicts you experience in a group will be disagreements like this one, and disagreements can become heated.

Myths about Conflict

There are a number of commonly-believed myths about conflict that we would like to dispel (see table 10.1).

1. **Conflict is harmful to a group and should be avoided.** We all have seen examples of how conflict can hurt a group. Minor misunderstandings can lead to hurt feelings, and a group may dissolve over a conflict. Clearly, conflict *can* be harmful to a group. However, many of our students see only the harm that can follow conflict. They don't realize that conflict can be beneficial to the group *if it is expressed and managed properly.* As we saw with the Bay of Pigs decision, the failure of decision makers to engage in open conflict contributed to the mission's failure.

   What are some of the benefits of conflict in a group? First, conflict can help a group understand the issues surrounding a decision or problem more completely than if the initial disagreements are not expressed. For example, one of us served on an advisory board for a voluntary organization. The administrative officer of the organization wanted to fire an employee immediately, without issuing a warning or giving the employee a chance to correct the offending behavior. One group member, experienced with personnel laws, disagreed strongly with what appeared to her to be a lack of due process in the proposed dismissal. When the other members of the advisory board understood the legal issues involved with discharging employees before giving them a chance to improve their performance, they agreed to present the employee with a clear set of guidelines and

Table 10.1　Myths about Conflict

Myth 1: Conflict Is Harmful and Should Be Avoided

Conflict can help members understand an issue more clearly.
Conflict can improve group decisions.
Conflict can increase member involvement.
Conflict can increase cohesiveness.

Myth 2: Conflict Represents a Misunderstanding or Breakdown in Communication

Some conflicts occur over differences in values, goals, methods of achieving goals, limited resources.

Myth 3: Conflicts Can Be Resolved if Parties Are Willing to Discuss the Issues

Conflicts over basic values and goals may not be resolvable.
Conflicts over limited resources and methods of achieving goals may be resolvable through
　communication if basic values and goals of the parties are compatible.

expectations to be followed. The willingness to disagree on the part of one group member enabled the others to understand the issue more completely. This type of disagreement illustrates *idea deviance* mentioned in chapter 6.

Second, conflict can improve a group's decision. A logical outcome of members understanding an issue more clearly is improved decision making. In the previous example, the dismissed employee could have sued the organization and the board for arbitrarily firing him. Not only was the decision the board reached fairer than immediate dismissal would have been, it also protected the organization against charges of capriciousness. Instead of dismissal, the board outlined exactly what they wanted him to do, thus clarifying his job duties and giving him the best possible chance to perform effectively. This action produced a much better outcome than the original proposal of the administrator.

Third, conflict tends to increase member involvement and participation. Group discussions can become boring and humdrum, but when a controversy occurs members perk up, pay attention, and voice their opinions. In the previous advisory board example, members who had begun to miss meetings started to come regularly again. Usually such an increase in interest comes whenever members feel their opinions can make a difference in the outcomes of the group.

Finally, conflict can increase cohesiveness. Have you ever had an argument with your boyfriend, girlfriend, or spouse, then observed how close you both feel after you have made up? If so, you have experienced the increase in positive feelings that can occur after a disagreement has been expressed and the conflict resolved. During the time when discharging the employee was being discussed, the advisory board members expressed strong feelings on several sides of the issue. However, after all members had the chance to air their views, the group came to a consensus decision. As consensus emerged, members became closer than ever before. Several members expressed their appreciation to the member who initially spoke up against the firing. They believed that her comments forced the group to anticipate the negative effects of its actions and create a better solution to the problem. Members realized that they could disagree, express themselves in forceful terms, and emerge more united than before the conflict. Secure that the group could withstand such disagreement, cohesiveness increased.

You can see from this discussion that although conflict *can* be harmful to a group, it doesn't have to be. Whether or not a conflict helps or harms a group depends on a number of other factors, including whether or not the conflict is resolvable in the first place.

2. **Conflicts stem from misunderstandings and breakdowns in communication.** Certainly *some* conflicts occur due to misunderstandings and communication failures. One of us chastised a subordinate for not providing a "detailed" outline of a proposal she was planning to submit. The subordinate countered—quite accurately—with the observation that a clear definition of "detailed" had not been provided, and she believed her proposal contained sufficient detail for the purpose. This conflict *did* stem from a failure to communicate clearly and produced a misunderstanding. But conflicts occur for a variety of other reasons, too.

Some conflicts occur when individuals understand each other quite well, but they disagree on basic values or the distribution of rewards. For example, a classroom group trying to come to agreement on whether to recommend the repeal of the *Roe v. Wade* court decision that made abortions legal in the United States was unable to arrive at an answer acceptable to all members. Several members believed that life begins at conception and that abortion is murder. Other members believed that a mother's life should take precedence over the fetus, at least until the fetus reaches a certain stage of development. Each subgroup understood accurately the position of the other subgroup. Misunderstanding and communication breakdown did not occur. However, the two subgroups' differing values and assumptions made agreement impossible.

Other conflicts occur over what goals the group will set, how to achieve those goals, or how the group will distribute limited resources like bonus money or access to computer time. In these cases, although misunderstandings may contribute to the conflict, the underlying reason for the conflict is much more basic than a communication breakdown. Such conflicts often reflect a struggle over power or wealth.

3. **All conflicts can be resolved if parties are willing to discuss the issues.** As you can see from the previous example, not all conflicts are resolvable. Whether or not a conflict can be resolved depends in part on the

underlying reason for the conflict. The conflict over basic values on the abortion question is not resolvable at the present time because it is based on differences in assumptions and values. The two assumptions represented—a fetus is a *person from conception* and has rights equal to that of the mother *versus* a fetus *becomes a person* sometime after conception, until which time a mother's rights take precedence—are not reconcilable. Both cannot be true simultaneously. A group experiencing such a conflict will not be able to come to consensus on a policy regarding abortion.

Conflicts that occur over scarce resources are also difficult, if not impossible, to resolve. For example, one of us serves on a library committee with representatives from many areas of the school. Meetings to distribute fairly the limited money available are usually full of argument and acrimony. Full agreement is rarely possible. Even members who acknowledge that one area deserves more money for books may vote against that proposal if it means their areas will receive less money. The problem, recognized by all members of the committee, is the fact that limited funds are available to support the legitimate requests of all areas.

Conflicts over goals can sometimes be difficult to resolve as well. For example, assume that you want an *A* on your group project and someone else is satisfied with a *C*. If you can't convince the other person of the value of striving for excellence and the other person can't persuade you to lighten up, you won't be able to resolve this conflict. If your goal of receiving an *A* is very important to you, you may end up having to do a lot of extra work on the project—yours *and* the other person's.

Conflicts over how to reach goals are sometimes easier to resolve than other types, especially if the basic values of the individuals are similar. In the project grade example, if you and the other member both want to get *A's,* but you prefer to show a movie and the other member prefers a skit, you may be able to come to a compromise or find a third alternative that satisfies you both. Because your basic values and goals are the same, you are more likely to see each other as allies, not enemies, which makes it easier to resolve the conflict.

Groupthink

By now you should recognize that conflict can help a group perform its best. Sometimes, though, it is not easy for members to express their disagreement with fellow group members. This is especially true in highly cohesive groups where a disagreement can be seen as disloyalty and a disagreeing member as a wet blanket on the group's plans. **Groupthink** refers to the tendency of cohesive groups *not* to examine critically all aspects of a decision or problem the group is considering.[2] Groupthink represents a specific failure in the group's critical thinking process—the failure to express doubts, disagreements, and conflict within the

Groupthink. (© 1987 King Features Syndicate, Inc. World rights reserved. Reprinted with special permission of King Features.)

group. As a result, the group's decision is flawed because it is made with partial information that has not been examined carefully. Although members may privately have their doubts about the group's decision, they keep their reservations to themselves. Thus the group is deprived of the full benefit of members' opinions and reasoning. The process leading to the Bay of Pigs decision is an example of groupthink because, as Arthur Schlesinger wrote, members failed to express their reservations.

Symptoms of Groupthink

Groupthink is most likely to occur in highly cohesive groups under pressure to achieve consensus. Here are three important symptoms to help you spot groupthink, followed by suggestions for preventing groupthink (see also table 10.2).

1. **The group overestimates its power and morality.** Group members believe their cause is right and assume that nothing can go wrong with their plans. For example, President Kennedy's advisors believed that the Cuban people wanted liberation from Castro. The advisors did not imagine that the Cuban people would prefer communism to democracy. This assumption was an important one upon which several of the invasion plans rested, but the advisors neglected to determine whether or not it was true. The belief, in fact, was completely in error.

Table 10.2   Symptoms of Groupthink

The Group Overestimates Its Power and Morality

Group believes its cause is *right.*
Members convince themselves they cannot fail.

The Group Becomes Closed-Minded

Group is selective in gathering information; chooses only information that supports its predisposition.
Group is biased in evaluating information.
Group excludes or ignores members and outsiders who seem to hold opposing views.

Group Members Experience Pressures to Conform

Members censor their own remarks.
Members who voice contradictory opinions receive pressure from other members to conform.
Members have the illusion that the group opinion is unanimous.

It is not just government policy groups who overestimate their power and the rightness of their causes. Many student groups we have observed have fallen into this trap as well. Sometimes we have seen classroom groups become so excited about one creative aspect of their performance that they ignore the rest of the presentation. For example, the members put all their efforts into preparing a lively skit but leave out key information relevant to their topic. However, they convince themselves that the presentation will be well received by the teacher: "She'll love it. No one else has tried anything like it. I just *know* we'll get an A." We have observed this behavior in meetings of a Board of Regents, a manufacturing company board, a university administration, a management group of a nuclear power plant, and many other situations.

2. **The group becomes closed-minded.** The group members have a preferred course of action and ignore any information that contradicts their preference. In the Bay of Pigs decision, group members (including President Kennedy) were predisposed in favor of carrying out the invasion for a variety of political reasons. Information that should have served as a warning was ignored if it contradicted the invasion plans. For example, Kennedy's advisors ignored intelligence reports about the strength of the Cuban air force and ground troops and the efficiency of the Cuban government. Closed-minded people are biased in their evaluation of information. Instead of looking open-mindedly at all relevant information, group members consider only information that supports their beliefs.

In a more ordinary example, one of us served on a faculty committee that recommended several major changes in the department's curriculum. The committee downplayed information about how upset some department members would be with the proposed changes: "Oh, it won't be a major problem." In fact, the proposed changes caused an uproar that could have been avoided if committee members had sought out disagreements to begin with instead of listening only to their own opinions, all of which supported the changes.

3. **Group members experience pressure to conform.** Group members experience both internal and external pressures to go along with the group. These pressures show up in several ways. First, members censor their own remarks without apparent pressure from other members. When all the other members of a group favor a certain course of action, most people are hesitant to express their doubts. Recently one of us served on an advisory board for a church. The board was in the process of making a very poorly thought-out decision. Your coauthor *knew* the decision had not been carefully made, but, as the only board member opposed to the action, hesitated for a long time before speaking out. This is quite natural—you want the people in your group to like and respect you, and you don't want to appear like someone "popping others' balloons." So, self-censorship often prevents conflicting opinions from reaching the group, to the detriment of the group's problem-solving process.

Second, a member who *does* voice a contradictory opinion is likely to be perceived as deviant and receive overt pressure from the group. Recall from chapter 6 that groups are uncomfortable with deviants (even idea deviants) and pressure them to go along with the group. During the Bay of Pigs decision, Robert Kennedy, brother of President Kennedy and one of his advisors, stopped Arthur Schlesinger from voicing his doubts about the invasion by telling Schlesinger that the president needed his support and loyalty, not his doubts and fears. This friendly warning, delivered at a social occasion, was effective in silencing Schlesinger's objections. Typically, groups will joke and tease other members to bring them into line with the rest of the group: "Why are you being such a worry wart, Pham? The rest of us think it's a great idea!" Usually, Pham will get the message and will join the bandwagon of support without expressing his reservations. Apparent "consensus" to avoid conflict comes at the cost of many poor decisions.

Finally, because self-censorship and group pressure operate to suppress disagreement and doubt, the group experiences the illusion that members unanimously support the decision or proposal. Assuming that the whole group must be in accord, the group proceeds to carry out the decision without testing to see whether the consensus is genuine. What *appears* to be an agreement may have little support from some individual members.

Preventing Groupthink

There are a number of steps you can take to prevent groupthink from occurring (see table 10.3). Here are suggestions for both leaders and members.

Table 10.3   Preventing Groupthink

Establish a Group Norm of Critical Evaluation

Encourage members to express disagreement.
Encourage critical thinking rather than the appearance of harmony.
Assign a devil's advocate to argue against popular proposals.
Leader must accept criticisms of his/her ideas open-mindedly.

Leader Should Not State Preferences at the Beginning of a Group's Session

Let other members express opinions first.
Offer an opinion only as another alternative (not *the* alternative) to be considered.
Encourage the group to meet without the designated leader present.

Prevent Insulation of the Group

Invite outside experts to present information.
Discuss tentative decisions with trusted outsiders to get an unbiased reaction.
Be alert to information that contradicts the prevailing opinion of the group.

1. **Establish a norm of critical evaluation.** The most important thing a group leader and other members can do to prevent groupthink is to establish a group norm to evaluate carefully and critically *all* information and reasoning. Such a norm can offset the proven human tendency to ignore or reject information that contradicts one's existing beliefs and values.

   In addition, it is helpful to develop a norm promoting members' expressions of all disagreements. If a group emphasizes getting along instead of critical thinking, members will feel hesitant to disagree. A norm supporting the expression of doubts and disagreements makes it okay for members to be in conflict with each other; then they can express doubts and challenge each other's evidence and reasoning.

   Another way of encouraging honest disagreements is to assign the role of *devil's advocate* to one or more members of the group. A **devil's advocate** is a person who has been assigned the task of arguing against a popular proposal. Thus, this person serves as an "official" idea deviant because the devil's advocate helps spot potential flaws in a plan or holes in arguments. If Josie agrees to be the group devil's advocate for a particular meeting, it is unlikely the other members will take her criticisms personally.

   It is extremely important that the norm of critical evaluation be supported by the leader's behavior. One of us worked on a staff with a boss who asked staff members to identify any problems we saw with a plan he had devised to improve the working environment. Taking the boss at his word, a couple of staff members began to question various elements of the plan. As they spoke, the boss became defensive, minimized their concerns, defended his proposal, and appeared to view the questioning members as disloyal. Soon the rest of the members became silent without voicing their objections to the plan. We concluded the meeting with the boss thinking the staff supported the plan, although we did not. In the future, whenever the boss asked for honest reactions to proposals he favored, no one was willing to go on the "hot seat" by expressing a criticism. Remember, what you do speaks louder than what you say!

2. **Leaders should not state their preferences at the beginning of a group's decision-making or problem-solving session.** One important source of groupthink is a strong or charismatic leader's preference. This was a factor in the Bay of Pigs decision. President Kennedy clearly favored the invasion and expressed his views at the beginning of the talks. The other members, who all admired him and wanted his respect, were hesitant to speak up against the invasion because they didn't want to appear disloyal. Thus, the presence of a strong, opinionated leader inhibited dissent and contributed to groupthink. Even if you don't have Kennedy charisma, when you are the group's leader you do have a position of power that may make it difficult for other members to disagree with your stated preferences.

In addition to not stating your preferences at the beginning of a group's discussion, consider asking the group to meet without you, especially if you are the supervisor rather than an elected chair. If you suspect that your presence or personality inhibits the group members from saying what they really feel and think, then schedule one or two meetings where you do not attend. This will make it easier for other members to express their opinions freely.

3. **Prevent the insulation of the group.** Groupthink often occurs when group members become so cohesive and so caught up in their own ideas that they become insulated from external opinion and expertise. In the Bay of Pigs decision, some experts on Cuba who had information relevant to the invasion plans were not consulted by the National Security Council. If they had been consulted, the Council might have scrapped the invasion and searched for a different way of dealing with Castro. Even ordinary groups can become insulated. The faculty committee mentioned earlier worked for an entire year developing a sweeping proposal to alter the school's curriculum. Members carried each other along with their enthusiasm for a shared vision. However, when the proposal was presented, it was greeted with dismay by other faculty members. The group had insulated itself from relevant external opinion. As a result, members misjudged how the rest of the faculty would react to their proposals. On the other hand, a faculty Constitution Committee to which one of us belonged did exactly the opposite. This committee sought out external opinions and conflicting views. Members then incorporated suggestions into the plan, which was overwhelmingly adopted by the faculty.

Leaders and members of the group can offset this tendency in several ways. They can encourage members to present tentative decisions to trusted associates outside the group, then report back to the group with the feedback. They can hold public hearings where any interested person can speak on the issues facing the group, such as zoning commissions do regularly. They can also arrange for outside experts to talk to the group. Most important, they can be alert themselves for any relevant information from outside the group. Instead of protecting the group from outside influence, they should ask repeatedly, "What objections might other people have to this proposal?"

Managing Conflict in the Group

Conflict is inevitable when people must reach decisions together and the value of expressing disagreement in a group is obvious. Trying to squash conflict does not eliminate it—it just sends it underground. But it is *also* true that conflict, if managed inappropriately, can *hurt* a group. In this next section we will discuss how to manage conflict productively.

Conflict Management Styles

There are many different ways of describing how people manage conflict. Several authors have different names for similar styles. The five styles we will discuss were described by Kenneth Thomas.[3] Whatever style an individual chooses is based upon the answer to two questions: (1) How important is it to satisfy your own needs? and (2) How important is it to satisfy the other person's needs? Figure 10.1 shows how these two dimensions intersect to produce the five common conflict management styles of avoidance, accommodation, competition, collaboration, and compromise. Table 10.4 gives examples of statements illustrating each style. *There is no one conflict style best to use in all circumstances.* Just as with leadership styles, the most appropriate conflict style depends upon the situation. Factors to consider include how important the issue is, how serious the consequences are if the group makes a mistake, whether the group is under any time pressure, and how important it is that the relationship between the conflicting parties be maintained. In most groups, preservation and enhancement of the relationship among the members is important. This means that conflict management styles incorporating the legitimate needs of all parties are preferable to those producing winners and losers.

Avoidance

Avoidance occurs when any group member chooses *not* to disagree or to bring up a conflicting point. It is the basis of groupthink. We have already talked about the dangers of avoiding conflict, but now we'd like to point out that the avoidance style is *sometimes* appropriate. If the issue is not very important and you are certain that the group's decision will not be hurt by your refusal to speak up,

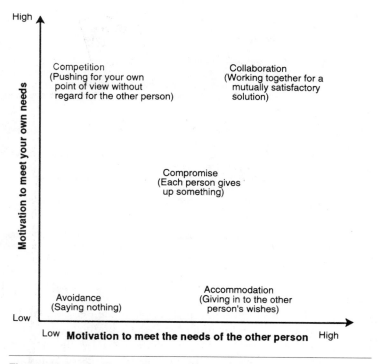

High

Motivation to meet your own needs

Competition
(Pushing for your own
   point of view without
   regard for the other person)

Collaboration
(Working together for a
   mutually satisfactory
   solution)

Compromise
(Each person gives
   up something)

Avoidance
(Saying nothing)

Accommodation
(Giving in to the other
   person's wishes)

Low

Low   **Motivation to meet the needs of the other person**   High

Figure 10.1   Conflict management styles. (Adapted from K. Thomas,
"Conflict and Conflict Management," *Handbook of Industrial and
Organizational Psychology*. Ed. by Marvin D. Dunnette, 1976. Used by
permission of Marvin D. Dunnette.)

avoidance of a possible conflict is appropriate. For example, one of us served on
a committee that was planning a banquet. The rest of the members favored a
different restaurant from the one your coauthor preferred. Both restaurants were
comparable in price, service, and atmosphere. Making an issue over this would
have been silly because there was no risk of making a serious mistake. This was
not an important enough issue to argue about.

Accommodation

Accommodation (also called "appeasement" or "giving in") occurs when one
person or faction gives in to the other without arguing strongly for a different
point of view. You should be honest with yourself if you choose to accommodate. Don't give in if the issue really *is* important to you. If you give in but
privately resent it, then you are likely to find yourself in the future arguing with
the other person for no apparent reason. This will hurt the group in the long run.
On the other hand, if the issue is not crucial to you but you know it *is* important

Table 10.4   Statements That Illustrate the Five Conflict Management Styles

Mary, the college financial director, wants the snack shop to close at 5 P.M. Roger, the evening student counselor, wants it to stay open until 8 P.M. Here are examples of how Roger might respond to Mary, using each of the conflict management styles discussed in the chapter:

	Mary:	We'll have to close the snack shop at 5. There isn't any money to keep it open later.
(Avoidance)	**Roger:**	[Says nothing; accepts Mary's statement.]
(Accommodation)	**Roger:**	I'd really like to keep it open, but if there's no money, I guess there's nothing else we can do.
(Competition)	**Roger:**	I won't accept that! We can't let the evening students down that way. Cut something else to get the money!
(Compromise)	**Roger:**	I would accept keeping it open just until 6:30 if you could cut some money from another program.
(Collaboration)	**Roger:**	I understand that it's necessary to contain costs. It's also important to serve evening students. Is there some way we can provide them food service without increasing costs?

[This was an actual problem faced by a student services committee. The solution? Provide vending machine service. This maintained constant labor costs, but gave students food service after 5:00 P.M.]

to the other person, then accommodation is appropriate. For example, a faculty/ student committee was charged with redecorating a student lounge. The chemistry professor did not like the color scheme recommended by the art professor and said so, but since the students liked it, the chemistry professor willingly accommodated their preferences. This is an appropriate use of accommodation to resolve conflict.

Competition

Competition, sometimes called the "win-lose" style, occurs when you fight hard to win and you don't care whether the other person is satisfied with the solution or not. Most of the time, highly competitive ways of handling conflict are harmful to a group. If one person tries to impose his or her will on a group, the other members will probably fight back. Competitive tactics often escalate a conflict, especially when people stop listening to understand each other. Each side tries harder and harder to force the other side to go along. Recently one of us attended an advisory board meeting where one member, Sherman, argued strongly for one solution to a particular problem. Two members disagreed with Sherman, who then began to use a variety of tactics to win the argument, starting with persuasion but moving quickly to attempted coercion and intimidation. Sherman's behavior indicated that he was more concerned about winning the argument than preserving the group. The visible conflict ended when the rest of the group reacted negatively to the intimidation tactics by voting against Sherman's suggestion.

When a group is doing something you believe is harmful, wrong, or against your values and beliefs, then competition is absolutely appropriate. You should not accommodate or avoid conflict if you think your basic values are being compromised or if you think the group is about to make a major mistake (as in the *Challenger* or Bay of Pigs cases). Remember, though, that if a conflict is resolved with one person winning and others losing, often the hurt feelings will damage teamwork in the future. You are better off to search for an alternative everyone can accept, if that is possible.

Collaboration

Collaboration, the *win-win* style of conflict management, occurs when the people in the conflict want to meet opposing parties' needs along with their own needs. Like competition, collaboration assumes individuals may argue strongly for their points of view. Unlike competitors, collaborators take care not to attack each other as people or to say or do anything that will harm the relationship. Instead, they invest a great deal of energy searching for a solution that will completely satisfy everyone. For example, during the Camp David talks it was obvious that both the leaders of Israel and Egypt wanted possession of the Sinai desert, which Israel had captured from Egypt during the Six-Day War. But the heads of each country were interested in satisfying each other's interests, too, so that lasting peace between Egypt and Israel could be established. Egypt wanted its ancestral lands returned and Israel wanted a buffer zone next to its border to protect it from a surprise attack. A collaborative solution was created whereby Israel would return the Sinai to Egypt but the Sinai would remain a demilitarized zone. This solution satisfied both parties—Egypt got its land back and Israel protected its border.[4]

You may be thinking that collaborative solutions are ideal for groups because they attempt to preserve relationships among conflicting parties while members hammer out mutually-acceptable solutions. However, collaborative solutions often require a great deal of time and energy, which groups don't always have. Not all decisions are important enough for the group to commit the time or energy to create a collaborative solution. And if basic values or assumptions differ, or trust is lacking, collaboration may be impossible.

Compromise

Compromise represents a middle-ground conflict management style that can be called a partial-win/partial-lose solution for each party. Unlike the collaborative style, parties using the compromise style give up something in order to get something in return. This type of horse-trading is typical of labor-management and government bargaining: "I'll settle for a $1-per-hour raise instead of $2 if you will agree to give up the demand for mandatory overtime," or "I'll vote for your bill if you support my amendment." If you know you are going to have to compromise,

"And this is the loyal opposition."

The right way to view someone who disagrees with you. (Drawing by Mankoff; © 1989 The New Yorker Magazine, Inc.)

you will be tempted to inflate your original demands. For instance, if you know you will have to settle for less money than you want, you'll ask at first for a higher figure than you really need.

Although there may be problems with using a compromise conflict management style, we believe it is appropriate for many conflicts. For example, when collaboration is impossible due to time pressures or differences in values, compromise may represent the best option available. Compromise solutions are partial solutions in the sense that each party does not receive completely what it wanted to begin with. However, if what each party had to give up seems balanced and the solution appears *fair* to all sides, then compromise can work quite well. *We cannot emphasize too strongly how important this concept of fairness is.* A compromise can work only if all parties *feel* the solution is fair, and that no one has *won*. But one party cannot assume to know what the other party will feel is fair. Instead, both parties should explain honestly what they believe is fair, and these individual conceptions of fairness should be included as absolute criteria by which to evaluate the final decision.

Expressing Disagreement

It should be apparent that *how* you express your disagreement with another group member has a major bearing on how the conflict will be resolved. We discussed earlier the importance of expressing your disagreements openly rather than keeping them to yourself (see table 10.5). However, there is an art to disagreeing. Even the most accurate and valid concern can be expressed so insensitively that the most rational of group members becomes defensive rather than open-minded. The following suggestions should help you express disagreements without damaging the relationships between you and other members.

1. **Express your disagreement.** As we have noted several times already, a disagreement has no chance whatsoever of helping a group if it is not expressed. An unexpressed disagreement does not disappear—it goes underground, to resurface in inappropriate ways. Avoiding a conflict may be only a temporary "solution" because the group is likely to later experience conflict over what seems to be a trivial issue. Issues can pile up so that eventually a large blow-up occurs when instead each issue could have been handled individually as a managed conflict. Try to keep in mind the principles that disagreements can help a group arrive at the best possible decision or solution, and that failure to express disagreements can lead to groupthink.

2. **Express your disagreement in a timely way.** Recent research demonstrates that *when* you disagree may be just as important as what you say.[5] When group members approach a deadline, they are less tolerant of a member who introduces a dissenting opinion. This suggests that you should express your doubts and disagreements early during the discussion. If you save them for later, when the rest of the members are ready to achieve closure, they will not thank you and probably will not heed your concerns.

3. **Express your disagreements with sensitivity toward the rest of the group.** One way to express your disagreement appropriately is to disagree with the idea, or parts of the idea, without criticizing the person. Suppose you have just suggested that your campus shut down its snack bar at 5:00 P.M. to cut costs. Which response would you rather hear: "That's stupid! What are the evening students supposed to do, starve?" or, "One problem I see is that your suggestion does not consider the needs of evening students for food service." The first response implies that the speaker is stupid, arouses defensiveness and cuts off further examination of the issue. The second response describes a major problem with the suggestion but leaves room for discussion regarding how to cut food service costs. The second response is helpful, the first is not. If you were the original speaker, you would hesitate to offer any further suggestions if somebody called *your* idea stupid.

Table 10.5   How to Disagree Productively

Express your Disagreement

Failure to express doubts and disagreements deprives the group of potentially valuable information and reasoning.
Express your disagreement in a timely way. Don't wait until the deadline is near to speak.

Express Disagreements with Sensitivity toward Others

Disagree with the idea, but do not criticize the person.
Use neutral, not emotionally charged, language.

React to Disagreement with a Spirit of Inquiry, Not Defensiveness

Ask for criticism of your ideas and opinions.
Show you are interested in the other's opinion by listening actively and sincerely.
Clarify misunderstandings that may have occurred.

Another way to show your sensitivity is to use neutral instead of emotionally-charged language. Name-calling or otherwise pushing people's emotional buttons is never helpful. One of us recently attended a meeting where one member, John, who disagreed with another member, Janos, made a snide play on words using Janos' last name. Naturally, Janos was offended and the atmosphere remained tense until John apologized. Disagreeing by making fun of others does *not* improve the group's decision-making process. Steer clear of words that you think might be offensive—be rhetorically sensitive.

4. **React to disagreement with a spirit of inquiry, not defensiveness.** Whether you are the group's leader or just a member, you have a lot of power to determine the atmosphere in your group. When someone disagrees with you, if you show that you are interested in what the other member is saying and the reasons he or she has for disagreeing, you are sending the right message to the rest of the group. Even if the disagreement was expressed poorly, you do not have to let someone else's insensitivity determine your reaction. Listen actively to the person who disagrees, make sure that person has understood your position accurately, clarify any misunderstandings that may have occurred, and show that you are willing to work together to find the best possible solution. For example, Kareema's committee had worked for several months on a proposal to change the criteria for promotion in her department. A new member, appointed to the committee to replace someone who had left the department, questioned the committee's preliminary investigation, saying, "I don't see how that's going to work. Seems to me you'll have more problems than you had before." Although Kareema *felt* defensive, she reacted calmly and asked, "Derek, what problems do you see with the proposal?" Derek explained his concerns, several of which uncovered problems Kareema's committee had

overlooked. The committee revised the proposal to accommodate Derek's concerns. The final proposal was now much stronger and was overwhelmingly approved by the rest of the department. Examples like this show how you can make disagreement and conflict work *for* your group rather than against it.

In addition to knowing how to express disagreements appropriately, group members also need tools to help them arrive at fair solutions. One such technique for managing serious intragroup conflict is named *principled negotiation*.

Steps in Principled Negotiation

Each member of the group, along with the group's leader, is responsible for helping manage the conflicts that arise within the group. However, even though you may want to resolve a conflict effectively, you may not know how to proceed. The following helpful steps are suggested by Fisher and Ury in their book *Getting to Yes: Negotiating Agreement without Giving In.*[6] Following these suggestions will help a group engage in **principled negotiation,** a conflict management procedure that encourages people to search for ways of meeting their own needs without damaging their relationships with others (see table 10.6).

1. **Separate the people from the problem.** Sometimes conflict can produce such strong emotions that people cannot be objective. What may start out as a disagreement about how to get something done becomes a personal declaration of war in which combatants try to hurt each other. Therefore, it is very important to separate the people from the issues. Remember that people believe and act in ways that make sense to them. Try not to take disagreement personally. Usually, it is not directed at you, but it is the result of strong beliefs that someone else holds. For example, the administrative headquarters of a church one of us belongs to recently experienced serious conflict among administrators. Members on both sides of the fence began to talk about the other side as *the enemy.* After several long sessions with a trained mediator, people on each side began to listen carefully to those on the other side. Each side learned that the other side cared deeply about the issues; they also realized that they shared many concerns. Eventually the conflict was resolved and the bad feelings healed. This occurred in part because both sides demonstrated that they cared about each other, and because they focused on the *issues* that divided them rather than personalities.

2. **Focus on interests, not positions.** Often group members are tempted to stake out positions from which they cannot be budged. If Roger says, "I insist that we keep the snack bar open in the evening," and Mary says, "We have to close the snack bar in the evening to save money," there is no way to reconcile those positions. They are incompatible, and the harder the

Table 10.6 Steps to Principled Negotiation

Separate the People from the Problem

1. Allow people to vent their emotions.
2. Deal with the issue separately from the people.
3. Do not personalize the issue.

Focus on Issues, Not Positions

1. Look for the reasons behind the positions people adopt.
2. Acknowledge people's interests as legitimate.
3. Look for ways to reconcile opposing interests.

Invent Options for Mutual Gain

1. Do not accept the options the conflicting parties give you as the only possible options from which to choose.
2. Look for creative solutions that combine the parties' interests.

Use Objective Criteria

1. Look for criteria that both parties accept as valid.
2. Encourage parties to suggest criteria they believe are fair.
3. Propose criteria if parties have not suggested them.

individuals cling to them, the more difficult it will be to resolve the conflict. Remember, though, that people stake out positions for reasons that seem good to them. It is the *reasons* for the positions (personal interests) that should be the focus of the negotiation. In our earlier example, Mary is interested in saving the campus money while Roger wants to make sure the evening students are provided with food service. *Both are legitimate interests.* One way to resolve them is to close the snack shop at 5 P.M. (thereby saving on labor and utility costs) but provide vending machines with a variety of sandwiches and snacks. In this way, the legitimate interests of each individual are served. In fact, this was a real-life example that faced a student services committee to which one of us belonged, and this was exactly how the conflict was resolved.

3. **Invent new options for mutual gain.** As the previous example illustrates, groups members should become creative at inventing alternatives. A number of techniques, such as brainstorming, are designed to help groups become more inventive. If the student services committee had assumed that there were only two available options—keeping the snack shop open past 5 P.M. or closing it—members could never have resolved the issue. The same student services committee later resolved a similar issue with the bookstore by inventing a solution which was not apparent when the committee first began to discuss the issue. Like us, you can probably remember other examples where a group was able to invent a *new* option that met everyone's interests.

4. **Insist on using objective criteria.** A great deal of wasted time can be saved if members use criteria they agree are fair and appropriate for judging among solutions. For example, the *Bluebook* establishes a price range that helps both used car buyers and sellers determine the fair price for a car. You may want $10,000 for your fifteen-year-old Chevette, but both you and potential buyers know that you won't receive such an inflated price. Using prices supplied by the *Bluebook* as criteria allows the negotiation to take place within narrower, more realistic limits.

The same use of objective criteria occurs in other situations, too. For example, one of us serves on a church finance committee charged with reviewing salaries and recommending adjustments. The salaries for the organist and choir director had not been reviewed in several years. The committee did not know whether these salaries were reasonable or not. A phone call to the local Council of Churches director provided information about how much organists and choir directors with comparable responsibilities received at other churches of similar size. This gave reasonable guidelines to the finance committee. When the finance committee presented the recommendations to the full board of directors, their recommendations were easy to defend because of the objective criteria they had used. This approach is often used in labor-management negotiating or in contract pricing.

Breaking a Deadlock

Even with the best of intentions, sometimes a group becomes deadlocked when it tries to resolve a conflict. There are a number of options groups can try if that happens. We will discuss two options here: mediation by the leader (see table 10.7), and arbitration by an objective third party. We recommend that groups try to resolve their own conflicts first before bringing in an outside arbitrator.

Mediation by the Leader

The leader can play an important and valuable part in helping a group resolve conflicts. The procedure we present here represents a kind of "last chance" process that can help to break a deadlock. It is appropriate for the leader to use *only when the leader is not one of the parties to the conflict*. If the leader has taken sides, it would be better to have another member, one who is trusted and respected by the conflicting parties, lead this procedure. The procedure assumes that before true resolution can occur each party involved in the conflict must first understand what the other party wants. This focus on *interests* is exactly what we suggested earlier in the *principled negotiation* procedure. The steps are as follows:

Table 10.7 Mediation by Leader or Other Trusted Group Member

Presenting the Alternatives

1. Side one presents its position and reasons.
2. Members of opposing side may ask for clarification.
3. Members of opposing side must explain the position to the satisfaction of side one.
4. Side two presents its position and reasons.
5. Members of side one may ask for clarification.
6. Members of side one must explain the position to the satisfaction of side two.

Charting the Alternatives

1. Group leader (or designated leader of this procedure) writes each position on a chart with pros and cons listed.
2. Leader and members look for areas of agreement.

Searching for Creative Alternatives

1. Leader reviews elements shared by both sides.
2. Leader asks members to collaborate or compromise in finding a solution that all can accept. Leader may suggest solutions also.

Resolution: A Consensus Alternative Is Adopted

1. Misunderstandings are uncovered and resolved.
2. Participants realize how much they have in common.
3. A solution is found that all members agree is the best they can all accept (although not necessarily everyone's favorite solution).
4. Group cohesiveness is increased.

---

1. **Presentation of alternatives.**
   a. One person from the first side presents exactly what that side wants and why. While this representative is speaking, the other members *from the same side* may clarify the statements, evidence, and claims. However, the members from the opposing side may say *nothing*.
   b. When the first side is finished presenting its case, members from the opposing side may now *ask* for clarification, restatements, explanations, or supporting evidence, but they *may not* disagree, argue, or propose any alternatives.
   c. A spokesperson for the opposing side is now required to explain the position just presented to the complete satisfaction of all the other group members, both those who originally presented that side and those who disagree. Only when this person has restated the original position to everyone's satisfaction is the group allowed to proceed. Note the requirement to listen actively, as explained in chapter 3. This step helps prevent misunderstandings from contributing to the conflict.
   d. Now a representative from the second side presents that side to the group. As before, members from that same side are allowed to clarify information, but members who disagree are not allowed to speak, except to ask for clarification. The group then follows the paraphrasing step in c.

How might accidents be reduced on National Ave?
Construct an overpass

Pro	Con
Would eliminate accidents, if used	Would be expensive
Would not impede traffic flow	Students might not use it (inconvenience)
Would not take long to complete (compared to underground tunnel)	People might throw things at cars below

Figure 10.2 Example of a chart of pros and cons.

e. If there are more than two sides or two alternatives being presented by various subgroups, then all are presented, clarified, paraphrased, and confirmed in exactly the same way.

2. **Charting the alternatives.**

a. The person designated to lead this particular procedure writes each position on a chalkboard or chart and lists underneath the benefits and advantages claimed by the supporters of each position. Then the leader lists the disadvantages or possible harmful effects of each position. An example of such a chart is shown in figure 10.2.

b. When all positions have been charted, group members look for areas of agreement about any of the statements on the chart. On what, if anything, do all members agree?

3. **Searching for creative alternatives.**

a. The leader reviews all elements of common ground shared by the group members. These include things like shared interest in solving the problem, similar elements in competing alternatives, cohesiveness and a shared sense of the group's history, and so forth. The leader then urges the group members to seek a collaborative solution that all could accept. If the leader has an idea or possible solution, this is the time to propose it.

b. The leader asks the group members to compromise and create an alternative that meets at least the minimum requirements of both (or all) sides of the conflict.

4. **Resolution occurs if and when a consensus alternative is adopted.**
Often this procedure is successful for any of several reasons. For example, it may uncover misunderstandings that interfere with the parties' ability to arrive at consensus. It frequently shows participants just how much they have in *agreement,* so they no longer have to focus on how much they disagree. Group members often find that the group develops increased

Managing Conflicts Productively

cohesiveness and team spirit. However, there will be some conflicts where a consensus or compromise solution cannot be reached with this procedure. In that case, the group may choose to call in an objective third party.

Third Party Arbitration

Third party arbitration occurs when an arbitrator who is not a member of the group is brought in to help resolve its differences. You probably have heard of arbitrators being used in labor-management or legal disputes. Arbitrators work in a variety of ways. Some are empowered to create their own solutions to the conflict, others are required to accept one or the other side, and still others are required to split the difference between the disputing parties. In some cases, called *binding arbitration,* the conflicting parties *must* accept the arbitrator's decision, but in other cases the parties may choose not to follow the arbitrator's suggestions. Sometimes just the threat of bringing in a third party arbitrator is enough to force conflicting parties to negotiate with each other in good faith, if they have not already been doing so. However, participants who accept solutions mandated by a third party arbitrator often feel dissatisfied with the outcome. For this reason, third party arbitration should be proposed only when the leader believes the conflict will remain unresolved without outside help. (Arbitration is a specialized field of its own. It has not been our intent to present detailed information, but rather to suggest an alternative when group-based communication procedures fail.)

Summary

We hope you have an appreciation of the benefits of conflict in the small group. Group decisions, such as the decision to invade Cuba in 1961, may be badly flawed if members are unwilling to express doubts and disagreements. Three common myths about conflict were discussed. One myth holds that conflict is harmful. Although this is sometimes true, it is also true that conflict can help a group understand an issue, improve the group's decisions, increase member involvement, and increase cohesiveness. In addition, while some conflicts are due to misunderstandings, others occur when participants understand each other very well; they simply disagree on basic goals, beliefs, or values. Finally, not all conflicts can be resolved through communication. Those stemming from value differences or competition for scarce resources may not be resolvable by ordinary discussion.

Groupthink refers to the tendency of highly cohesive groups *not* to examine critically all aspects of a decision. Groups experiencing groupthink tend to overestimate their power and morality, become closed-minded and biased in evaluating information, and members experience pressures to conform rather than question prevailing group opinions. Groupthink can be prevented if a group establishes a norm of critical evaluation, if leaders reserve their opinions until *after* others have expressed themselves, and if the group makes a point of seeking opinions and information from individuals outside the group.

Five common conflict management styles include avoidance, accommodation, competition, collaboration, and compromise. Each one is appropriate in certain circumstances. It is usually important for relationships among group members to be preserved. For this reason, we recommend collaboration and compromise, which encourage the group to search for ways to satisfy all participants in the conflict. If parties to conflict remain unsatisfied or believe they have been treated unfairly, the conflict is likely to recur. It is important for group members to express their disagreements constructively by timing their disagreements appropriately, being rhetorically sensitive toward the other members, and reacting to disagreement with a spirit of inquiry and openness.

Procedures were given for *principled negotiation,* where individuals try to meet their needs without damaging their relationships with other group members. These include separating the people from the issues, focusing on the underlying interests behind the positions people take, inventing options that satisfy both parties, and using objective criteria acceptable to all. When a group is deadlocked, a neutral group member can lead the group through a mediation procedure that includes asking each side to present its alternatives while the other side engages in active listening, mapping the alternatives on the board so that all can see the pros and cons, searching for inventive solutions that combine key elements of the alternatives, and seeking a consensus alternative. If a group remains deadlocked, it can invite a third party arbitrator to provide a solution. In summary, conflict can help the group make wise decisions, but only if it is expressed and managed appropriately.

Review Questions

1. Explain three myths about conflict and show how believing each of these myths can hurt a group.
2. Define *groupthink* and give an example from your own experience of a group experiencing groupthink. What might the group have done to prevent groupthink in this instance?
3. Describe five conflict management styles and situations where each is appropriate. From your own experience, give an example of how you have used each of the styles.
4. What advice would you give to someone who wants to express disagreement in a productive way?
5. Describe the principled negotiation procedure and give examples of how you have used (or could have used) each of these suggestions.
6. Describe the steps a group can take to help a group break a deadlock. How are these suggestions related to the concept of *active listening* described in chapter 3?

Bibliography

Fisher, Roger, and Brown, Scott. *Getting Together: Building a Relationship That Gets to Yes.* Boston: Houghton Mifflin, 1988.

Fisher, Roger, and Ury, William. *Getting to Yes: Negotiating Agreement without Giving In.* New York: Penguin Books, 1983.

Janis, Irving L. *Groupthink: Psychological Studies of Policy Decisions and Fiascoes.* 2d ed. rev. Boston: Houghton Mifflin, 1983.

Thomas, Kenneth W. "Conflict and Conflict Management." In Marvin Dunnette (ed.), *Handbook of Industrial and Organizational Psychology.* Chicago: Rand McNally, 1976: 890–934.

References

1. The following information about the Bay of Pigs invasion is taken from Irving L. Janis, *Groupthink,* 2d ed. rev. (Boston: Houghton Mifflin, 1983).
2. Janis, *Groupthink.*
3. Kenneth Thomas, "Conflict and Conflict Management," in *Handbook of Industrial and Organizational Psychology,* ed. Marvin Dunnette (Chicago: Rand McNally, 1976): 890–934.
4. Roger Fisher and William Ury, *Getting to Yes: Negotiating Agreement without Giving In* (New York: Penguin Books, 1983).
5. Kruglanski, Arie W. and Donna M. Webster, "Group Members' Reactions to Opinion Deviates and Conformists at Varying Degrees of Proximity to Decision Deadline and of Environmental Noise," *Journal of Personality and Social Psychology,* 61 (1991): 212–226.
6. Fisher and Ury, *Getting to Yes.*

PART FOUR

Special Techniques for Small Groups

Throughout your reading of this book, you have been learning valuable information about how you can improve your participation as a group member. Part Four presents specific techniques you can use to help the groups you belong to. Chapter 11 describes in detail a variety of special group procedures that are easy to use. Each procedure is designed to accomplish a specific objective or overcome a problem in a group. Chapter 12 provides a number of techniques and standardized forms to use when you function as a group's observer. Using these techniques will enhance your value as a group member.

CHAPTER ELEVEN

Group Techniques in Organizations

CHAPTER OUTLINE

Generating Information and Ideas
Brainstorming
Focus Groups
Buzz Groups
Identifying Problems
Problem Census
RISK Technique
Solving Problems and Making Decisions Effectively
Nominal Group Technique
Implementing Group Solutions
PERT
Improving Organizational Effectiveness
Quality Circles
Self-Managed Work Teams
When Members Cannot Meet Face-to-Face
Delphi Technique
Teleconferencing

KEY TERMS AND CONCEPTS

Brainstorming
Buzz Group
Delphi Technique
Focus Group
Nominal Group Technique
PERT
Problem Census
Quality Circle
RISK Technique
Self-Managed Work Team
Teleconference

STUDY QUESTIONS

1. What are three group techniques especially useful for generating information and ideas, and what are the special features of each technique?
2. What are two group techniques useful in identifying organizational problems, and how can they be used?
3. What group techniques can be used to improve organizational effectiveness, and what are the unique features of each one?
4. What techniques are available when members cannot meet face-to-face?

In the late 1980s, an international hotel chain was looking for ways to save money in an increasingly competitive market.[1] Managers asked quality circle members for help. Group members brainstormed, identified areas where they perceived waste, and studied these areas for three months. They discovered the most serious financial losses—over $6000 during the study period—occurred due to unused fruit baskets, especially those on the hotel's two corporate floors. The quality circle members brainstormed again, this time to discover the causes of the waste. They found that many corporate guests with reservations were no-shows, corporate guests were not always assigned to corporate floors, the room temperature was too warm to maintain the fruit, and even when the fruit *was* fresh, guests thought it was not, or thought they would be charged for eating it.

Once the underlying reasons for the fruit basket problem were detected, the quality circle members decided they could reduce the waste by 90 percent. For example, instead of placing baskets in the rooms on the corporate floors in advance, the circle members recommended that the hotel do away with the corporate floors and, as a personalized service, place baskets in rooms only after a corporate guest had checked in. They suggested simple procedures whereby the front desk clerks and room service personnel could coordinate their efforts to ensure that fruit baskets were delivered to the right guests in a timely fashion. During another three month study period to observe the effects of the changes, the quality circle members noted that fruit basket costs were reduced from $6196 to $409.50. In addition, fruit did not spoil because of improvements in the way it was maintained, and guests were pleased with the personalized service.

This true story illustrates two important points. First, the techniques and procedures presented in this chapter are designed to work in ordinary, everyday situations. Many of the examples we have presented in this book have dealt with life or death matters such as the *Challenger* decision, but most of the problems you and we face are less momentous. Even so, our problems are important to us and to the organizations we work for! The group techniques we present here can be helpful no matter how significant the problem. Second, group techniques and procedures may be combined in innovative ways to help organizations of all kinds. In the story we presented, the quality circle and brainstorming procedures were combined. This combination helped the hotel come to grips with its fruit basket problem.

We caution you about two things as you learn about the variety of group procedures available to you. First, *no* technique is a cure-all for every problem that occurs in an organization. For example, quality circles can be helpful and cost effective; however, an organization with a history of mistrust and poor employee relations cannot expect quality circles to solve serious organizational problems. In that case, it would be better to combine quality circles or other group techniques with an appropriate organization-wide development program. Second, for any technique to succeed, systematic advanced planning is required. Some procedures require only a brief explanation before they are introduced to the group, but others (such as quality circle programs) require extensive participant training. Participants must know what they are supposed to do before they begin, what they can expect from any particular group technique, and what the group is supposed to accomplish for the organization. Otherwise, group members will find the procedure to be a boring waste of time. Successful use of group techniques takes planning, participant training, commitment by the organization, and skillful procedural leadership.

In this chapter we present a variety of group techniques and procedures, each designed to accomplish specific objectives. We have arranged the techniques by their major organizational functions, but in fact each of these techniques can be used in a variety of ways. In addition, any technique can be modified or combined with another technique to suit a particular organizational purpose, as we illustrated in the introductory example. We encourage you to use your creativity in applying the procedures we present by adapting them to fit *your* purpose.

Generating Information and Ideas

One of the most important functions groups provide for organizations is to allow members to present information the organization can use. If used properly, groups can supply much more information than can a single individual working alone. Several techniques capitalize on this feature of groups: *brainstorming, focus groups,* and *buzz groups.*

Brainstorming

Brainstorming is a procedure designed especially to release a group's creativity.[2] It is impossible to be creative and critical at the same time, so brainstorming separates the idea-creation from the idea-evaluation process by not allowing any criticism to take place while the group is generating ideas. Later, the group evaluates the ideas, combines or modifies them, and selects the best ones. As you saw with the hotel chain in our earlier example, brainstorming is often combined with other techniques. The basic procedure is as follows:

1. **The group is presented with a problem to solve.** The problem can range from something specific and concrete (How can we get rid of our inventory of last year's car models?) to something abstract and intangible (How can we improve the quality of work life for employees?).
2. **Members are encouraged to come up with as many solutions as possible to the problem.** Several rules must be followed. The most important of these is that NO EVALUATION IS PERMITTED DURING BRAINSTORMING. With judgment and evaluation temporarily suspended, members are encouraged to turn their imaginations loose, to encourage wild and crazy ideas to surface, to build on each other's ideas, to combine ideas, and to strive for quantity.

3. **All ideas are recorded so that the whole group can see them.** Often the group's recorder will write ideas on a large pad of paper. As the top sheet is filled, it is posted on the wall so that all ideas are clearly visible at all times. Visibility of previous ideas often triggers new ideas.

4. **The ideas are evaluated at another session.** Just because brainstorming requires temporarily suspending critical evaluation does not mean that the critical thinking function is unimportant. *After* brainstorming has generated a lot of ideas, critical thinking is employed to evaluate each idea, and to modify or combine ideas into workable solutions to the problem. Figure 11.1 and table 11.1 present a summary of the brainstorming guidelines and a sample list of creative ideas from a brainstorming session.

Sometimes it may be more productive for each person to brainstorm silently rather than openly in a group. In this form of brainstorming, each person quietly tries to think of as many new and different solutions as possible and writes them on a notepad. Then each person's ideas are posted on a chart that everyone can see and members are encouraged to add to the list as new ideas occur to them.

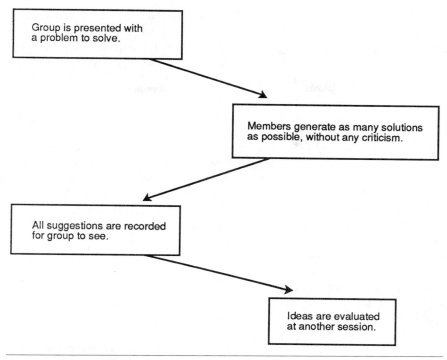

Figure 11.1 Guidelines for brainstorming.

Table 11.1 A List of Students' Ideas Generated by Brainstorming

---

How Can Car/Pedestrian Accidents Be Reduced on National Avenue?

Put up warning signs for traffic that a crosswalk is coming.
Put up a traffic light where the crosswalk is now.
Make traffic slow to 20 since it's a school zone.
Ticket all drivers going faster than 20.
Station a safety patrol to help students cross.
Put in an underpass, like on Grand Avenue.
Build a barrier to prevent students from crossing National Avenue at all.
Use stun guns to stop students from crossing.

Use stun guns on drivers who are going too fast.
Throw thumbtacks on the street so cars will go another way.
Build a giant trampoline so students can jump across without having to walk.
Issue each student a jetpack so they can fly across the street.
Build an overpass so students don't have to cross against traffic.

Frequently our student groups use brainstorming when they want to come up with an innovative class presentation. Knowing that their ideas will not be criticized frees students' inhibitions and allows creativity to surface. This, of course, is the whole point of brainstorming. The technique is widely used by a variety of corporate groups such as advertising agencies, manufacturers, and city councils.

Focus Groups

The **focus group** technique, which encourages unstructured discussion about a given topic, is often used to analyze people's interests and values. In a focus group discussion, the facilitator introduces a topic to the group and instructs group members to discuss the topic any way they choose. The facilitator gives no further direction to the group, but may probe or ask questions. Usually, the group discussion is tape recorded for later analysis. After the group is finished, the facilitator or another researcher listens to the tape for usable ideas.

Although focus groups were originally created within the advertising industry, they have been used in a variety of creative ways by many other types of organizations. For example, when Gloria was a public relations officer at a small campus, she used a focus group to discover more effective ways of scheduling and promoting evening classes. A group of evening students was given instructions simply to talk about what it was like to be an evening student. From the discussion it was clear that evening students were often trying to juggle full-time jobs, families, and other responsibilities in addition to school. The school's schedule was forcing them to come to the campus for four nights a week to complete two courses. But the focus group discussion indicated that the students would be happy to stay later each evening if they could take the same two courses by coming to the campus only two nights a week. Campus officials found a way to "stack" the evening classes to allow this. In addition, the student comments spurred many imaginative ideas for advertising and promoting the evening offerings.

This technique has proved exceptionally adaptable. For example, a beauty parlor owner with management problems used focus groups to discover that employees took little pride in their work because they believed she was playing favorites. When she offered employees a company-wide benefits program and let the stylists have their own business cards, morale improved.[3] In another example, law firms sometimes "pre-try" cases using focus groups. A lawyer will present both sides of a firm's case. The focus group members are tape recorded as they discuss the case. In this way, the lawyer is able to discover in advance the strengths and weaknesses of the case, which evidence is credible and which isn't, and which arguments are, or are not, persuasive. The lawyer can then sharpen the presentation for the audience that counts—the actual jury. Focus groups have been used to investigate customers' feelings about products, reactions to company actions, suggestions for improving morale, ideas for employee activities, and so forth.

Buzz Groups

In the **buzz group** procedure, a large group is subdivided into smaller groups of six people each who discuss an assigned question, then report their answers to the entire larger group. This technique is ideal when you want to encourage participation and involvement but it isn't feasible to have all the people working together in one large group. It also gives everyone the chance to participate. The technique may be used to identify problems or issues, generate questions to be studied, compile a list of ideas or solutions, or stimulate personal involvement. After the facilitator assigns the target question, the large group is split into smaller groups. These groups then discuss the question, record their agreements, and present these ideas or findings to the larger group. The following steps detail this procedure, which is summarized in figure 11.2.

1. **The facilitator presents a target question to the entire large group.** The question is posted in writing so all can see. Examples of concise target questions are: What techniques can we use to publicize the Glover Program to citizens of each county or city? What can be done to reduce parking problems between 9:00 A.M. and 2:00 P.M. on campus? What courses should an accounting student be required to take?

2. **The large group is divided into smaller groups of six each.** The audience in a buzz session may be seated in an auditorium with fixed or movable seats or at tables. If the audience is seated in fixed seats, have them count off by threes in each row, then have people in alternate rows turn in their seats to face each other.

3. **Each group is given a copy of the target question on an index card and a recorder-spokesperson is selected by seating.** For example, the facilitator might say, "The person in each group sitting in the forward left-hand seat will be the recorder." This individual then writes all ideas on the index card.

4. **The group spends six minutes thinking of and evaluating ideas.** First, group members are asked to record as many ideas as they can in five minutes. If the group seems really involved, they may be allowed an extra minute to wrap up the discussion. Then, group members spend one final minute evaluating the items, deciding which to eliminate, and rank ordering the rest. (Because this procedure occurs in groups of six for six minutes it is sometimes called "Phillips' 66" after the man who developed the technique.)

5. **The group then reports its list to the entire assembly.** Reporting the findings can be done in a variety of ways, depending upon the group size and meeting format. One possibility is for the index cards to be collected and edited to remove duplications, and a tally made of how many times each item was mentioned. The overall list can then be duplicated and distributed to the whole group or to a special group for processing. Another

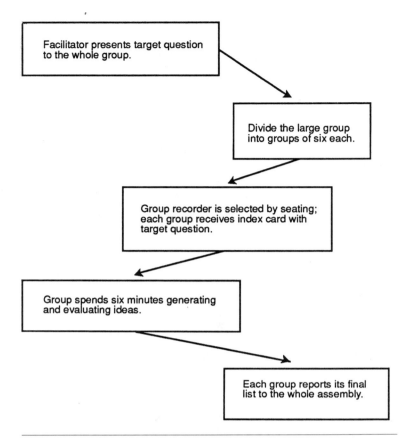

Figure 11.2 Steps for conducting buzz groups.

possibility is for the facilitator to call upon each spokesperson to report orally from the audience by listing one *new* item from the list without explanation until all items are recorded. Someone writes all the items on a chart or board visible to the whole audience.

Many variations of the buzz group technique are possible. It is a useful procedure for discussing policy questions of all kinds. For example, one of us was a participant among 500 educational leaders in Kentucky who were charged with promoting a "minimum foundation program" for public education. This controversial program meant higher taxes and a flow of money from wealthier to poorer districts. Conference organizers were seeking ways of promoting the program within the state. The buzz technique helped identify specific local problems, inexpensive advertising and promotional techniques, arguments for the program, and so forth. Although the conference was large, every participant was involved in the discussion and the enthusiasm was remarkable.

Identifying Problems

There are a number of techniques that are specifically designed to help identify problems with a particular policy or course of action. You will recall that identifying potential negative consequences of a decision is a key factor in effective decision making. Two procedures that will help you do this are the *problem census* and the *RISK technique*.

Problem Census

The **problem census** is a "posting" technique for identifying important problems or issues. It can be used to discover problems encountered by a group of employees or to establish agenda items for future meetings. Sometimes a group leader wants to encourage participation and make group processes more democratic, but doesn't know exactly where to begin. The problem census is ideal for this purpose, because it requires all the members of a group to take responsibility for creating the group's work agenda. Members often become more committed to the group's task because they are enthused about working on items they perceive as important to them. For example, a university department where one of us worked periodically conducted a problem census that became the department's agenda in a series of future meetings. As various departmental problems were listed, different faculty members committed themselves to investigating the problems and preparing an outline for discussing each problem as it came up. Sales staffs frequently use this technique to establish priorities based on what salespeople in the field need. The following are detailed steps for conducting a problem census. These are summarized in figure 11.3.

1. **Seat the group in a semicircle facing a chart or board.**
2. **Explain the purpose of the technique, which is to bring out any problems, concerns, questions, or difficulties any member wants to discuss.**
3. **Ask each participant to present one problem or concern.** This is done in *round-robin* fashion as the first person presents one problem, the second presents one, and so forth. Anyone who does not have a problem to list may pass. This continues until all problems are identified.
4. **Post each problem on a board or chart as it is presented.** As each page of the chart is filled, it is taped to the wall so that all problems are visible at all times. The group's recorder must never challenge or disagree, but may

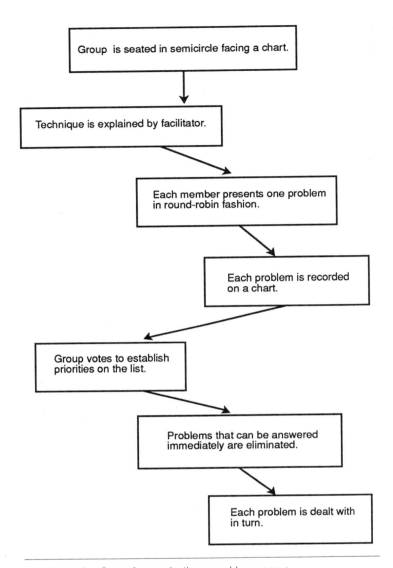

Figure 11.3 Steps for conducting a problem census.

ask for clarification or elaboration. The recorder may have to restate long problems more concisely, but should always ask the speaker whether the rephrasing accurately reflects the speaker's intent.

5. **The group votes to establish priorities on the list.** Usually, each member votes individually for three or four top choices. The items are then ranked from most to least votes received. *All* items remain on the list; voting just prioritizes the agenda.

6. **Problems that can be answered immediately are eliminated.** Sometimes, group members can answer questions or solve problems to the satisfaction of the person who initially presented the problem. Such questions or issues are removed from the list; the others remain for future consideration.

7. **Each problem is dealt with in turn.** Some issues may call for an investigation and report, a lecture, or other informational presentation such as a brochure. Some will require the services of outside consultants. However, major problems should be handled and analyzed by the entire group or a subcommittee, following an appropriate problem-solving procedure.

RISK Technique

The **RISK technique** is designed to help an organization assess how a proposed change or new policy will affect the individuals and groups involved. RISK focuses on possible negative consequences of the proposed change. Suppose you are responsible for implementing a new employee benefits program at your company. Before you start putting the plan into effect, you want to make sure all problems that could come up have been identified and, if possible, dealt with in advance. RISK will help you do this. The steps are presented below and summarized in figure 11.4.

1. **The proposed solution or change is presented in detail and members are asked to think of any risks, fears, or problems they see with the proposal.** Members may generate their list of problems by brainstorming in a group or using the solo brainstorming step of the nominal group technique (explained later).

2. **The problems are posted in round-robin fashion on a clearly visible chart or board.** As with the problem census, it is crucial that the person recording the ideas remain nonjudgmental and accepting. If this doesn't happen, people will be reluctant to mention their *real* concerns and the technique won't work. Once all the initial concerns are posted, the recorder asks members to add to the list. Often, the most serious risks do not surface until the very end of this process.

3. **A master list of risks is compiled and circulated to participants, who are again encouraged to add anything else that occurs to them.**

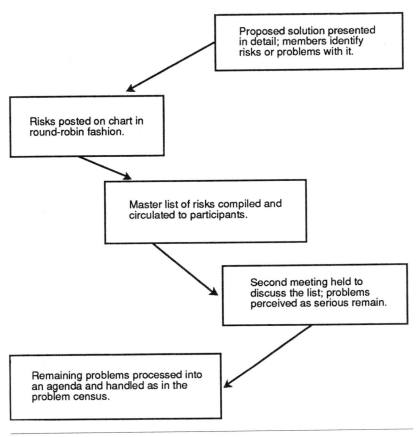

Figure 11.4 Steps for conducting the RISK technique.

4. **A second meeting is held to discuss the list.** First, members are asked to add any additional risks to the list. Then, as each risk is discussed, members decide whether it represents a serious problem or one that can be resolved readily and removed from the list. At this meeting, members should be encouraged to share their feelings, fears, and worries.

5. **The risks remaining on the list are processed into an agenda to be handled in the same way as items from the problem census.**

Solving Problems and Making Decisions Effectively

A major advantage of group over individual problem solving is that several heads can be better than one. But, as we have indicated, capitalizing on that advantage can be difficult. Groups consistently make better decisions when they use systematic decision-making procedures than when they don't. There are a number of procedures designed to foster orderly, methodical decision making. Most of these techniques are based on the belief that before a group can create and select the best alternatives to solve its problem, it must first thoroughly understand the problem. No one technique has been shown to be better than another in helping a group create the best possible solution; what *has* been demonstrated is that using *any* procedure usually produces better decisions than *not* following a procedure. In chapter 9 we presented in detail a framework for organizing problem-solving discussions: the General Procedural Model for Problem Solving. We now present a technique suitable for use during any phase of problem solving: the *Nominal Group Technique.*

Nominal Group Technique

Nominal means "in name only." The **Nominal Group Technique** capitalizes on the finding that sometimes people working individually while in the presence of others generate more ideas than while interacting as a group. In addition, sometimes dominant members inhibit the participation of quieter members. The nominal group technique attempts to get around this potential problem by alternating between solitary work and group interaction. Also, the technique can enable members to reach a decision on a controversial issue without leaving a residue of bitterness from win-lose conflict. For example, one complex organization used the nominal group technique as part of a detailed decision analysis procedure to decide what type of computer system to buy. This organization consisted of many different units and subunits that coordinated work with each other, but also had unique needs that must be satisfied. Making this decision could have created hard feelings among the organizational units, but the nominal group technique helped the organization achieve consensus about the best computer system. Participants were satisfied with both the process and the outcome.[4]

In the nominal group technique, members (usually six to nine) work individually in each other's presence by writing their ideas. Then, members record the ideas on a chart, discuss them as a group, and finally evaluate them by a ranking procedure until members reach a decision. The following steps comprise the process, which is summarized in figure 11.5

1. **The problem, situation, or question is stated clearly and concisely.**
   Elements of the problem or question are described, and discrepancies between what is desired and what currently exists are explained, often by a member of top management. Care must be taken *not* to mention possible solutions. Group members can ask questions to clarify or add information about the problem. If the group is large, it may be subdivided into smaller groups, each with its own facilitator.

2. **The coordinator asks participants to generate a list of the features or characteristics of the problem or question.** Steps 1 and 2 may be combined, with the facilitator presenting the problem and moving the group directly into step 3.

3. **The coordinator gives the group five to fifteen minutes to work silently.** Each person, brainstorming silently, lists on paper as many solutions or answers to the original question as possible.

4. **Each suggestion is recorded on a chart visible to all members.** Suggestions are listed in round-robin fashion. The first person gives *one* item from his or her list and the recorder lists the item on the chart. Then the next person gives one item, and so forth, until the master list is complete. If any additional ideas or items occur to people while the list is being compiled, they should add them to the master list. During this step, no discussion is permitted.

5. **Members clarify the items but do not yet evaluate them.** The group discusses each item on the list, but only to clarify or elaborate upon it. Any member may ask what a particular item means, but arguing, criticizing, or disagreeing are not permitted during step 5.

6. **Each person chooses his or her top-ranked items.** Each person is given a set of note cards on which to write the five items he or she most prefers. These cards are rank-ordered. A rating of 5 is written on the top card, 4 on the next, and so on, and collected by the facilitator. The individual ratings are tallied for each item and divided by the number of participants. The five items with the highest average ratings become the agenda items for the group's discussion.

7. **The group engages in full discussion of the top-rated items.** This discussion should be a freewheeling and thorough evaluative discussion. Critical thinking, disagreement, and exhaustive analysis of the items are encouraged.

8. **A decision is reached.** Often, the discussion in step 7 will produce a consensus decision. If so, the group's work is completed. If not, group members can re-vote on the items and continue their discussion. Steps 6 and 7 may be repeated as often as necessary until support for one idea, or for a combination of ideas, emerges. The decision is then acted upon by the group itself or the parent organization that established the group.

You can see that this technique tries to minimize the disadvantages of group discussion and take advantage of the benefits. By encouraging members to work alone, the stifling effect of domineering members is neutralized, and the tendency for some lazy or shy members to let others carry the ball is minimized. On the other hand, the technique also uses the open discussion that frequently produces well-thought-out group decisions. However, we caution you not to overuse this

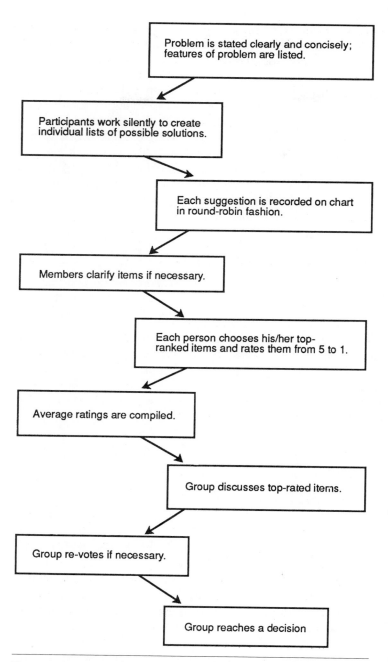

Figure 11.5 Steps for conducting the nominal group technique.

technique when you wish to create a sense of teamwork. The nominal group technique may not create a sense of cohesiveness and sometimes produces lower satisfaction ratings than normal discussion.

Both of us have used this technique, or modifications of it, with great success. One of us employed it to help a major manufacturer identify problems with package instructions for a product and suggest possible solutions for these problems. Recently, we used a modification of the nominal group technique to help plan changes to the communication curriculum. Students were asked first to identify the strengths of the communication major, then to identify the weaknesses. Each list was rank-ordered by the students and used by the faculty to help plan curricular and other departmental changes. In each example, it was not important for the group members providing the information to develop a sense of cohesiveness; thus, the nominal group technique was ideally suited for the situations.

Implementing Group Solutions

The final step in group problem solving is implementing the solution. Sometimes this can be quite a complicated procedure if the solution is a complex one involving many people and numerous assignments. Special techniques can help groups monitor the implementation process.

PERT

PERT (*Program Evaluation and Review Technique*) is a set of concrete suggestions to help a group keep track of who will do what by when. Here are the main points:

1. Determine the final step by describing how the solution should appear when it is fully implemented.
2. List all the events that must occur before the final goal is realized.
3. Order these steps chronologically.
4. For complicated solutions, develop a flow diagram of the procedure and all the steps in it.
5. Generate a list of all the activities, materials, and people needed to accomplish each step.
6. Estimate the time needed to accomplish each step, then add all the estimates to find the total time needed for implementation of the plan.
7. Compare the total time estimate with deadlines or expectations and correct as necessary by assigning more or less time and people to complete a given step.
8. Determine which members will be responsible for each step.[5]

We recommend PERT, or modifications of it, to our students when they work on group projects. Figure 11.6 contains an example of a PERT-like chart developed by a group of students working on a project that involved library research and observation of another group.

Improving Organizational Effectiveness

Most human beings have the need to influence events that affect their lives. Because we spend almost one-third of our time at work, most of us want to participate in decisions that affect our work. We also want the chance to use our creativity and knowledge to improve products, programs, and procedures where we work. Group techniques provide a way for us to participate in many decisions that affect our working lives. Two group procedures that help involve employees in the decision-making loops of their organizations are *quality circles* and *self-managed work teams.*

Quality Circles

A **quality circle** is a small group of employees who meet at regular intervals on company time to discuss work-related matters. They are sometimes called *work effectiveness teams.* If instituted properly, quality circles can improve company effectiveness by increasing worker productivity, identifying quality control problems and possible solutions, and enhancing worker involvement. However, whether quality circles actually do produce these benefits depends a great deal on how well the organization has prepared for the introduction of quality circles, the training the employees have received regarding their own participation, and how much employees trust the organization's management.

Quality circles can be effective, but careful planning is required. In addition, a number of consistent problems have occurred with quality circles. Sometimes unions see them as a ploy to increase production without improving wages or benefits, and thus as a threat to job security. Top managers and stockholders may benefit, but the quality circle members may suffer in the long run. Managers can be threatened if they perceive that suggestions from quality circles sabotage their managerial prerogatives. Quality circle programs stagnate if the company fails to act promptly on all suggestions the groups produce or give sufficient explanation as to why a suggestion is not being implemented, or fails to reward employees for quality circle suggestions. It is extremely important that quality circles *not* be used as a panacea to overcome deep-seated organizational problems or inadequate management. They often work best in conjunction with an overall organizational development program that supports the concept of employee participation. Table 11.2 presents suggestions that improve the probability of having a successful quality circle program.

Date	Aretha	Barney	Candy	Denzil	Group
Tues Apr. 4	Report on Prelim. Observ.		Report on Prelim Obsv.		Decide Which Group to Observe; Decide Variables
Thu Apr. 6		Prelim. Report on Conflict	Prelim. Report on LDSHP	Prelim. Report on roles	Discuss Prelim. Reports; Decide Methods of Analysis
Tues Apr. 11		Complete Lib Research, Conflict	Complete Lib Research, LDSHP	Complete Lib Research, Roles	
Thu Apr. 13		Observe GRP, 8 PM	Observe GRP, 8 PM	Have Materials Ready for Observation; Cont. Analysis; Questionnaire	
Tues Apr. 18		Complete SYMLOG of GRP	Complete SYMLOG of GRP		Meet After Class, Discuss Prelim. Findings
Thu Apr. 20			Observe GRP, 8 P.M.	Observe GRP, 8 P.M. Have Tape Recording Materials Ready	
Tues Apr. 25					Discuss Overall Observations Listen to Tape
Thu Apr. 27		Complete First Draft, Conflict	Complete First Draft, LDSHP	Complete First Draft, Roles	
Mon May 1	Begin Overall Editing/Typing	Final Draft of Conflict, & Intro. Done	Final Draft of LDSHP, & Conclusion Done	Final Draft of Roles, Done	Look at Each Others' Section to Improve Content/Style
Tues May 2					
Wed May 3					
Thu May 4					
Fri May 5	Editing Completed; Typing Done	Tables/Charts To Aretha (Conflict)	Tables/Charts To Aretha (Leadership)	Tables/Charts To Aretha (Roles)	
Sat May 6	Proofing; Make copies			Proofreading Done; Make copies	
Sun May 7	Distribute Copies to All By 8 P.M.	Assemble Full Report By 5 P.M.	Assemble Full Report By 5 P.M.	Make Large Charts for Class Presentation	
Mon May 8		Read Full Paper	Read Full Paper	Read Full Paper	"Rehearsal" at Aretha's House, 7 P.M.
Tues May 9					Final Presentation to Class

Figure 11.6 Sample PERT chart for a student group project.

Table 11.2   Suggestions for Helping a Quality Circle Program Succeed

1. Make sure the CEO and other top managers support the program and are actively involved; these people must serve as appropriate role models and must establish a climate of care and support.
2. Help middle managers see the program as a part of good supervision.
3. Make the program voluntary, but be sure to educate every person in the organization about the program.
4. Provide education and training for participants on how to operate as a group; provide special training for leaders.
5. Narrow the scope of the quality circles to relatively simple problems at first, until the circles develop into mature teams.
6. Involve line personnel and experienced operations people; make them group leaders whenever appropriate.
7. Continue to provide additional training, as needed, to supplement the initial quality circle training.

Quality circles are used by diverse American, foreign, and multinational companies, including Xerox, Procter & Gamble, Westinghouse, Ford, General Motors, Dow Chemical, Paul Revere Insurance Group, and countless others. They can be found in all types of organizations, ranging from manufacturing and service organizations to state governments, to school systems, to voluntary organizations, and sometimes to individual families. Participants may be white collar, blue collar, pink collar, or some combination. Sometimes quality circle participants work on relatively ordinary problems, such as the hotel that wanted to eliminate waste on its fruit baskets. Other times, participants tackle major issues such as how to develop a country's exports.

What do quality circle programs actually *do?* With the procedural guidance of a group leader (who may be a manager or supervisor), the quality circle members meet to discuss work-related problems. Typically, they focus on problems they observe within their own areas of responsibility. For example, a quality circle made up of factory line workers is more likely to focus on how to streamline the assembly procedures than on how to improve the company's advertising message. The group generates lists of problems and identifies possible solutions for them. These problems and solutions are presented to managers by the quality circle leader. In turn, the managers report back to the quality circle regarding how the suggestions were used, or why they were not implemented. Often, quality circle members who propose a cost-saving idea are rewarded with bonuses as well as recognition. Some of the techniques we have presented thus far, including brainstorming and problem census, can be used by a quality circle. Clearly, knowledge of group processes is important for an effective quality circle program.

Self-Managed Work Teams

Self-managed work teams, sometimes called autonomous work groups or modules, are groups of peers who manage their own work schedules and procedures within certain prescribed limits. Members are highly trained and cross-trained—each of them is able to perform several types of tasks for the team. Ed Musselwhite, who has both trained and written about such teams, says that the process is similar to having a team of people building a house: "When you need more carpenters, the painters can put down their brushes and pick up hammers for a couple of hours. Or the carpenter goes and helps the plumber when he's behind."[6] Not only is this efficient, but it also helps workers develop a variety of skills, reduces boredom and frustration. For example, at Volvo, the Swedish auto manufacturer, self-managed teams assemble each car. Team members decide who will perform what job, and the jobs are rotated regularly. Self-managed work teams have been used with great success at such companies as Procter & Gamble, Sherwin-Williams, GM and TRW and, of course, Saturn.

A self-managed work team elects its own leader, who is a coworker, not a supervisor or manager. The leader acts as a coordinator, not a boss. The organization establishes the work group's area of freedom, but often these groups have a great deal of latitude in how they operate. Some work groups establish their own schedules and annual budgets, prepare their own reports, develop specifications for jobs and procedures, solve technical problems that occur in the course of completing jobs, and even prepare bids in attempting to attract new company business. For example, at Executive Offices, Inc., an office furniture manufacturer, the custom-orders team has complete authority to bid jobs under $10,000, custom-design the furniture for the client, and schedule its manufacture. The team originally included a salesperson skilled at pricing, a furniture designer, a craftsperson adept at creating specialized parts, and three skilled assemblers. Now, however, members have cross-trained each other so each knows what the other does. For complex jobs, the whole team goes to the client's offices to listen and offer suggestions. The team's success has made the custom-order portion of the business extremely profitable.[7]

Several of the same concerns exist with autonomous work groups as with quality circles. Middle managers and unions, in particular, can feel threatened by them. Coordinators can act like bosses. However, companies that have instituted such programs report that self-managing work teams give a 20 to 40 percent edge in productivity over more traditional work systems.[8] They require less supervision and surveillance, produce higher quality products, have less lost time, and generally produce high morale and job satisfaction.

When Members Cannot Meet Face-to-Face

Sometimes an organization will need to secure the opinions of employees or members who are widely scattered geographically, or whose varying work schedules make it impossible for them to meet face-to-face. Nevertheless, there are options that a creative manager can use to get group-type information. Several of the techniques we have already presented can be modified so that members never have to meet together in the same place. In addition, two techniques are tailor-made to solve such problems: the *Delphi technique* and *teleconferencing*.

Delphi Technique

Strictly speaking, the Delphi technique is not a group discussion technique at all. However, we present it here because it can help you obtain grouplike information without having to go to the expense of convening a group of geographically distant people. This technique can require a lot of time to complete, so it is not used for urgent problems or crises.

The **Delphi technique** involves presenting a problem or issue to the appropriate individuals, asking them to list their ideas or solutions, compiling a master list, circulating this master list to all participants, and asking them to comment in writing to each item on the list. Often the "comment" is a rating number on a scale of 1 to 7. The list, with comments, is then circulated and participants are asked again to supply their comments. This procedure is continued until a decision is reached. The steps are detailed in the list that follows, and summarized in figure 11.7.

1. **A Delphi panel is selected by the facilitator.** Panel members are generally selected for their expertise, interest, and involvement. Only the facilitator knows who the panel is; identities are kept confidential throughout the procedure in order to minimize the influence of status or personality. You can see that the panel is not a *group* as defined earlier.

2. **The problem or issue is stated concisely in writing and sent to each member of the Delphi panel for individual work.** Examples of problem statements include the following: "How can we reduce the number of course drops and adds during the first week of the semester?" "How can we eliminate waste with the complimentary fruit baskets?" "Why are our competitors able to market innovative products sooner than we do?" and "Why are so many parts installed incorrectly in our cars?" Each member writes down his or her position regarding the issue and sends the written comments back to the facilitator.

3. **The facilitator compiles another document that details all the individual positions taken by the panel and distributes a copy to each member.** Each member may then comment, in writing, regarding the positions taken by the others. In addition, each person may modify his or

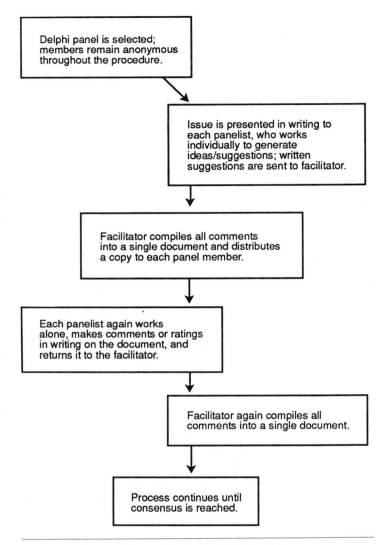

Figure 11.7 Steps for conducting the Delphi technique.

her original position and give reasons for the modifications. The comments are returned to the facilitator. Identities are kept secret; no one knows who made which comments.

4. **This procedure, with the facilitator compiling the individual comments into a single document and distributing it to the group, continues until consensus is reached.** Not only is the Delphi technique useful when members cannot meet, it provides anonymity and therefore minimizes the

differences in speaking skills, status, and personality that can cause problems in face-to-face groups. This makes it easier for members to express themselves honestly and to change their minds without fear of "losing face." In addition, the technique can be modified in a number of ways, or combined with other techniques, to suit specific needs of individual groups and organizations.

Teleconferencing

Ideal for meetings of individuals who are geographically separated, a **teleconference** is an electronically-mediated meeting that can take several forms. In a video conference, participants can both see and hear each other. In an audio conference, which can be as simple as a telephone conference call, participants can hear but not see each other. In a computer conference, participants can send messages that appear on computer terminals. Currently, these techniques vary in expense and usefulness, but as the expense of travel for executives to attend face-to-face meetings continues to increase, even expensive video teleconferences will eventually pay off.

Most companies have the capacity now to conduct conference calls via telephone. The advantages are lowered travel costs, including money and time, although these advantages are somewhat offset by the fact that many nonverbal cues (such as facial expressions and body language) are missing. Also, the sense of sharing, involvement, and team spirit can be low. Video conferencing solves some of these problems, but costs are generally prohibitive with current technology.

With current technology, computer conferencing holds promise as a meeting technique that can be employed relatively inexpensively. The preferred computer conferencing method allows each participant to view simultaneously on a personal computer terminal the responses of all other participants. This *window* method is more similar to face-to-face interaction and produces higher quality decisions than a different system where participants have to complete a message before they can interact.[9]

Several factors will improve the effectiveness of teleconferences.[10] Face-to-face meetings of participants before and after the teleconference meetings enhance the sense of *groupness*. Using a trained moderator improves the process. So does making sure that participants are aware of the rules and guidelines for speaking, and they agree to abide by specified time limits. Teleconferences are most useful for certain types of tasks, such as routine meetings and information sharing. For complex tasks where many disagreements are likely to occur, face-to-face meetings are still preferable. A comparison of strengths of face-to-face and teleconference meetings is contained in table 11.3.

Table 11.3 Comparison of Strengths

___

Teleconferences

Can be useful for information sharing, routine meetings
Quantity and quality of ideas is equal to face-to-face meetings
In negotiations, evidence is more persuasive than personality
Participants may pay more attention to what is said
In conflict, more opinion change may occur than in face-to-face meetings
Audioconferences/computer conferences are cost effective

Face-to-face Meetings

Better where group cohesiveness, interpersonal relationships are important
Easier to maintain the organization of the group
Can exchange more messages, more quickly
Important nonverbal information (facial expressions, uses of space) is available
People generally prefer face-to-face meetings
Participants are more confident of their perceptions in face-to-face meetings

___

Adapted from Gene D. Fowler and Marilyn E. Wackerbarth, "Audio Teleconferencing versus Face-to-Face Conferencing: A Synthesis of the Literature," *Western Journal of Speech Communication* 44 (Summer, 1980): 236–252.

Summary

This chapter discussed a variety of group techniques designed to address a number of organizational problems. Most of these techniques can be modified and adapted for different uses. The first set of techniques we presented are especially helpful for generating information and ideas. Buzz groups help members of a large assembly give input on an issue; relatively unstructured focus groups permit the members to focus on items of importance to them; and brainstorming, with its rule of deferred evaluation, helps group members release their creativity. Two techniques help identify problems: the problem census is useful for establishing an agenda for a group's future problem solving, and the RISK technique is a kind of *second chance* procedure that helps spot problems before a solution is implemented.

Group decision making is improved when members use a systematic procedure. The nominal group technique can be used during any phase of group problem solving, especially for solving major problems likely to involve extensive conflicts. It capitalizes on the fact that members working alone in the presence of others often work harder. Once a solution has been developed, procedures like PERT help groups plan and keep track of the implementation.

Organizations have found that group techniques, appropriately planned and implemented, can improve organizational effectiveness. Quality circles are voluntary groups of employees who meet regularly on company time to identify and solve job-related problems. Self-managed work teams are groups of peers who work as a team, developing their own goals, procedures, and work schedules within broad limitations set by the company.

Finally, just because group members cannot meet face-to-face doesn't prevent an organization from taking advantage of the benefits that group discussion can provide. Two procedures can help: in the Delphi technique, members remain anonymous and the interaction is conducted in writing as a facilitator compiles individual responses into a master list; with teleconferencing, participants are able to communicate directly with each other via audio, video, or computer link-ups.

Review Questions

1. Describe the purposes and limitations of each of the three techniques that are useful for generating information and ideas: brainstorming, focus groups, and buzz groups.
2. List the steps of the problem census and the RISK technique, then describe what happens during each step. From your own experience, give examples of how these techniques can be used.
3. List the steps of the Nominal Group Technique and describe what occurs during each step. For what kinds of questions might you use the Nominal Group Technique?
4. Design a PERT chart for yourself to help you plan and complete a current project.
5. Describe the small group techniques an organization can use to increase employee participation and improve effectiveness. What guidelines would you suggest for a company that wanted to implement such procedures?
6. Describe the techniques a corporation can use to overcome the problem of group members who are scattered geographically, work different shifts, or have schedules that make face-to-face meetings difficult.

Bibliography

Cathcart, Robert S. and Samovar, Larry A. (eds.). *Small Group Communication: A Reader*. 6th ed. Dubuque, IA: Wm. C. Brown, 1992, Section 2: 33–125.

Goodall, H. Lloyd, Jr. *Small Group Communication in Organizations*. Dubuque, IA: Wm. C. Brown, 1985.

Ross, Raymond S. *Small Groups in Organizational Settings*. Englewood Cliffs, NJ: Prentice-Hall, 1989.

References

1. The following information comes from Joseph M. Putti and Wong K. Cheong, "Singapore's Positive Experience with Quality Circles," *National Productivity Review* 9 (Spring, 1990): 193–200.

2. Alex Osborn, *Applied Imagination,* rev. ed. (New York: Charles Scribner's Sons, 1957).

3. Easy Klein, "What you can—and can't—learn from focus groups," *D & B Reports* (July/August, 1989): 26–28.

4. James B. Thomas, Reuben R. McDaniel, Jr., and Michael J. Dooris, "Strategic Issue Analysis: NGT and Decision Analysis for Resolving Strategic Issues," *Journal of Applied Behavioral Science* 25 (May, 1989): 189–201.

5. David R. Siebold, "Making Meetings More Successful: Plans, Formats, and Procedures for Group Problem Solving," in *Small Group Communication: A Reader,* 5th ed., eds. Robert S. Cathcart and Larry A. Samovar (Dubuque, IA: Wm. C. Brown, 1988): 219–220.

6. Ed Musselwhite, quoted by Thomas Owen, "The Self-Managing Work Team," *Small Business Reports* (February, 1991): 54.

7. Thomas Owen, "Self-Managing Work Team," *Small Business Reports* (February, 1991): 53–65.

8. Henry P. Sims, Jr. and James W. Dean, Jr., "Beyond Quality Circles: Self-Managing Teams," *Personnel Journal* (1985): 25–32.

9. Sharon L. Murrell, "The Impact of Communicating through Computers," (Unpublished doctoral dissertation, State University of New York at Stony Brook, 1983).

10. Compiled from Larry L. Barker, Kathy J. Wahlers, Kittie W. Watson, and Robert J. Kibler, *Groups in Process: An Introduction to Small Group Communication,* 3d ed. (Englewood Cliffs, NJ: Prentice-Hall, 1987): 208; Robert J. Johansen, J. Vallee, and K. Spangler, *Electronic Meetings: Technical Alternatives and Social Choices* (Reading, Mass.: Addison-Wesley, 1979): 113–115.

CHAPTER TWELVE

Techniques for Observing
Problem-Solving Groups

CHAPTER OUTLINE

The Role of the Observer

Observation Instruments and Techniques

Verbal Interaction Analysis

Content Analysis Procedures

SYMLOG

Member/Observer Rating Scales

Rating Scales for General Evaluation
Postmeeting Reaction Forms
Evaluating Individual Participants
Evaluating Group Leadership

KEY TERMS AND CONCEPTS

Consultant Observer

Content Analysis Procedures

Postmeeting Reaction Forms (PMRs)

Rating Scales

SYMLOG

Verbal Interaction Analysis

STUDY QUESTIONS

1. Describe two types of observers who can help a problem-solving group improve its procedures.
2. How can an observer gather and analyze data about a group's verbal interaction patterns?
3. How can an observer gather and analyze data about the content of what is discussed in a group?
4. What is a SYMLOG diagram and how can it help a group?
5. What are two types of rating scales, and how can each be used to help a group?

The technical college's executive committee meetings were boring. While all the members agreed that communication among the various departments was essential for the college to function effectively, the weekly staff meetings somehow were not satisfying this need. The real communication about problems, solutions, and goals of the various departments was done outside the meetings. Members were not complaining much, but they showed little enthusiasm for the meetings. The chair of the committee, Basil, was concerned. He asked Gloria to observe the meetings, figure out what was wrong, make recommendations for improvement, and conduct training sessions to help members interact more effectively during the meetings.

For two months, Gloria systematically observed, analyzed, and evaluated the staff meetings. First, she attended meetings, took notes, and completed a content analysis that showed Basil doing most of the talking. He was almost the only member to initiate new ideas during the meetings. Other members contributed only when addressed directly by Basil. Thus, a *wheel* interaction pattern (with Basil as the hub and everyone else as an individual spoke) had become the group's norm. Gloria then gave each member a questionnaire that asked how effective the meetings were and whether people felt free to contribute to the discussion or to disagree. The results indicated that Basil believed the meetings were very effective, most other members thought they were moderately effective, and two members rated them completely ineffective. Gloria then followed up the questionnaire by interviewing each staff member to determine what they would like to see the meetings accomplish and how they thought the meetings could be improved. She paid particular attention to the comments of the two dissatisfied members.

Gloria concluded that the meetings were dominated by Basil, but that he was completely unaware he was dominating. Members felt stifled during the meetings, but didn't know how to express those feelings to Basil or to change the pattern of their meetings. Members wanted to discuss freely the problems that had come up in their respective departments, and they hoped the staff meetings would provide an open forum for exchanging information and ideas. The two members who were most dissatisfied were quite knowledgeable about college operations, so they felt slighted when Basil treated them as if they were incompetent. Members were suppressing disagreements for fear of retribution by Basil; although Basil was not a tyrant, he made it clear from his behavior (rolling his eyes, interrupting people, speaking sarcastically) that he did not like it when others disagreed with his ideas. In short, this committee displayed some obvious and some hidden problems, all of which could be overcome with training and desire.

This true story highlights the value of having someone observe a group, describe its behavior, evaluate that behavior, and make recommendations to improve the functioning of the group. In this chapter we will present a variety of techniques to help you do that.

The Role of the Observer

The role of observer in the group can be a valuable and helpful one if the observer knows how to function. But most group members have not been trained to be effective group participants. This makes it especially important for those who *do* know something about small group communication to monitor the group's discussions and help the group perform as well as possible. The knowledgeable observer can function like an athletic coach who helps players improve their performance as a team.

In chapter 1, we introduced the concept of the participant observer, a group member who makes available his or her knowledge and skills to help a group perform more effectively. A second type of observer is the **consultant observer.** This person is an outsider brought in to observe, evaluate, and make recommendations to the group. The consultant observer may be a member of the organization the group belongs to or an outside consultant specifically trained in small group communication. When executives learn that someone within the organization has small group communication expertise, they often ask that person to apply his or her skills to help the group. That was Gloria's situation when she observed the technical college executive staff, and that may also be your position someday.

Both kinds of observers use their knowledge to improve a group's performance, but each has unique advantages and disadvantages. The consultant observer may be able to maintain more objectivity regarding group members and group processes, but the participant observer may have inside information that gives insight regarding what is happening in the group. If the group has been experiencing serious conflict, some members may suspect that the consultant observer has been brought in to serve as a *hatchet person* for an executive. On the other hand, a participant observer may be seen as biased rather than objective, thereby undermining his or her effectiveness as an advisor to the group.

What do observers look for? In trying to help the group do its best, they seek to answer two general questions: "How well is this group performing?" and "How can it improve?" However, those are broad questions! You already have learned that many elements contribute to how well a group system functions. As an observer, if you try to look at everything at once you will become overwhelmed. We recommend that you cope with this possibility by planning your observation strategy in advance. Table 12.1 contains a list of questions you can use as a general guide for observing. We are *not* recommending that you try to answer all the questions; instead, use the list to screen out those elements that seem to be working well so you can concentrate observation on those that can be improved.

Table 12.1   Questions to Guide Your Observations

Group Goals

Are there clear and accepted group goals?
How well does the group understand its charge?
Does the group know and accept limits on its area of freedom?
Do members know what output they are supposed to produce?

Setting

Does the physical environment (seating arrangements, privacy, attractiveness) facilitate group
   discussions?

Communication Skills and Interaction Patterns

How clearly do members express their ideas and opinions?
How well do members listen to each other?
Do members complete one topic before they switch to another?
Is verbal participation balanced equally among all members?
Is the pattern of interaction all-channel or unduly restricted?

Communication Climate and Norms

Does the group climate seem supportive and cooperative or defensive and competitive?
What attitudes do the members exhibit toward themselves and each other?
Do any hidden agenda items seem to interfere with group progress?
Do any norms seem to interfere with group progress or cohesiveness?

Leadership and Member Roles

What style of leadership is the designated leader providing?
Is the leadership appropriate for the group's needs?
Are the roles performed by members appropriate both for their skills and the needs of the group?
Are there any needed functions not being provided by anyone?

Decision-Making and Problem-Solving Procedures

Are members adequately prepared for meetings?
Is the group using an agenda? If so, how well is it being followed? Does it serve the group's needs?
Is anyone providing periodic internal summaries so members can keep track of major points of
   discussion?
Are decisions, assignments, and proposals being recorded?
How are decisions being made?
Has the group defined and analyzed the problem before members begin developing solutions?
Do members understand and agree upon criteria in making decisions?
How creative is the group in generating potential solutions?
Are members deferring judgment until all solutions have been listed and understood?
Are information and ideas being evaluated critically or accepted at face value?
Do you see any tendency toward groupthink?
Has the group made adequate plans to implement decisions?
Are special procedures (brainstorming, problem census, etc.) being used as needed?
Could procedural changes benefit the group?

Whether you are a participant observer or a consultant observer, there are several guidelines you should follow when you are giving feedback to the group about its performance:

1. *Stress the positive* and point out what the group or the leader is doing well.
2. *Do not overwhelm the group* by telling the members each and every thing you think should be improved. Instead, emphasize one or two things that most need improvement.
3. *Avoid arguing* when you present your observations, opinions, and advice, and make sure they are understood. Leave the group members free to decide whether and how your advice will be used.
4. *Do not interrupt the whole meeting* if you want to give advice to the group's leader while a meeting is in progress. Instead, whisper or write your suggestions.
5. *Speak clearly and concisely* when you are giving feedback. Do not ramble or belabor your points. Consider the following remarks by Larry, who observed that group members were switching to new topics without completing the original one:

> One of the problems I see is that you are having trouble staying on track with your discussion! In the past five minutes, you have talked about a pedestrian overpass at Grand and National, why money was spent on artificial turf instead of library books, how you can handle a landlord who won't repair plumbing, and several other topics. Your discussion would be more efficient if you helped each other focus on the original question: how can pedestrian/car accidents be eliminated on National Avenue?

In this example of giving feedback, Larry states the problem he has observed, gives a few (rather than ten or twenty) examples to clarify what he means, and provides a suggestion that makes the whole group responsible for solving the problem. He doesn't ramble endlessly about the problem or blame individual members.

6. *Prepare members for any special procedures* you may be asked to lead by explaining the procedure or giving members a handout that outlines the key steps. (We encourage you to use the figures in this book, so long as you give credit to the source.)
7. *Make individual critical comments in private* to the appropriate person so he or she will not feel attacked or publicly humiliated.

Now that you have some idea of what observers look for and how they present their findings in a rhetorically sensitive way, we present a variety of instruments to help you gather information about your group.

Observation Instruments and Techniques

The techniques and instruments we present may be used by group members themselves as part of an evaluation of the group or by observers. Many of the instruments were developed especially for classes in small group communication, discussion, and leadership. They can be used as is or adapted to suit particular situations and groups.

Verbal Interaction Analysis

A **verbal interaction analysis** shows who talks to whom, how often each member speaks, and whether the group participation is balanced or dominated by one or more individuals. A model interaction diagram is shown in figure 12.1. The names of all participants are located around the circle in the same order in which they sit during the discussion. Whenever a person speaks, an arrow is drawn from that person's position toward the individual to whom the remark was addressed. Subsequent remarks in the same direction are indicated by the short cross marks on the base of the arrow. (For example, Gallo addressed 3 remarks to Brown in the model diagram.) The longer arrow pointing toward the center indicates remarks made to the group as a whole.

An interaction diagram can look messy or confusing. For ease of interpretation, the numbers and percentages can be displayed in a chart such as the one in figure 12.2. From the frequency of participation to the group as a whole and to specific members, who might you guess is the leader of this group? Do you consider the participation balanced or not? Does anyone appear to dominate the discussion?

Content Analysis Procedures

Content analysis procedures help you analyze the *type* of remarks being made by specific members, as well as how often such remarks were made. The example in figure 12.3 uses the member role designations (task, maintenance, and self-centered) to help the observer identify who is performing which behaviors and how often. The specific behaviors are listed along the left margin and the participants' names across the top. Each time a member speaks, the observer places a mark in the appropriate box according to the type of remark made. Later, the tally marks are converted to percentages as shown in figure 12.4. Can you tell who is probably the task leader of this group? Who is the maintenance leader? Are any individuals acting in self-centered ways?

Group _____

Time _____

    Begin _____

    End _____

Place _____

Observer _____

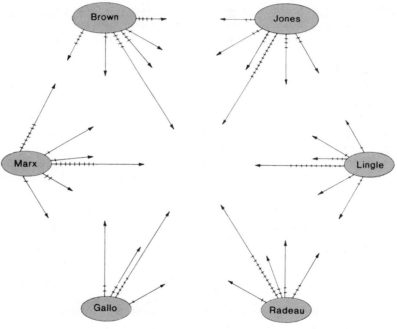

**Frequency and Direction
of Participation**

Figure 12.1 Verbal interaction diagram.

Group __CURRICULUM COMMITTEE_____ Place __CRAIG HALL_____

Observer __SMITH_____ Date __8-28-90_____

Beginning time ___9:00 A.M._____ Ending time __10:30 A.M._____

TO:

FROM:	Brown	Jones	Lingle	Radeau	Gallo	Marx	Group	Total
Brown	—	5	2	4	2	5	5	23 / 16.1
Jones	3	—	3	4	4	3	13	30 / 21
Lingle	2	2	—	3	2	4	12	25 / 17.5
Radeau	3	3	4	—	0	2	12	24 / 16.8
Gallo	3	3	2	0	—	0	6	14 / 9.8
Marx	8	2	2	3	2	—	10	27 / 18.9
Total number / percent	19 / 13.3	15 / 10.5	13 / 9.1	14 / 9.8	10 / 7	14 / 9.8	58 / 40.6	143 / 100

Figure 12.2 How to display data from a verbal interaction diagram.

Any category system can be used to construct a content analysis diagram. For example, you may want to focus on the defensive and supportive behaviors described in chapter 6 (see table 6.9). In that case, you would record all the individual defensive and supportive communication categories (i.e., control, superiority, provisionalism, empathy, etc.) along the left side.

There are other types of content analyses that can be performed. For example, you might want to trace the development of any fantasy chains in the group, the progression of an idea from its original introduction by one member through all its modifications by the rest of the group, types of conflicts, or the types of arguments members use to support their ideas. It will make your job much easier if you tape-record (with permission, of course) the group's interaction first.

SYMLOG

SYMLOG is an acronym that stands for the *Systematic Multiple-Level Observation of Groups;* it is both a comprehensive theory and a methodology that produces a diagram, like a three-dimensional snapshot, of relationships among group members[1]. Developed by Bales, SYMLOG theory is quite complicated. We are presenting a simplified explanation here so you can understand how SYMLOG can be used to describe a group. (Detailed instructions for completing a SYMLOG diagram may be found in the *SYMLOG Case Study Kit,* a workbook that explains SYMLOG theory and provides special forms for constructing a diagram.)

Group _____ Place _____ Observer _____

Date _____ Beginning time _____ Ending time _____

Participants' Names

Behavioral Functions						
1. Initiating and orienting						
2. Information giving						
3. Information seeking						
4. Opinion giving						
5. Opinion seeking						
6. Clarifying and elaborating						
7. Evaluating						
8. Summarizing						
9. Coordinating						
10. Consensus testing						
11. Recording						
12. Suggesting procedure						
13. Gatekeeping						
14. Supporting						
15. Harmonizing						
16. Tension relieving						
17. Dramatizing						
18. Norming						
19. Withdrawing						
20. Blocking						
21. Status and recognition seeking						

Figure 12.3 Content analysis of task, maintenance, and self-centered behaviors.

Group _EXECUTIVE COMMITTEE_   Place _CU LOBBY_
Observer _ANDY_   Date _8-28-90_
Beginning time _4:30 P.M._   Ending time _6:30 P.M._

Participants' Names

Behavioral Functions	Mary	John	Edna	Dave	Jodi	Total number / percent
1. Initiating and orienting	5	3				8 / 5.7
2. Information giving	6	5		2	3	16 / 11.4
3. Information seeking			3			3 / 2.1
4. Opinion giving	8	8	4	2	1	23 / 16.4
5. Opinion seeking			2			2 / 1.4
6. Clarifying and elaborating			3			3 / 2.1
7. Evaluating	2	4			1	7 / 5
8. Summarizing	2					2 / 1.4
9. Coordinating	8					8 / 5.7
10. Consensus testing				3		3 / 2.1
11. Recording			5			5 / 3.6
12. Suggesting procedure	3	6				9 / 6.4
13. Gatekeeping			1	5		6 / 4.3
14. Supporting	2		2	6		10 / 7.1
15. Harmonizing				3	2	5 / 3.6
16. Tension relieving					6	6 / 4.3
17. Dramatizing		5			3	8 / 5.7
18. Norming				4		4 / 2.9
19. Withdrawing		1				1 / .7
20. Blocking	2	5				7 / 5
21. Status and recognition seeking		4				4 / 2.9
Total number / percent	38 / 27.1	35 / 25	26 / 18.6	25 / 17.9	16 / 11.4	140 / 100

Figure 12.4   How to display data from content analysis of member behaviors.

SYMLOG theory assumes that behaviors in a group can be classified along each of three dimensions: dominant versus submissive; friendly versus unfriendly; and task-oriented versus emotionally expressive. An observer uses a twenty-six item rating scale to categorize each member's behavior; the rating scale is then tallied in a special way so that each member can be placed on the SYMLOG diagram. An example of a SYMLOG diagram, or "map," is shown in figure 12.5. The more a member is task-oriented, the closer he or she is to the top of the diagram; the more emotionally expressive, the closer to the bottom. (The *F* stands for *forward,* or task-oriented behavior, and the *B* stands for *backward,* or emotionally expressive behavior.) The friendlier a member is toward the other members of the group, the closer she or he is to the right; the more unfriendly, the closer to the left. (The *P* stands for *positive* or friendly behavior, the *N* for *negative* or unfriendly behavior.) The third dimension, dominance or submissiveness, is shown by the size of the circle; a dominant member has a large circle while a submissive one has a small circle.

Notice the individuals on the SYMLOG diagram in figure 12.5. Ann is very dominant, task-oriented, and negative toward other members of the group. (This is how authoritarian leaders often appear in SYMLOG diagrams.) In contrast, Bob is friendly and emotionally expressive, although he also is dominant. It is likely that a group with two such strong, but opposite, individuals will experience conflict during their group meetings. Notice where Charlie is located. He is moderately dominant, positive, and task-oriented. (This is how democratic leaders and members of productive, democratic groups often appear on SYMLOG diagrams.) If you were asked to describe this group, you would probably say it is unproductive, lacks cohesiveness, and members appear to waste a lot of time during meetings.

Now look at figure 12.6. This is a SYMLOG diagram showing a unified, cohesive group. All the members are in or near the upper right-hand quadrant (Bales calls this the *decision-making quadrant*), which shows that they are task-oriented enough to make progress toward the group's goal, but friendly enough toward each other that interpersonal relationships are probably harmonious. This group is likely to be productive and efficient.

A SYMLOG analysis encourages you to view the group as a whole system whose component parts (the members) are interdependent. It helps you visualize and think about members' behaviors, and how these behaviors are related. For example, assume you observe a group with both a highly task-oriented and a highly expressive member. What is likely to be the effect these two members will have on each other? Will their different behaviors in the group complement each other or pull the group in opposite directions? What difference will it make if both members are dominant? If one is negative and the other positive? How can you use SYMLOG to "map" these possible effects? Thinking in SYMLOG terminology helps you manage the complexity of group interaction as you create a "snapshot" that captures the essence of a group.

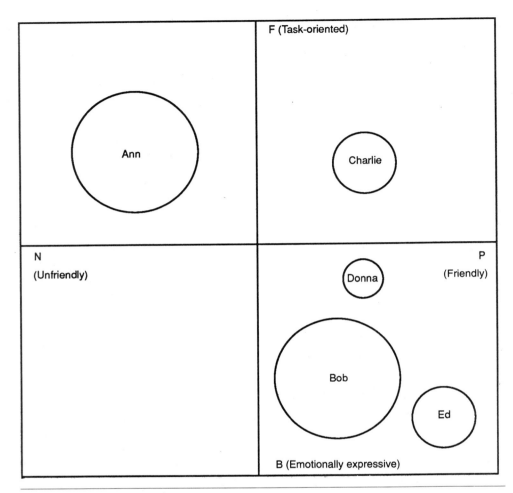

Figure 12.5 SYMLOG diagram of a noncohesive group.

There are a variety of ways to use SYMLOG, and several computer programs have been created to make its use easier.[2] However, it is possible to construct a SYMLOG diagram by hand. If this analysis appeals to you, we recommend that you purchase the *SYMLOG Case Study Kit,* which contains all the instructions and forms you need to produce a diagram by hand.

Member/Observer Rating Scales

Rating scales are used by either a group member or an observer to evaluate some aspect of a group. For example, the question "How well did the committee chair keep the discussion organized?" is asking you to rate the leader's ability to

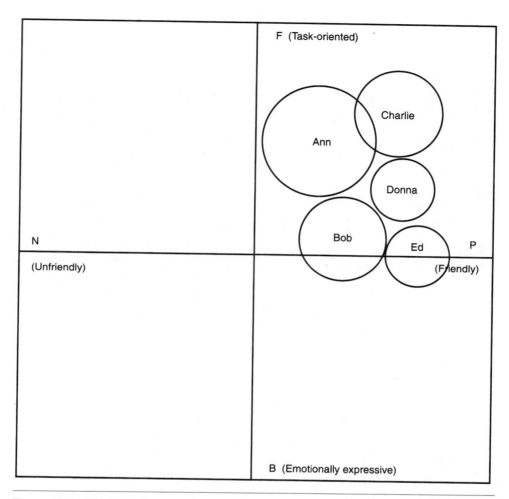

Figure 12.6 SYMLOG diagram of a unified, productive group.

conduct a systematic discussion. Such questions may be closed-ended, where the responses are already provided for you (such as *very well, adequately,* and *very poorly*) or they may be open-ended, where you are free to respond any way you choose. A questionnaire with several such questions is called a *rating instrument.* Many different rating scales and instruments have been prepared to serve a variety of purposes. We have used these instruments on a number of occasions. Feel free to copy ours, create your own, or modify any of these to suit your specific purposes.

Date _____   Group _____

Time _____   Observer _____

Group Characteristic	5 Excellent	4 Good	3 Average	2 Fair	1 Poor
Organization of discussion					
Equality of opportunity to speak					
Cooperative group orientation					
Listening to understand					
Evaluation of ideas					

Comments:

Figure 12.7   All-purpose discussion rating scale.

Rating Scales for General Evaluation

Rating scales can be used by participants or outside observers to evaluate any aspect of a group and its discussion, including group climate, cohesiveness, efficiency, satisfaction, freedom to express disagreement, and organization of discussion. We encourage you to devise your own scales or modify the ones presented here. Figure 12.7 is a general scale that can be used to evaluate any group discussion, and figure 12.8 is a scale adapted from one developed by Patton and Giffin to identify deficiencies in problem-solving procedures. Figure 12.9 is the Seashore Index of Group Cohesiveness, designed to measure cohesiveness of a work group.[3]

Postmeeting Reaction Forms

Postmeeting reaction forms (PMRs) are questionnaires designed to get objective feedback from members about what they thought of a particular meeting. PMRs may focus on a particular aspect of a meeting (such as leadership) or may deal with several broad aspects (such as how effective members believe the meetings are). The PMR forms are distributed by the leader, a member, or an observer; they

Instructions: Indicate the degree to which the group accomplished each identified behavior. Use the following scale for your evaluations:

Poor	Fair	Average	Good	Excellent
1	2	3	4	5

Circle the appropriate number in front of each item.

1 2 3 4 5   1. The concern of each member was identified regarding the problem the group attempted to solve.

1 2 3 4 5   2. This concern was identified *before* the problem was analyzed.

1 2 3 4 5   3. In problem analysis, the present condition was carefully compared with the specific condition desired.

1 2 3 4 5   4. The goal was carefully defined and agreed to by all members.

1 2 3 4 5   5. Valid (and relevant) information was secured when needed.

1 2 3 4 5   6. Possible solutions were listed and clarified before they were evaluated.

1 2 3 4 5   7. Criteria for evaluating proposed solutions were clearly identified and accepted by the group.

1 2 3 4 5   8. Predictions were made regarding the probable effectiveness of each proposed solution, using the available information and criteria.

1 2 3 4 5   9. Consensus was achieved on the most desirable solution.

1 2 3 4 5   10. A detailed plan to implement the solution was developed.

1 2 3 4 5   11. The problem-solving process was systematic and orderly.

Figure 12.8   Problem-solving process rating scale.

are completed *anonymously* by members, results are tallied, and findings are reported to the group as soon as possible. The findings provide a basis for the group to discuss how to improve its communication and effectiveness. If Basil, the group leader in our introductory example, had not had the services of an observer, he could have used PMRs to get feedback from the other members about how the group's discussions could be improved.

Check one response for each question.

1. Do you feel that you are really a part of your work group?
   - _____ Really a part of my work group
   - _____ Included in most ways
   - _____ Included in some ways, but not in others
   - _____ Don't feel I really belong
   - _____ Don't work with any one group of people
   - _____ Not ascertained

2. If you had a chance to do the same kind of work for the same pay in another work group, how would you feel about moving?
   - _____ Would want very much to move
   - _____ Would rather move than stay where I am
   - _____ Would make no difference to me
   - _____ Would want very much to stay where I am
   - _____ Not ascertained

3. How does your group compare with other similar groups on each of the following points?

	Better Than Most	About the Same as Most	Not as Good as Most	Not Ascertained
a. The way the members get along together	_____	_____	_____	_____
b. The way the members stick together	_____	_____	_____	_____
c. The way the members help each other on the job	_____	_____	_____	_____

Figure 12.9 Seashore Index of Group Cohesiveness. Source: Stanley E. Seashore, *Group Cohesiveness in the Industrial Work Group*, (Institute for Social Research, The University of Michigan, Ann Arbor, 1954).

1. How do you feel about today's discussion?

    excellent _____ good _____ all right _____ so-so _____ bad _____

2. What were the strong points of the discussion?

3. What were the weaknesses?

4. What changes would you suggest for future meetings?

(You need not sign your name.)

Figure 12.10   Postmeeting reaction form.

PMRs are tailored to fit the purposes and needs of the group. Questions may concern substantive items, interpersonal relationships, matters of procedure, or a mixture of all three. Two different examples of PMRs are shown in figures 12.10 and 12.11.

Evaluating Individual Participants

In addition to evaluating general group processes, it is often useful to evaluate behaviors of outside individual participants. The following forms may be completed by an observer or by the members themselves. Figure 12.12 shows a simple rating form, written by a group of students, that focuses on some of the most important aspects of participation. A more detailed form is shown in figure 12.13.

Evaluating Group Leadership

Leading small group interaction often warrants special attention. The following forms are designed especially to evaluate leadership. Figure 12.14 is the Barnlund-Haiman Leadership Rating Scale that evaluates several aspects of group leadership[4] and figure 12.15 is a self-rating scale that a discussion leader may use for self-evaluation.

Instruction: Circle the number that best indicates your reactions to the following questions about the discussion in which you participated:

1. *Adequacy of Communication.* To what extent do you feel members were understanding each others' statements and positions?

   0   1   2   3   4   5   6   7   8   9   10

   Talked past each other;   Communicated directly with
   misunderstanding   each other; understanding well

2. *Opportunity to Speak* To what extent did you feel free to speak?

   0   1   2   3   4   5   6   7   8   9   10

   Never had a   Had all the opportunity to
   chance to speak   talk I wanted

3. *Climate of Acceptance.* How well did members support each other, show acceptance of individuals?

   0   1   2   3   4   5   6   7   8   9   10

   Highly critical   Supportive and receptive
   and punishing

4. *Interpersonal Relations.* How pleasant and concerned were members with interpersonal relations?

   0   1   2   3   4   5   6   7   8   9   10

   Quarrelsome, status   Pleasant, empathic,
   differences emphasized   concerned with persons

5. *Leadership.* How adequate was the leader (or leadership) of the group?

   0   1   2   3   4   5   6   7   8   9   10

   Too weak ( ) or   Shared, group-centered,
   dominating ( )   and sufficient

6. *Satisfaction with Role.* How satisfied are you with your personal participation in the discussion?

   0   1   2   3   4   5   6   7   8   9   10

   Very dissatisfied   Very satisfied

7. *Quality of Product.* How satisfied are you with the discussions, solutions, or learnings that came out of this discussion?

   0   1   2   3   4   5   6   7   8   9   10

   Very displeased   Very satisfied

8. *Overall.* How do you rate the discussion as a whole apart from any specific aspect of it?

   0   1   2   3   4   5   6   7   8   9   10

   Awful; waste of time   Superb; time well spent

Figure 12.11 Postmeeting reaction form.

Date _____

_____   Observer _____
(Name of participant)

1. Contributions to the *content of the discussion*? (well prepared, supplied information, adequate reasoning, etc.)

5	4	3	2	1

Outstanding in   Fair share   Few or
quality and quantity   none

2. Contributions to *efficient group procedures*? (agenda planning, relevant comments, summaries, keeping on track)

5	4	3	2	1

Always relevant,   Relevant, no   Sidetracked,
aided organization   aid in order   confused group

3. Degree of *cooperating*. (listening to understand, responsible, agreeable, group centered, open-minded)

5	4	3	2	1

Very responsible   Self-centered
and constructive

4. *Speaking*. (clear, to group, one point at a time, concise)

5	4	3	2	1

Brief, clear,   Vague, indirect,
to group   wordy

5. *Value* to the group? (overall rating)

5	4	3	2	1

Most valuable   Least valuable

Suggestions:

Figure 12.12   Participant rating scale.

Participant's name _____

Instruction: Circle the number that best reflects your evaluation of the discussant's participation on each scale.

Superior Poor

1	2	3	4	5	1. Was prepared and informed.
1	2	3	4	5	2. Contributions were brief and clear.
1	2	3	4	5	3. Comments relevant and well timed.
1	2	3	4	5	4. Spoke distinctly and audibly to all.
1	2	3.	4	5	5. Contributions made readily and voluntarily.
1	2	3	4	5	6. Frequency of participation (if poor, too low ( ) or high ( ).
1	2	3	4	5	7. Nonverbal responses were clear and constant.
1	2	3	4	5	8. Listened to understand and follow discussion.
1	2	3	4	5	9. Open-minded.
1	2	3	4	5	10. Cooperative and constructive.
1	2	3	4	5	11. Helped keep discussion organized, following outline.
1	2	3	4	5	12. Contributed to evaluation of information and ideas.
1	2	3	4	5	13. Respectful and tactful with others.
1	2	3	4	5	14. Encouraged others to participate.
1	2	3	4	5	15. Overall rating in relation to other discussants.

Comments: Evaluator _____

Figure 12.13 Participant rating scale.

Instructions: This rating scale may be used to evaluate leadership in groups with or without official leaders. In the latter case (the leaderless group), use part A of each item only. When evaluating the actions of an official leader, use parts A and B of each item on the scale.

INFLUENCE IN PROCEDURE

Initiating Discussion

A. 3   2   1   0   1   2   3

Group needed more help in getting started	Group got right amount of help	Group needed less help in getting started

B. The quality of the introductory remarks was:

Excellent	Good	Adequate	Fair	Poor

Organizing Group Thinking

A. 3   2   1   0   1   2   3

Group needed more direction in thinking	Group got right amount of help	Group needed less direction in thinking

B. If and when attempts were made to organize group thinking, they were:

Excellent	Good	Adequate	Fair	Poor

Clarifying Communication

A. 3   2   1   0   1   2   3

Group needed more help in clarifying communication	Group got right amount of help	Group needed less help in clarifying communication

B. If and when attempts were made to clarify communication, they were:

Excellent	Good	Adequate	Fair	Poor

Summarizing and Verbalizing Agreements

A. 3   2   1   0   1   2   3

Group needed more help in summarizing and verbalizing agreements	Group got right amount of help	Group needed less help in summarizing and verbalizing agreements

B. If and when attempts were made to summarize and verbalize, they were:

Excellent	Good	Adequate	Fair	Poor

Resolving Conflict

A. 3   2   1   0   1   2   3

Group needed more help in resolving conflict	Group got right amount of help	Group needed less help in resolving conflict

B. If and when attempts were made to resolve conflict, they were:

Excellent	Good	Adequate	Fair	Poor

Figure 12.14 Barnlund-Haiman Leadership Rating Scale. From D. C. Barnlund and F. S. Haiman, *The Dynamics of Discussion* pp. 401–404, (Houghton-Mifflin, 1960.) Used by permission of Robert Goldsmith, M.D., executor of Barnlund estate.

Techniques for Observing Problem-Solving Groups

INFLUENCE IN CREATIVE AND CRITICAL THINKING

Stimulating Critical Thinking

A. 3 2 1 0 1 2 3

| Group needed more stimulation in creative thinking | Group got right amount of help | Group needed less stimulation creative thinking |

B. If and when attempts were made to stimulate ideas, they were:

| Excellent | Good | Adequate | Fair | Poor |

Encouraging Criticism

A. 3 2 1 0 1 2 3

| Group needed more encouragement to be critical | Group got right amount of help | Group needed less encouragement to be critical |

B. If and when attempts were made to encourage criticism, they were:

| Excellent | Good | Adequate | Fair | Poor |

Balancing Abstract and Concrete Thought

A. 3 2 1 0 1 2 3

| Group needed to be more concrete | Group achieved proper balance | Group needed to be more abstract |

B. If and when attempts were made to balance abstract and concrete, they were:

| Excellent | Good | Adequate | Fair | Poor |

INFLUENCE IN INTERPERSONAL RELATIONS

Climate-Making

A. 3 2 1 0 1 2 3

| Group needed more help in securing a permissive atmosphere | Group got right amount of help | Group needed less help in securing a permissive atmosphere |

B. If and when attempts were made to establish a permissive atmosphere, they were:

| Excellent | Good | Adequate | Fair | Poor |

Regulating Participation

A. 3 2 1 0 1 2 3

| Group needed more regulation of participation | Group got right amount of help | Group needed less regulation of participation |

B. If and when attempts were made to regulate participation, they were:

| Excellent | Good | Adequate | Fair | Poor |

Overall Leadership

A. 3 2 1 0 1 2 3

| Group needed more control | Group got right amount of control | Group needed less control |

B. If and when attempts were made to control the group, they were:

| Excellent | Good | Adequate | Fair | Poor |

Figure 12.14—*Continued*

Instructions: Rate yourself on each item by putting a check mark in the "Yes" or "No" column. Your score is five times the number of items marked "Yes." Rating: *excellent*, 90 or higher; *good*, 80–85; *fair*, 70–75; *inadequate*, 65 or lower.

	Yes	No
1. I prepared all needed facilities.	____	____
2. I started the meeting promptly and ended on time.	____	____
3. I established an atmosphere of permissiveness and informality; I was open and responsive to all ideas.	____	____
4. I clearly oriented the group to its purpose and area of freedom.	____	____
5. I encouraged all members to participate and maintained equal opportunity for all to speak.	____	____
6. I used a plan for leading the group in an organized consideration of all major phases of the problem.	____	____
7. I listened actively, and (if needed) encouraged all members to do so.	____	____
8. I saw to it that the problem was discussed thoroughly before solutions were considered.	____	____
9. I integrated related ideas or suggestions and urged the group to arrive at consensus on a solution.	____	____
10. My questions were clear and brief.	____	____
11. I saw to it that unclear statements were paraphrased or otherwise clarified.	____	____
12. I prompted open discussion of substantive conflicts.	____	____
13. I maintained order and organization, promptly pointing out tangents, making transitions, and keeping track of the passage of time.	____	____
14. I saw to it that the meeting produced definite assignments or plans for action, and that any subsequent meeting was arranged.	____	____
15. All important information, ideas, and decisions were promptly and accurately recorded.	____	____
16. I actively encouraged creative thinking.	____	____
17. I encouraged thorough evaluation of information and all ideas for solutions.	____	____
18. I was able to remain neutral during constructive arguments, and otherwise encourage teamwork.	____	____
19. I suggested or urged establishment of needed norms and standards.	____	____
20. I encouraged members to discuss how they felt about the group process and resolve any blocks to progress.	____	____

Figure 12.15   Leader self-rating scale.

Summary

We began this chapter by presenting a real-life situation to show you how valuable you can be if you know how to observe a small group, describe how it functions, evaluate it, and make recommendations to improve its effectiveness. These observations may be conducted by a participant observer or a consultant observer. Whichever you are, it is wise to plan your observations so you won't become overwhelmed. It is also important to follow certain guidelines when you present your evaluations and recommendations to the group to minimize the chance of arousing defensive reactions or otherwise disrupting the group.

We presented a variety of methods that observers and members may use to gather information. These include verbal interaction analyses, content analyses, SYMLOG, and a variety of rating scales. The information provided by these methods can help group members improve their performances during group discussions.

Review Questions

1. Explain the difference between a participant observer and a consultant observer and list advantages and disadvantages of each type to a group being observed.
2. When you plan to observe a group, how can you focus your observations so that you do not become overwhelmed with information?
3. How would you conduct a verbal interaction analysis of a discussion group, prepare the data so they can be readily interpreted, and explain what the data reveal about the group?
4. How would you conduct a content analysis of a discussion group using the role categories presented in this chapter, prepare the data so they can be readily interpreted, and explain what the data reveal about the group?
5. Select an area of small group communication (such as leadership, group climate, conflict management, etc.) and construct a rating instrument to evaluate this with respect to a specific group. If possible, distribute your questionnaire and tally the completed forms. How could you improve the instrument for future use?

References

1. Complete information on constructing a SYMLOG diagram, along with an abbreviated explanation of SYMLOG theory, may be found in a workbook, *SYMLOG Case Study Kit,* R. F. Bales (New York: The Free Press, 1980). For the readers who are interested in details of both the theory and methodology, we refer them to R. F. Bales and Stephen P. Cohen, *SYMLOG: A System for the Multiple-Level Observation of Groups* (New York: The Free Press, 1979).
2. Richard V. Polley, SYMLOG computer software, Lewis and Clark University, Portland, OR.
3. Stanley Seashore, *Group Cohesiveness in the Industrial Work Group* (Ann Arbor, MI: University of Michigan Institute for Social Research, 1954).
4. Dean C. Barnlund and Franklyn S. Haiman, *The Dynamics of Discussion* (Boston: Houghton Mifflin, 1960): 401–404.

INDEX

A

Abstract-concrete, 74–75, 80, 83
Acceptance level, 211
Accommodation, 241–42
Active listening, 61–63, 246, 250
Ad hominem attack, 111
Administrative duties of leader, 179–96
    developing group, 189–91
    following up, 181
    leading discussion, 182–89
    managing written communication, 191–96
    planning, 179–80
Affect, level of meaning, 71
Agenda, democratic leader and, 164
Ambiguity, tolerance for, 100
Ambiguous terms, 106–7
Analogy, 113
Anderson, P. A., 93
Appearance, as nonverbal message, 87–88
Appeasement. *See* Accommodation
Arbitration, 252
Area of freedom, 212
Arguments
    critical thinking and, 97
    evaluation of, 104–5
    leader neutral during, 186
Assembly effect, 207
Assignments, of members, 181
Assuming meaning, 59
Attitudes
    critical thinker's, 98–99
    member's, 29–31
Authoritarian, 30, 165
Autocratic leader, 164
Autonomous work group. *See* Self-managed
    work team
Avoidance, 240–41

B

Bach, G. R., 60, 66
Backchannel sounds, 90–91
Bales, R. F., 128, 149, 227, 292, 309
Barker, L. L., 53, 66, 282
Barnlund, D. C., 305, 309
Bayless, O. L., 227
Bay of Pigs invasion, 230, 231, 235, 236, 237,
    239, 243
Behavioral role, 136–39
Behaviors, 32
    content analysis of, 288
    leader modifying, 189
    leadership as, 163–64
Berg, D. M., 60, 66
Berkowitz, L., 211, 227
Beyer, B. K., 119, 120
Bibliography, compiling, 30
Birdwhistell, R. L., 93
Blanchard, K. H., 168, 169, 174
Block, M. W., 226
Bormann, E. G., 149, 150, 161, 174
Brainstorming, 211, 216
    leader stimulating, 187–88
    procedure, 259–62
Breakdowns in communication, 233
The Breakfast Club, 124–26, 130, 137, 145
Brilhart, J. K., 21, 65, 93, 149, 201, 202, 227
Brockriede, W., 120
Brown, S., 254
Browne, M. N., 104, 119
Burgoon, J. K., 93, 116
Burleson, B. R., 227
Buzz groups, 263–65
Bylaws, and rules of small groups, 130
Bypassing, 73–74

C

Campbell, S. K., 119
Camp David talks, 243
Cartwright, D., 22
Cassota, L. L., 56, 66
Cathcart, R. S., 65, 66, 93, 174, 201, 281, 282
Causal relationships, 112
Causes, 36, 112
Chair, title or role of, 158
Challenger disaster, 96, 99–100, 107, 114–15, 118, 230, 243, 258
Charisma, 157
Charting
    alternative solutions during mediation, 251
    pros and cons of solutions, 219
Chemers, M., 168, 170
Cheong, W. K., 282
Cissna, K. N. L., 66
Climate of group, 144–47
Closed-mindedness, 117, 236. *See also* Dogmatism
Closed system, 33
Coch, L., 226
Coercion, 156
Cohen, S. P., 309
Cohesiveness
    conflict producing, 232–33
    eye contact and, 89
    increasing, 146
    problem solving and, 207
    Seashore Index of Group Cohesiveness, 300
    shared leadership and, 166
    trust and, 145
Collaboration, 243
Committee
    ad hoc, 17
    conference, 17
    defined, 16
    standing, 17
    task force, 17
Communication, Part Two
    breakdowns in, 233
    cycle, 46
    defined, 13–14, 47–48
    intercultural, 55
    leadership and, 155, 161
    process, 47–48
    written, in group, 191–96
Communication apprehension. *See* Willingness to communicate
Communication competence, of leader, 161
Communication networks, 32

Competition
    conflict style, 242–43
    eye contact, seating and, 89
Completer, leader as, 167
Compromise
    conflict management style, 243–46
    leader facilitating, 191
Compulsive talker, control of, 185–86
Computer conference, 279
Conference, 17
Conflict
    avoidance of, 220
    benefits of, 231–32
    communication breakdown and, 52
    expressing disagreement during, 245–49
    issues of, 125
    management by leader, 190–91
    managing, 240–52
    myths about, 231–34
    over goals, 234
    phase in decision making, 219
    styles of, 240–44
Cook, W. B., 21
Coons, A. E., 174
Consensus
    decision making by, 4, 220–21, 251
    defined, 220
Content analysis, 290, 293
Context, as dimension of culture, 57
Context level of meaning, 71
Contingency concept (theory) of leadership, 168–72
Coordinator, 158, 159, 160, 161, 189
Creative thinking, 187, 216
Credibility of source of opinion, 107
Criteria, 188
    absolute versus important, 218
    defined, 217
    objective, 249
Critical thinking, chapter 5
    asking questions and, 83
    attitudes of critical thinker, 99–100
    behaviors counterproductive to, 115–18
    defined, 96–97
    effort required, 118
    groupthink and, 234–35
    leader stimulating, 187
    norms favoring, 238–39
    in problem solving, 98, 208–9
Criticism of solutions, 217–19
Crosby, P. V., 22

Culture of group, 141–49
    defined, 54, 141
    effects on communication process, 54–58
    nonverbal signals and, 88–91
    norms and, 132
Curtis, D. B., 66

D

Davitz, J. D., 93
Davitz, L., 93
Dean, J. W., Jr., 282
Decision emergence phase, 219
Decision making
    conflict and, 231–34
    leader involvement in, 239
    methods of, 220–21
    phases in, 219–20
    problem solving versus, 210
Defensive climate, 146–47
Defensive responding, 60–61, 246
Delegating leader style, 170
Delphi technique, 277–79
Deming, E. W., 16–19
Democratic decision making, 10
Democratic leadership, power distance and, 56.
        See also Group-centered democratic
        leadership
Designated leader, 158–61
Developing a group, by leader, 189–91
Deviants, group pressure on, 133, 134, 237
Devil's advocate, 238
DeVito, J. A., 93
Dewey, J. E., 213, 226, 227
Dialect, credibility related to, 73
Direct observation for information, 102
Disagreement
    conflict arising from, 231
    expressing, 245–46
    tolerance for, 126. See also Conflict
Discussion questions, 80–83
Division of labor, 178. See also Roles
Dogmatism, 117–18
    leader emergence and, 161
Dooris, M. J., 282
Doublespeak, 74, 107
Dramatizing, 138
Dunnette, M., 254
Dyad, 12–13

E

Eckman, P., 93
Egalitarianism, 30
Ehninger, D., 120
Either-or thinking, 112–13, 115, 117
Ellis, D. G., 149
Ellsworth, P., 93
Emergent leader, 161–62
Emotive words, 75–76
Environment, 33
Equalizing opportunity to speak, 185–86
Equilibrium problem, 128
Ethnocentrism, 55
Evaluation, following brainstorming, 260
Evidence
    critical thinking and, 97, 105
    evaluating, 108–10
Expert power, 157, 161
Eye contact, 89

F

Facial expression, 89–90
Facilitator
    of Delphi technique, 277–78
    title of, 158
Fact, 106
Fairness, in conflict resolution, 244
Fallacies, 110–11
Fantasy themes and chains, 142–44
Feedback, 36, 52
    giving as observer, 289
Feldman, D., 149
Fiedler, F., 174
Fisher, B. A., 149, 219, 227
Fisher, R., 247, 254
Focused listening, 63–64
Focus groups, 262
Focusing on irrelevancies, 60
Formal role, 136
Formation phase, 128
French, J. R. P., 156, 174, 226
Friesen, W. V., 93
Functional theory of leadership, 166

G

Galanes, G. J., 21, 65, 93, 149, 201, 202
Gatekeeping, 137, 138, 166, 167
Geier, J. C., 174
Gender and cultural rules, 57–58

General Procedural Model for Problem Solving, 213–25
General systems theory, 27–37
Gibb, J. R., 150
Glaser, E., 97, 98
Goal
    component of problem, 209
    conflict about, 233, 234
    improvement of group, 188
    of meeting, 179
Goodall, H. L., 174, 281
Gouran, D. S., 22, 107, 114, 120
Group, defined, 11–12
Group-centered democratic leadership, 162, 197–200
Group dynamics, 13
Groupthink, 234–40
    defined, 234
    preventing, 115, 237–40
    probing questions and, 114–15
    symptoms of, 235–37
Gruner, C., 120
Gudykunst, W. B., 66
Gwynne, S. C., 21

H

Hackman, M. Z., 156, 174
Haiman, F. S., 305, 309
Hall, E. T., 88, 93
Hall, J., 226
Handouts, 183
Harper, R. G., 93
Hersey, P., 168–69, 174
Hidden agenda, 139–40, 190
Hirokawa, R. Y., 22, 120, 226, 227
Hoffman, L. R., 226
Hofstede, G., 66
Human potential movement, 13
Huseman, R., 120

I

Ideal solution procedure, 213
Identification. *See* Referent power
Implementation of solution, 221
Improvement, leader fostering, 188–89
Impulsiveness, 116
Incomplete comparisons, fallacy of, 113
Individualism-collectivism dimension, 56
Individualistic culture, 18, 56
Individual roles, 137, 139–40

Inference, 106
Influence. *See* Leadership
Informal role, 136
Information
    assessing need for, 101–2, 114
    evaluating, 103–14
    gathering, 100–103
Initiating discussion, 183
Inputs, 28–31
Inquiry, spirit of, 246
Insulation of group, 239
Integrative systems/process model of leadership, 170–72
Interaction, 11, 14, 31. *See also* Communication
Intercultural communication, 55
Interdependence, 11, 14, 35–36
Interdependent goal, 35–36
Interpersonal communication, versus small group, 14
Interviews, 103
Intrapersonal communication, 14
Intrinsic interest, 211
Intuition, in problem solving, 208
Inventions, 206
Ishikawa, K., 18
Issues, in critical thinking, 98

J

Janis, I. L., 226, 230, 231, 254
Jaynes, W. F., 174
Jochem, L. M., 227
Johansen, R. J., 282
Johnson, C. E., 156, 174
Jonas, A., 120
Juran, J., 18

K

Kahn, R., 42
Katz, D., 42
Keeley, S. M., 104, 119
Kennedy, President John F., 158, 230, 231, 235, 236, 237
Kibler, R. J., 282
King, S. W., 66
Klein, E., 282
Kruglanski, A. W., 254

L

Lack of confidence, uncritical thinking and, 116
LaFasto, F. M. J., 150, 174, 201, 202, 227
Laissez-faire leader, 164
Language
    expressing disagreement, 246
    using to help group progress, 71–83
Larson, C. E., 150, 174, 201, 202, 227
Leader
    adaptability of, 155, 199
    as completer, 167
    defined, 155–56, 158
    designated, 158–61
    expectations of, by members, 178–96
    preferences and decision making, 239
    seating, space and, 89
    self-rating scale, 307
    types of, 158–62
        autocratic, 164
        coordinator, 160, 161
        democratic, 164, 197–200
        emergent, 161–62
        laissez faire, 164
        peer, 159–60
        supervisory, 159
Leaderless groups, 161
Leadership, 8, 152–73
    adaptability and, 154
    communication and, 155–56
    current ideas about, 166–72
    defined, 155
    functional, 166–67
    group-centered democratic, 197–200
    myths about, 162–66
    rating scales, 305–7
    style, 163–66
    traits, 162–63
Leading discussion, 181–89
Learning groups, 16
Leathers, D. A., 93, 120
Leavitt, H., 150
Legitimate power, 156
Levels of meaning in messages, 71
Levine, B. J., 227
Liaison, leader serving as, 181
Life cycles in systems, 37–38
Listening, 53–54
    actively, 61–63
    focused, 63
    habits, 58–61
Lustig, M. W., 56, 66

M

Mabry, E. A., 90, 93
McCroskey, J. R., 116
McDaniel, R. R., Jr., 282
Maintenance roles (behaviors), 133, 138
Mapping, during problem solving, 211–12, 214
Martz, A. E., 120
Massarik, F., 174
Matarazzo, J. D., 93
Meaning
    determining, 104–5
    of speaker versus words, 73
Mediation, 249–52
Meeting notice, 195
Member familiarity, 21
Message, 47
    defined, 70
    verbal and nonverbal, chapter 4
Meyers, C., 120
Miesing, P., 227
Mind raping, 59–60
Minutes, 64, 193–94
Misunderstanding and conflict, 232
Moderator, 158
Morocco, C. C., 150
Motion, by committee, 196
Movements, as nonverbal signals, 90
Multiple causes, 36–37
Multiple paths, 37
Murrell, S. L., 282
Musselwhite, E., 282
Myths about communication, 51–52

N

Naisbitt, J., 5, 9, 21
Nominal group technique, 269–72
Nonverbal communication, principles of, 84–86
Nonverbal signals, 84–91
    categories of, 87–91
    functions of, 86–87
    peer pressure and, 132
Norms, 32, 129–36, 238
    changing, 135
    cultural, 132
    defined, 129–30
    development of, 130–32
    problem solving, 207
    trust and, 189
Notes, leader's personal, 188
Notice of meeting, 179–80, 195

O

Observation
  feedback of, 289
  instruments and techniques for, 290–307
Observer
  participant as, 19–20
  role of, 19, 287–89
Obstacles to change, 209–10
Open-mindedness
  critical thinker and, 98–100
  defined, 98
  leader emergence and, 161
Open system, 33–35
Opinions, evaluating, 106–7
Organizational groups, 5, 6, 16–19, 38–40
Organizing remarks, 77–80
Orientation phase, 219
Osborn, A., 282
Outputs, 32–33
Overdependence, 116
Overgeneralization, 111
Owen, T., 282

P

Paraphrase, 54
Parnes, S. J., 227
Parsons, T., 149
Participant-observer perspective, 19–20
Participant rating scales, 303–4
Participating, leader style of, 170
Patience, in critical thinkers, 100
Peer leader, 159–60
Peer pressure, 130, 132
Personal notes, 192–93
PERT (Program Evaluation and Review
    Technique), 272–74
Phases
  in decision making, 219–20
  in group development, 128–29
Phillips, G., 116
Planning for meetings, 179
Planning stage of problem solving, 7
Plato, 162
Polley, R. V., 309
Poole, M. S., 22, 214, 220, 227
Positional role, 136
Postmeeting reaction forms (PMRs), 298–302
Power, sources and types, 156–58
Power distance, 56–57
Pratt, J. M., 150

Preble, J. F., 227
Pressure to conform in groupthink, 237
Primacy and norms, 131
Primary groups, 15
Primary tension, 124–25, 129, 183
Principled negotiation, 247–49
Probes (questions), 99–100, 114–15
Problem
  characteristics of, 210–13
  defined, 209
  describing and analyzing, 214–16
  separating people from, 247
Problem census, 265–67
Problem question, 215
Problem solving, 205–25
  critical thinking in, 98
  decision making versus, 210
  groups and, 6–10
  group versus individuals, 8–10, 207–8
  process rating scale, 299
Procedures, 32
  leader suggesting, 183
  observer preparing members for, 289
  problem solving, 207–23. *See also* General
      Procedural Model for Problem Solving
Production phase, 128
Profile of role, 140–41
Pseudolistening, 58–59
Purpose, groups classified by, 14–19
Putnam, L. L., 150
Putti, J. M., 282

Q

Quality (control) circle, 18, 258–59, 273–75
Questions
  for analysis of problem, 216
  for discussion, 80–83
  implementation, 221
  leader asking, 183
  leader responding to, 186
  target in buzz groups, 263
Quiet members, encouraging, 186

R

Raths, L. E., 120
Rating possible solutions, 219
Rating scales, 296–99
Raven, B., 156, 174
Reading for information, 102–3
Reasoning, checking for errors in, 110–13

Reasons in support of claims, 105
Records of group, 193–95, 219, 260
    during Nominal Group Technique, 270
    during problem census, 265–66. *See also*
        Minutes
Referent power, 157, 161
Reflective thinking, 213
Reinforcement, 220
Relationship
    among members, 128
    level of meaning, 71
Remland, M., 93
Reports, 195. *See also* Minutes, Records of group
Resource persons, 180
Response to questions, 82
Responsibility
    of chair for communication, 51
    of members, 30–31
Reticence. *See* Willingness to communicate
Reward power, 157, 161
Rewards, sharing by leader, 191
RISK technique, 267–68
Robert, Henry M., 201
Robert's Rules of Order, 130, 183, 196
Rogers commission, 96
Rokeach, M., 120
Role in group
    development of, 128
    emergence of, 140
    functions of, 137–38
    profile, 140–41
    types of, 136–38
    special, 183
Ross, R. G., 281
Rost, K. M., 227
Rothstein, A., 120
Ruch, W. V., 21, 22
Rules
    defined, 129–30
    formal, construction of, 130
    group, 125
    leader following, 200
Rules of communication
    culture and, 55
    of language usage, 72–73

S

Saine, T., 93
Samovar, L. A., 65, 66, 93, 174, 201, 281, 282
Samter, W., 227
Saturn Corporation, 4–6, 9, 19, 38, 276

Schacter, S., 150
Scheffler, A. E., 90, 93
Schutz, W. C., 14, 22, 174
Scientific method, 109, 213
    as basis for problem solving, 208–9
Scott, W. L., 174
Seashore, S., 309
Secondary groups, 15–19
Secondary tension, 125
Secretary of small group, 136
Self-managed work team, 18–19, 31, 38, 276
Selling, leader style of, 169
Sensitivity in expressing disagreement, 245
Shartle, C. L., 174
Shaw, M. E., 11, 21
Shils, E. A., 149
Shyness. *See* Willingness to communicate
Sidetracking, 60
Siebold, D. R., 282
Sieburg, E., 66
Sign, 48
Signal, in communication, 47
Silent arguing, 59
Sims, H. P., Jr., 282
Situational leadership model, 169
Size, of small group, 12–13
Skeptical inquiry, attitude of, 98
Small group, defined, 12–13
Small group communication, defined, 14
Social distance, 88
Solidarity, 133
Solution multiplicity, 211
Solution question, 215
Solutions
    collaborative, 251
    generating and explaining, 216–17. *See also*
        Solution multiplicity, Solution question
Space (and seating) as nonverbal signal, 88–89
Spangler, K., 282
Stages
    in group life, 13, 37–38
    of problem solving, 7. *See also* Life cycles in
        systems
Standard agenda procedure, 213
Statistical reasoning, evaluating, 109
Status and nonverbal signals, 89–91
Steil, L. K., 53, 66
Stogdill, R. M., 174
Structuring discussion, 183–85
Style theory of leadership, 164–65
Subcultures, 54. *See also* Culture
Summarizing, by leader, 185
Supervisory leader, 159

Supportive climate, 146–47
Symbol, 47–50, 71, 190
SYMLOG, 292, 295–96
System
    defined, 28
    model of, 34
    subsystems of, 40
    theory of, 27–37

T

Tables, for discussion, 89
Tannenbaum, R., 174
Task difficulty, 211
Task force, 17
Task roles (behaviors), 133, 138
Team, 38. *See also* Self-managed work team
Teamwork, developing, 190–91
Teleconferences, 279–80
Telling, as leader style, 169
Tensions
    inevitability of, 7
    managing, 126–27
    types of, 124–26
        primary, 124, 129, 131
        secondary, 125
        tertiary, 125–29
Thomas, J. B., 282
Thomas, K. W., 240, 254
Throughput processes, 31–32
Time cues, 91
Ting-Toomey, S., 66
Topic changes, controlling, 183–84
Trait theory of leadership, 162–63
Transactional, 50–51
Treece, J. B., 21
Trigger words. *See* Emotive words
Tropman, J. E., 201
Trust
    climate of, 144–45
    defined, 144
    establishing, 189–90

U

Ury, W., 247, 254

V

Vallee, J., 282
Verbal interaction analysis, 290–92
Voice, nonverbal signals of, 90–91
Von Bertalanffy, L., 42
Voting
    to decide, 220–21
    to narrow list of solutions, 218
    to test consensus, 220

W

Wahlers, K. J., 282
Ware, G., 120
Wasserman, S., 120
Watson, G., 97, 98, 120
Watson, K. W., 53, 66, 282
Watson, W. H., 226
Webster, D. M., 254
Wechsler, I. R., 174
Weins, A. N., 93
Williams, D., 21
Willingness to communicate, 116–17
Win-lose. *See* Competition
Win-win. *See* Collaboration
Work effectiveness team. *See* Quality circle
Work team, 19, 38, 73. *See also* Self-managed work team
Written communication, 191–96
Wyden, P., 66

Z

Zander, A., 22
Zimbardo, P., 116